Sino-Soviet Relations Since Mao

The Chairman's Legacy

(Carl G.)

C. G. Jacobsen

PRAEGER

PRAEGER SPECIAL STUDIES • PRAEGER SCIENTIFIC

Library of Congress Cataloging in Publication Data

Jacobsen, Carl G
  Sino-Soviet relations since Mao.

  Bibliography: p.
  Includes index.
    1. China--Foreign relations--Russia.
2. Russia--Foreign relations--China. I. Title.
DS740.5.R8J33   327.51047   80-27319
ISBN 0-03-058346-2

Published in 1981 by Praeger Publishers
CBS Educational and Professional Publishing
A Division of CBS, Inc.
521 Fifth Avenue, New York, New York 10175 U.S.A.

© 1981 by Praeger Publishers

123456789   145   987654321

Printed in the United States of America

TABLE OF CONTENTS

List of Tables

List of Maps

NOTE ON CHINESE NAMES

On January 1, 1979, China adopted the pinyin system of transcription from the Chinese to the English. Below is a list of major names and places that are mentioned in the text in accordance with the pinyin system. The older, traditional English versions appear in parenthesis.

Chen Xilian (Chen Hsi-lien)
Deng Xiaoping (Teng Hsiao-ping)
Hu Yaobang (Hu Yao-pang)
Hua Guofeng (Hua Kuo-feng)
Ji Dengkui (Chi Teng-kuei)
Jiang Qing (Chiang Ching)
Lin Biao (Lin Piao)
Liu Shaoqui (Liu Shao-chi)
Mao Zedong (Mao Tse-tung)
Wang Dongxing (Wang Tung-hsing)
Wang Hongwen (Wang Hung-wen)
Wu De (Wu Teh)
Yao Wenyuan (Yao Wen-yuan)
Zhang Chunqiao (Chang Chun-Chiao)
Zhao Ziyang (Chao Tsu-yang)
Zhou Enlai (Chou En-lai)

Beijing (Peking)
Fuzhou (Foochow)
Guangxi Zhuang (Kwangsi Chuang)
Guangzhou (Canton)
Jiangxi (Kiangsi)
Jinan (Tsinan)
Lanzhou (Lanchow)
Nanjing (Nanking)
Nei Monggol (Inner Mongolia)
Shanghai (Shanghai)
Sichuan (Szechwan)
Xinjiang (Sinkiang)
Yanan (Yenan)

Historical references have not been altered. Thus the Treaty of Peking of 1860, for example, has not been renamed the Treaty of Beijing. Similarily, the Battle of Stalingrad remains known as the Battle of Stalingrad even though the city after which it was named is now called Volgograd. Also, quotations that employ the old system of transcription have not been changed.

INTRODUCTION: SINO-SOVIET RELATIONS SINCE MAO

The state of relations between the two giants of the Eurasian landmass, the Soviet Union and China, looms as a crucial determinant of the future health of the world's body politic. Indeed, one might well argue that the disputes, fears, and uncertainties that so bedeviled Sino-Soviet ties through the 1960s and 1970s still add up today to the single most potent question undermining prognoses of future alignments and stability. It may, furthermore, be the one question whose resolution is the most difficult to predict.

That may be one reason why Western scholars have shied away from confronting the issue. The 1950s and 1960s saw a flood of literature, much of which could be divided chronologically between early exposes of the presumed dangers flowing from Sino-Soviet alliance and later treatises on the explosive potential of Sino-Soviet rancor. Little serious work emerged during the 1970s. Some potential authors may have been deterred by their belief that both the essence and the potential consequences of Sino-Soviet confrontation remained as described in earlier studies. Others may be presumed to have been deterred through dawning realization of the greater complexities now involved and appreciation of the limitations of available knowledge. While observers who concentrated on the outward manifestations of Sino-Soviet relations noted a frosty glacier interrupted only occasionally by cracks or ripples, those familiar with the more tumultuous domestic political scene in China began to see a correlation between interstate nuances and the ebb and flow of Beijing politics. (See "Note on Chinese Names" at the beginning of this book.) Looked at from this perspective the hiccups jarring the surface of Sino-Soviet hostility began to look rather like the tips of domestic Chinese icebergs. Indeed, accumulating evidence presents a powerful case for the argument that Sino-Soviet relations were in effect suspended through the 1970s, hostage to the vagaries of a continuing and fundamental struggle for power within China's leadership hierarchy. To some extent all foreign policies are of course hostage to domestic perceptions and requirements. But the depth and longevity of Chinese factional antagonisms, and the different symbolisms assigned to ties with Moscow by the contending factions, served to make this particularly true in the Sino-Soviet case.

The recognition that the superficialities of the Sino-Soviet relationship floated on a cauldron of domestic Chinese turmoil, and that any attempt to illuminate the former must therefore of necessity rest on an analysis of the latter, forced the aspiring scholar to confront also the inadequacies of Western "Sinology." U.S. commentary on Chinese affairs has been particularly prone to simpler notions of good and bad. The tendency has long roots. Missionary successes were said to demonstrate the innate goodness of heathens eager to be taught the virtues of "civilization"; occasional attacks on missionaries were ascribed to ignorance and barbarism, confirming both the need for a missionary presence and the glory of its purpose. Later, Chiang Kaichek's anticommunism and pro-Americanism were all too often thought to be synonymous with legitimacy and competence as concerned his stewardship of the Chinese nation. The few who were skeptical of that assumption, who saw Mao Zedong as perhaps more representative of Chinese realities, and who ventured the thought that his historical independence of Soviet communism augured well for U.S. interests, were to find their voices drowned by the rhetoric of the emerging Cold War. The very pragmatic Sino-Soviet alliance of the 1950s was thought to prove perceptions of world communist unity and conspiracy. The rupture of Sino-Soviet ties in the early 1960s forced recognition of the existence of two communist "camps." But the ascribed irrationality of the Cultural Revolution launched by Mao a few years later imbedded and inflamed the hostility previously nurtured. Most Western comment of this era could be divided between an establishment concensus that echoed the "Yellow Peril" phobia associated with earlier instances of "antisocial" behaviour on the part of Chinese leaders or population and the lonely idolatery of those who chose to define themselves as Maoists.

Establishment attitudes toward Mao underwent an extraordinary osmosis during the 1970s. Sino-U.S. rapprochement and Mao's 1972 reception of U.S. President Nixon in Beijing tended to be attributed to the steadying influence of the moderate, pragmatic, and therefore approachable Premier Zhou Enlai. The bouts of anti-Americanism that intermittently surfaced during subsequent years were alternately seen as the relapse of a sick patient (Mao) and the machinations of wild-eyed fringe extremists whose professed loyalty to Maoist tenets earned them a degree of immunity at times when their supposed mentor was too enfeebled or senile to keep them on leash. The ouster of radical leaders (the "Gang of Four") after Mao's death was greeted as the removal of a cancerous cell; the end of the decade emergence of Zhou Enlai's "heir apparent," Deng Xiaoping, was equated with the triumph of U.S. (and Western) interests—and greeted with despair by the "Maoists." Establishment commentary on Mao and the radicals was as devoid of understanding of their aspirations and goals as "Maoist" commentary was of their failings. But establishment commentary on Deng was as much a prisoner of rapture as that on Mao had been of enmity. There was little appreciation of the fact that Moscow had also heaved a sigh of relief at the eclipse of the Gang of Four and that Moscow viewed the prospect of a Deng-dominated regime in Beijing with a measure of relief; nor was there much appreciation of the reasons for this state of affairs.

The present work addresses itself both to the task of charting the recent course of Sino-Soviet relations and to the challenge of illuminating the domestic determinants that have shaped the course. It focuses on the evolving military-strategic and political arenas, yet deals also with ideological, economic, and other themes. It analyzes the complex and diverse sources of tension and mistrust, the historical, cultural, territorial, and sociopolitical issues that have divided the antagonists, and juxtaposes these to the arguments and logic of those striving to soothe the discord. The approach may be described as interdisciplinary, and rooted in history. The ambition, and the hope, rests on the conviction that such an approach promises to provide a more comprehensive and subtle account of the conflicting themes affecting Sino-Soviet relations of the 1980s than has hitherto been available. The intent is not to present a day to day chronology of events, but to illuminate the concerns, prejudices, and predilections that molded past events and that provide the conceptual parameters likely to define future action and reaction patterns.

Chapter 1 looks at "The Strategic Context," the realities of the Sino-Soviet balance of power. The potency of China's military capabilities has frequently been overestimated by Western analysts, government, military, and academic (perhaps a residue of the Yellow Peril phobia of old). Hindsight mocks earlier projections of Chinese strategic forces for the 1970s and 1980s. Exaggeration of Chinese power was evident in most scenarios for Sino-Soviet war, and it was evident in the dread, the awe, and the fear that the possibility of Sino-Soviet accommodation conjured up in the minds and columns of Western defence writers. Sometimes the fault could be ascribed to the all-too-natural tendency to project from personal experience or bias. More often it reflected a narrowness of focus, whether such revolve around People's Liberation Army (PLA) doctrine or ambition, particular border squirmishes, or some other question or event. Chinese abilities were rarely seen in the full context of Soviet and U.S. power. China's strengths or advantages have often not been sufficiently juxtaposed to her weaknesses, to limitations both of the present and of the foreseeable future. This chapter therefore addresses itself to the essential task or presenting a larger picture of China's military potential relative to that of the Soviet Union and, indirectly, the United States.

The post-World War II evolution of the Soviet-U.S. balance of power is first sketched, to establish the yardstick against which Chinese capabilities and prospects must be judged. This is followed by a review of China's past and present efforts in the strategic arena. The various elements of China's strategic forces are described and assessed. China's strategic force potential of the early 1980s is shown to be analagous to that of the Soviet Union in the mid and late 1950s. China's supporting industrial infrastructure is in fact less developed than was that of the Soviet Union during those years. Beijing's military-technological inferiority vis a vis Moscow in 1980 was greater than that of Moscow vis a vis Washington two and a half decades earlier. The United States had then possessed neither missile defences nor very accurate offensive strike means; this meant that primitive Soviet missiles could be expected to reach target areas when and if fired and that silos and dispersal methods might otherwise ensure their invulnerability. By 1980, on the other hand, the Soviet Union had a deployed Ballistic Missile Defence system around Moscow that would likely ensure the sanctity of the heartland against Chinese attack through the 1980s, and she had established a research and testing program designed to ensure that the advantage would be extended. The Soviet Union had, furthermore, like the United States, developed missiles accurate enough to destroy an opponent's silos and a general intelligence and fast reaction potential that must daunt Chinese strategic planners. Notwithstanding post-Mao advocacies, his prescription for a limited "force de frappe" sufficient to inject an element of uncertainty into an opponent's calculations remained the optimum towards which realistic Chinese defence planning strove. Full superpower status appeared unattainable before the turn of the century, and even that timescale would demand an extraordinarily costly diversion of scarce skills and equipment.

The conventional balance was scarcely less lopsided. The People's Liberation Army of 1980 was probably less potent and certainly less mobile than the Soviet armed forces of 1945. Its logistical capability is flattered by the analogy. In a sense this mattered less as long as doctrine centred on Mao's "People's War" theories, as long as defence by attrition remained the overriding concern. The deficiencies became more glaring and more acute when his successors' preference for "traditional" force structures came to the fore. The buildup to China's 1979 attack on Vietnam and the less than glorious prosecution of that conflict highlighted enduring problems of major proportions.

China had one advantage when compared to the Soviet Union of the 1950s, namely, access to military equipment and technology from abroad. But the access was limited. The United States remained at least somewhat leery of high-technology sales (much as the Soviet Union had been during the days of the Sino-Soviet "alliance"). More importantly, perhaps, was the fact that high technology foreign inputs could not easily be digested by China's military-industrial defence complex. China's production, repair, and servicing capacities could not absorb any major influx, nor could her pool of trained manpower. Finally, there was the point that at least some Chinese leaders continued to look askance at developmental strategies that entailed indebtedness and dependence, whether in the civilian or military spheres. This type of concern was muted after the 1976 ouster of the Gang of Four, but it was not forgotten.

Chapter 2 analyzes "The Roots of Friction: Cultural, Territorial, Geopolitical, and Ideological"—the historical record. It becomes apparent that the irony of 1969, when the border incidents of that year spawned propaganda in both nations depicting the other as the modern reincarnation of the Mongol "scourge," was but one manifestation of a centuries old litany of misunderstandings, fears, and uncertainties. The element of the blind talking to the deaf was evident as early as 1619 when Russian envoys first reached Beijing (offering no tribute, they received no audience).

The maze of territorial disputes, and the conflicting perspectives that have spawned or exacerbated them, is dealt with at some length. This section of Chapter 2 goes back to the late sixteenth century and early seventeenth century Russian settlement of Far East lands and the territories' 1649 annexation by Tsarist fiat; it looks at the Treaties of Nerchinsk (1689) and Kyakhta (1728) when the expanding Manchu empire rolled back the sway of Romanov writ, and discusses the "unequal" Treaties of Aigun and Peking (1858 and 1860), through which Moscow wrested back most of the "lost" territories. The

Karakhan Manifesto of 1919, the Lenin government's renunciation of Tsarist exploitation, is dealt with, as are later interpretations and changes of official postures. The increasingly fervent and personalized anti-Sovietism of Mao was to be a significant factor in the extremism of attitudes adopted by both sides during the late 1960s and early 1970s. Chinese maps made grandiose claims of sovereignty over Soviet Far Eastern and Siberian reaches; the Soviet Union suggested that her version of history would justify further Soviet claims on China. With the enfeeblement and subsequent death of Mao and the ouster of his radical followers during the mid and later 1970s, both Moscow and Beijing reverted to their more moderate stance of late 1964, early 1965. This period, after the removal of Khrushchev and before Mao succeeded in reestablishing his dominance (through the turmoil of the Cultural Revolution), when de facto policy control in Beijing remained in the hands of Liu Shaoqui and Deng Xiaoping, was a time of pragmatic deideologized and depersonalized search for a modus vivendi that would be mutually acceptable. Similarly, by the end of the 1970s Chinese sources put an end to the more extravagant claims of the intervening years; Moscow, for its part, set aside the not too veiled hints of the past that she retained irredentist aspirations of her own. The focus narrowed to stretches of the border that had not been precisely delineated and to Chinese allegations that there were in fact areas where Moscow had encroached beyond 1860 boundary lines. With both sides professing basic acceptance of these lines, however, the disputes appeared eminently negotiable in principle. On the other hand, there remained certain locales, such as the Amur-Ussuri confluence, where particular circumstances and different interpretations and interests ensured that negotiations would not be problem free. The international environment had also changed since the mid 1960s, further complicating prospects for compromise.

Having covered the question of territorial disputes the analysis turns to the sometimes overlooked factor of geographical determinants. Geography played a significant role in fashioning aspirations and demands, especially as concerns Pacific border lands. The Amur-Ussuri river basins and Sakhalin Island (said to have the dairying potential of Denmark) are the only truly fertile regions possessed by the Soviet Union east of Lake Baikal. The permafrost, mountains, and severe climatic conditions of Siberia proper place near-prohibitive penalties on ventures for permanent settlement. The limited acreage favoring habitation therefore became and remains crucially important, as a base and as a processing and transshipment center, to Soviet designs to exploit Siberian resources (on the other hand, it should be noted that the area's size is not sufficient to support the population scale suggested by those who advocate or fear a Chinese assault for purposes of "lebensraum"). The location of Vladivostok and Moscow's reluctance to countenance Japanese claims to the southernmost islands of the Kurile chain reflect on another dictate of geography. Ice limits pose major difficulties for coastal activities further north.

The final section of the chapter delves into the ideological and practical disputes that have affected relations between the Communist Party of the Soviet Union (CPSU) and the Communist Party of China (CPC). Going back to the 1920s, it traces Mao's independent organizing of a peasant nucleus in Hunan; the disapproval of the city-based and Stalin supported CPC "apparat"; the decimation of the latter by Chiang Kaishek forces in the late 1920s and the subsequent flight of many CPC leaders to the sanctuary offered by Mao, the so recently castigated renegade; Chiang's "extermination campaigns" (aided by Nazi officers), and the Long March to Yanan. Mao's estrangement from Moscow ran deep. Stalin had little faith in his chances for success and little liking for his independence of thought and organization. Aid was diverted to Chiang Kaishek's Kuomintang, on the premise that a bourgeois, nationalist, and hence "anticolonial" China was the realizable alternative most likely to serve Soviet interests. Bets were hedged after the Second World War, when Moscow facilitated the establishment of Maoist/CPC control in Manchuria and began a program of more significant material and financial support, but the flow of aid to Chiang was to continue right up until the collapse of his regime in 1949.

When Mao arrived in Moscow to sign the "alliance" treaty he was forced to suffer a rather humiliating wait before the actual start of negotiations; when they finally began, bargaining was hard and pragmatic. Both sides needed the appearance of alliance and fraternity, for the purpose of security against perceived imperialist threats. Lengthy horse trading led to extensive Soviet material, personnel, financial, educational, and military aid, but at a cost in terms of products and produce and also extraterritorial privileges for Moscow that many Chinese considered to be excessive. And while the latter privileges were terminated by Stalin's heirs, the relationship continued to reflect pragmatic bargaining rather than comraderie.

Points of friction accumulated, across the ideological, economic, security, and foreign policy spectrums, until the alliance deathknell was sounded by the Great Leap Forward, unleashed by Mao in 1958. The peasant focus, the drive to decentralize political and economic power ("a smelter in every backyard"), and the frenzied pace of that program—a pace which inevitably led to jolting disruptions and shortages in many sectors of the economy—confirmed all of Moscow's prejudices. Mao came to be seen as a dangerously naive, agrarian, even "petty-bourgeois" zealot whose policies sabotaged the effectiveness of the Soviet-modelled centralized economic structure (and Soviet aid) and whose instincts moreover threatened the control and stability of the (largely Soviet-trained) Party apparat; the program's flagrant disregard for Soviet advice furthermore confirmed Mao's personal unreliability as far as Soviet interests were concerned. With the exception of the final consideration, Moscow's objections and exasperation echoed the attitudes of more traditional CPC leaders, the apparat, the survivors of the original CPC structure, and their allies. Led by Liu Shaoqui and Deng Xiaoping, they succeeded by the early 1960s in maneuvering Mao into de facto retirement by playing on the chaos and ultimate failure of the Great Leap Forward. The degree of entrenchment of their control of Party, governmental, and economic affairs was to be reflected in the fact that Mao's Cultural Revolution comeback some years later had to be engineered from outside and in opposition to CPC organs under the banner of "storm the Party headquarters." Yet Mao's victory was not to be complete. The next decade and a half, until the final reemergence of Deng Xiaoping, was to be wracked by the ebbs and flows of what can best be characterized as a quasi civil war for the body and soul of the Party. That, and the intimately interwoven theme of attitudes toward the Soviet Union, is the topic of Chapter 3.

A related concern, the antecedents of which are studied in Chapter 2, with later manifestations and consequences treated in Chapter 3, is that of ideology—the ideological antipathy between Mao and Soviet leaders, between Mao and his domestic rivals. The ideological struggle was to a large extent the same in both cases, as reflected in Mao's castigation of Liu as "China's Khrushchev," and of Deng, later, as "the new Khrushchev." Equally revealing was Moscow's semi-official commentary after the ouster of the Gang of Four following Mao's death: "the majority of the leaders hostile to the Soviet Union have now been removed from power" (see Chapter 3's note 54).

A concentration on the two antipodes, Mao Zedong and his nemesis and successor Deng Xiaoping, and a stretched but useful analogy with early Soviet leaders and experience serve to place the issues in sharp relief. All analogies are in a sense caricatures, since no two individuals or situations can be exactly alike; yet, a good caricature does highlight essential characteristics and features (even though artists may differ as to the relative importance of particular traits and hence accord them different emphasis or prominence).

A Mao-Lenin analogy inevitably skirts at least some obvious differences. There is no evidence that Mao was as well versed in Marxist thought as was Lenin, nor that he was fully conversant with Leninist dictas. Thus, although he accepted Lenin's prescription for a vanguard Party to funnel, organize, and direct revolutionary aspirations, his impulses always retained a streak of voluntarism reminiscent of the Taiping rebels of the 1850s and 1860s (notwithstanding the fact that Mao himself had seen their voluntarism, and "subjectivism," as the prime cause for their ultimate demise). Mao's stress on the peasantry as the main revolutionary class also went well beyond Lenin's prescriptions. Yet one might see it as but a natural extension of Lenin's original inclusion of the peasantry into his "workers, soldiers, and peasants" trilogy of allies in the cause of Russian revolution, an extension similarly dictated by the circumstances of the time, by the fact that China's "proletariat" was even more miniscule than Russia's of 1917. Mao also was less condemnatory of Han Chinese chauvinism than was Lenin of "Great Russian" tendencies, and his inclinations were less "internationalist." The latter point also distinguishes his radical/fundamentalist allies from their Soviet counterparts, Trotsky and his supporters. (This particular analogy, first developed by this author towards the end of 1975, was later to creep into official Chinese press commentary, after the ouster of the Gang.) Without detracting from that statement, however, one should perhaps point out the degree to which China is, as indeed it has always perceived itself to be, a world apart.

The similarities between the Maoist vision and that of Lenin, between the aspirations of the Chinese radical/fundamentalists and Trotsky, and between the policies (political, economic, and social) of Deng Xiaoping and the early Stalin regime are startling. Mao's push for decentralization echoed Lenin's emphatic stress on government by local councils, Soviets, rather than a central Party apparat. (Stalin's leadership of the emergent apparat after the Revolution occurred largely by default, because Lenin and his more prominent associates chose to exercise their authority through the Council of Ministers, or Commissars, the apex of the Soviet hierarchy.) Both came increasingly to rail against the apparat, Lenin in his "Last Testament" call for Stalin's dismissal, Mao in vituparative diatribes against Deng (and, earlier, against Liu); both saw the dangers of the apparat evolving into a self-serving "new class" of mandarins (Yoguslav critic M. Djilas' categorization of Stalinist reality). As Lenin came to accept most elements of Trotsky's call for "permanent revolution," so Mao accepted the similar thesis of China's radicals. The call for mini Cultural Revolutions every seven years or so became perhaps the most important clarion call of his final decade. To Mao, it came to stand as the absolute, necessary requirement for the future success of his revolution, to avoid the degeneration implied by "new class," to keep revolutionary ideals alive, and to extend the sway and permanence of revolutionary conviction. Finally, there was the related focus on egalitarianism. This point should not be overplayed, since both Mao and Lenin proved capable of ruthlessly exploiting the power of their stature and position against perceived class enemies and counterrevolutionaries (one thinks, for example, of Cultural Revolution excesses and Lenin's suppression of the Kronstadt revolt). In fact, the sometime arrogant, haughty, and dictatorial fashion with which China's radicals sought to speed, direct, and implement egalitarian democracy at the grass roots level has been seen by some as ironic cause of the alienation that in the end gave the advantage to their opponents. Yet, the goal and the conviction are important in themselves, and they are important differentiators between what was and what was to be.

Deng, like Stalin, believed in central Party control, centralized government, and centralized economy. As Stalin replaced vibrant artistic freedom and seeking with more sycophantic "socialist realism," so Deng in 1980 struck down Mao's constitutionally guaranteed "Four Freedoms,"—the rights to "speak out freely, air views fully, hold great debates, and write big character posters." Freedom became an elitist, earned right—a right of the professional, artistic, and governmental elite that supported the regime. Elitism, in fact, became a central characteristic of both reigns. Both introduced greater wage differentiations, a greater reliance on financial bonuses as work incentives, and a more hardnosed attitude towards unemployment. Production took priority over ideology and social goals. Where Mao, as Lenin before him, sought to combine "red and expert," Deng impatiently asserted that it mattered not what color a cat was as long as it caught mice. Stalin would have agreed. Discipline became the cardinal rule, discipline and production—for production's sake. Other criteria were seen as utopian and disruptive to the requirements of future power.

Like Stalin, Deng was confident enough of his control (and hence of his future ability to change course) to encourage extensive foreign investment. On this point Lenin had been more cautious, although appreciative of the advantages to be gained from capitalists' inherent proclivity to compete among themselves, while Mao had been sensitive about the dependence corollary attendant upon foreign financing. Still, the early Deng-dominated government, as that of Stalin during the late 1920s and early and mid 1930s, went beyond established precedence in this regard. And they were both sufficiently rewarded and encouraged by the consequent conversion of their capitalist "partners" to the theory that they therefore represented "moderate" succession regimes. In the words of *The Times Atlas of World History* (published by *The Times* of London, the paragon of traditional conservative values): "Labelled an extremist, by 1925 Trotsky had been manouvered out... Stalin and Bukharin now dominated Soviet politics. Moderation, it seemed, had triumphed." By substituting "radicals" for Trotsky, and Deng Xiaoping and Hua Guofeng for the other gentlemen named, the statement stood as a quintessential summary of Western establishment attitudes to events in China during the latter 1970s and early 1980s.

The parallel between Deng and Stalin has a limitation. The Deng regime did institute a ruthless purge from office of radical-fundamentalist officials and followers, yet the perverse paranoia and death rates of the Stalinist purges appeared to be absent—a not immaterial difference. On the other hand, there can be no question that the policies of the two regimes showed astounding similarities in practically every field of Party and government endeavor. And that suggests a final point of some import, namely that Deng's efforts echoed the Stalinist concept of "socialism in one country." The noteworthy aspect of that concept lies in its explicit emphasis on nationalism, as opposed to internationalism, on self-interest rather than extended solidarity. This meant that while governing theory and practice in Deng's China parallelled that of early Stalinist Russia, and to a significant extent also that of post-Stalinist Russia, total communion of interest was neither automatic nor likely. With pragmatic self-interest ensconced at both sides of the table accommodation was possible and perhaps probable; full unity of interest or purpose was not.

In effect, Chapter 3 charts the evolution of domestic Chinese power struggles, the fortunes of various factional interests, their policy programs, and their compromises, with particular attention paid throughout to the intimate role played by Sino-Soviet relations—both as substance and, perhaps more to the point, as symbol. Soviet reaction to this phenomenon, Soviet exasperation at the impotence implied by its corollary that interstate relations remained hostage to currents over which little control could be exercised, and the ramifications of this on Soviet politics, is traced in some detail. China's limited rapprochement with Washington after 1971 and the degree to which that relationship was a function of and dependent on the course of more basic policy debates in Beijing is also dealt with. The chapter ends with an analysis of Deng's final rehabilitation in 1977 and the subsequent establishment of a not always harmonious Hua Guofeng-Deng Xiaoping compromise regime. One intriguing aspect of the political maneuvering on which that compromise floated is suggested by evidence that Hua Guofeng, the pro forma architect of the arrest of the Gang of Four in 1976, was now seeking to rally residual radical/fundamentalist strength to his cause in order to stem the tide favoring Deng preeminence. Again, the prominence and importance of Sino-Soviet symbolism as a tool and weathervane of domestic Chinese politics is evident.

Chapter 4 looks at ramifications on and for the external environment. Concentrating on the late 1970s after the death of the Chairman, it traces the impact of the Moscow-Beijing interaction on the two actors' policies towards third countries and areas, towards Europe, towards Africa and the Near and Middle East, towards Japan, and towards Southeast Asia. It deals with Moscow's increasing impatience at the fact that Mao's death did not solve the impasse, at the fact that the domestic Chinese struggle for power, though clearly shifting ground, nevertheless remained fluid and unresolved, and at the fact that her ability to influence events remained minimal. Soviet impatience was reflected in evidence of renewed interest in containment-type policies and the preparation of contingency options. The spectre of possible Sino-U.S. alliance led to increased Soviet assertiveness (rather than hamstringing, as envisaged by Washington proponents of such alliance prospects). A "China-consideration" could be discerned in forward Soviet policies in Yemen, Afghanistan, other peripheral locales, and, most notably, in Indochina. Alliance with Vietnam allowed Moscow for the first time to present to Chinese strategic planners the kind of two-front spectre that China's geopolitical locale had posited to Soviet planners. Furthermore, while Soviet military options along the border had previously been restricted to the largely ineffectual (border skirmishes) or to the overly dramatic (major incursions, whether nuclear or non-nuclear), the Vietnam tie opened a pandora's box of potential as concerns medium-level action and pressure possibilities.

The analysis then focuses on the events leading up to China's February 1979 invasion of northern Vietnam, the course of that campaign, and its eventual termination. It looks at the many motives that underlay China's action and juxtaposes these rationales to the final outcome, weighing achievement and failure. The extent, success, and cost of Moscow's aid to its ally is similarly assessed, as is the performance of the Vietnamese. The detailed analysis of the conflict leads inexorably to the conclusion that China's main ambitions were not realized (she did not succeed in changing the course of events in

Laos or Cambodia, nor in weakening the Soviet-Vietnamese alliance); Vietnam succeeded again in teaching a larger power not to presume on apparent power discrepancies (the cost was substantial, but offset by the fact that the conflict diverted attention from economic failures and legitimized the reestablishment of a war economy, a mobilized command economy); Moscow, on the other hand, appears to have involved herself just enough to prove she would not desert an ally in need, just enough to live up to her own obligations without sullying the useful propaganda image of Chinese aggression. Yet while China's main ambitions may have been thwarted, there is evidence that at least some of her leaders expected failure and, in fact, found the domestic repercussions of such failure to justify the venture. Clearly the demonstration of "will" (as opposed to capability) was also thought to have intrinsic value. The net result is a plausible case for the proposition that this was one of those unique wars of history from which apparent victors and apparent vanquished could both draw satisfaction, from which both sides could claim a degree of victory.

Chapter 5 covers the "Phoney War" state of political-military maneuvering that followed China's withdrawal from Vietnam, the resumption and floundering of Sino-Soviet and Sino-Vietnamese negotiations, and the apparently stepped-up jostling for position within Chinese policy-making councils that unfolded as 1979 progressed. China's conditional pursuit of the relationship with Washington is discussed, as is the impact of certain not-so-extraneous events, most notably the Soviet intervention in Afghanistan. Soviet motives for and action in Afghanistan are analyzed, with due regard to the primary determinants of internal Afghan (and Soviet) events, but with special attention paid also to the role of and consequences for Moscow's posture vis a vis China and the United States. The ensuing quasi Cold War polarization of the international environment is treated at some length, with particular reference to China's cautious alignment with U.S. interests. The chapter ends with a discussion of the events of early 1980 when Deng finally succeeded in appointing many of his closest associates to central Politburo, Party Secretariat, and governmental posts; there followed a slight though distinct chilling of attitudes towards Washington and a declaration that renewed talks with Moscow was a definite possibility. The 1980s thus opened with the ensconcement in Beijing of perhaps the most self-assuredly pragmatic and independent Chinese regime of modern history.

Chapter 6 diverts attention to "The Third Actor: The Soviet Far East-Manchuria-Japan Triangle." As noted in the opening paragraph: "Japan is the joker in the Sino-Soviet pack, the third actor who for geopolitical, economic, and other reasons could become the most crucial external variable affecting the future course of Sino-Soviet relations." The presentation sketches the turbulent history of Japan's relations with her continental neighbors and analyzes the legacy of that history in residual territorial disputes and cultural antipathies. It is a legacy that can stand as a classic case of how the process of ethnocentric interpretation can provide different nations with diametrically opposed views of the historical record. Self-serving, selective, chauvinist prisms ensured not only that versions of events differed, but led also to a near total lack of empathy or understanding for different perceptions.

The treatment of the historical record and its continued relevance for contemporary disputes and attitudes is followed by an in-depth look at economic and security-related problems and issues. Japan's extraordinary resource dependence and vulnerability, especially as concerns energy requirements, is the subject of lengthy discussion. The analysis looks at the scale and character of Japan's fuel dependence, the political uncertainties plaguing Mid East sources of oil, the restrictions imposed on uranium availability by the United States, Canada, and Australia, and Japan's attempts to lessen its exposure to the vagaries of extraneous political currents through diversification of both exports and imports. The extent and limits of compatibility between Japan's economy and those of the Soviet Union and China is scrutinized. On purely economic grounds there is scant doubt that a stable coupling of Japan's scientific-technological prowess to her continental neighbors' resource and labour abundance (the former most pronounced in the Soviet Union, the latter in China) would warrant the most grandiose expectations. And while certain caveats might be attached to the prognosis as concerns Sino-Japanese complementarity, caveats derived both from China's present sociopolitical, developmental realities and from the nature of her current modernization plans, Soviet-Japanese prospects are not similarly encumbered. But while the economic vistas conjured up by the possibility of further Soviet-Japanese convergence are alluring and indeed compelling when viewed in isolation, they remain stymied by fundamental differences in other spheres of policy. The investigation consequently proceeds to a focus on the political and security-related issues that continue to exert major influence on the pace and nature of Japan's relations with Moscow and, to a lesser extent, Beijing.

The final section of the book—"Conclusion: Future Prospects"—draws together the threads of the preceding coverage of historical, territorial, cultural, ideological, sociopolitical, economic, security, and foreign policy issues that have affected and continue to affect the Sino-Soviet relationship. It looks at the implications of Deng Xiaoping's emerging preeminence, his early 1980s dominance of Beijing policy and appointments (the composite picutre that emerges evokes comparisons with the France of General de Gaulle), and at the relevance and repurcussions of succession in Moscow. The Conclusion seeks to establish the parameters likely to shape future Sino-Soviet ties. Probable and possible areas of accommodation and compromise are delineated, as are areas conducive to continuing friction and discord. The major determinants of policy are shown to be internal and bilateral. The attitude and posture of the United States, though far from irrelevant, appeared to have become less central when seen through the eyes of Moscow or Beijing than when viewed through U.S. lenses. As concerns Sino-U.S. ties, this implied that China felt freer to play the "American card" for tactical advantage and reason; China's attitude towards her "American card" appeared more calculatingly manipulative than was Washington's stance vis a vis its "China card." A strong argument could be made for the proposition that China in particular, but also the Soviet Union, entered the 1980s with governments that perceived themselves as freer to pursue policies of pragmatic self-interest than had previously been the case. It was a perception that extended both to policies towards each . other, and to their posture towards third countries.

Finally, a note on sources. Some topics covered rest on a wealth of easily accessible source material: Soviet, Chinese, U.S., Japanese, and other. This is especially true of the survey of strategic realities, of the historical sections, the treatment of economic considerations, and the discussion of ideological precepts. Other parts of the study, such as that which treats the Sino-Vietnamese War of 1979, are more difficult to document. Where official reports are thought too encumbered by particular biases, by narrow political interests of the moment, the search for balance has led to a greater weight being assigned to the reports of the better journalists in the field and to extensive personal interviews—interviews which by their nature must remain confidential. Even the best journalism, the most diligent and widely-cast search for corroborative evidence and the acutest of personal observations, cannot suffice to fill every gap of knowledge as concerns more recent events. But a full composite of available sources does bring the picture into clearer focus than would be possible on the basis of any one source or any one type of source. Final judgment awaits later history.

MAP 1.   East Asia

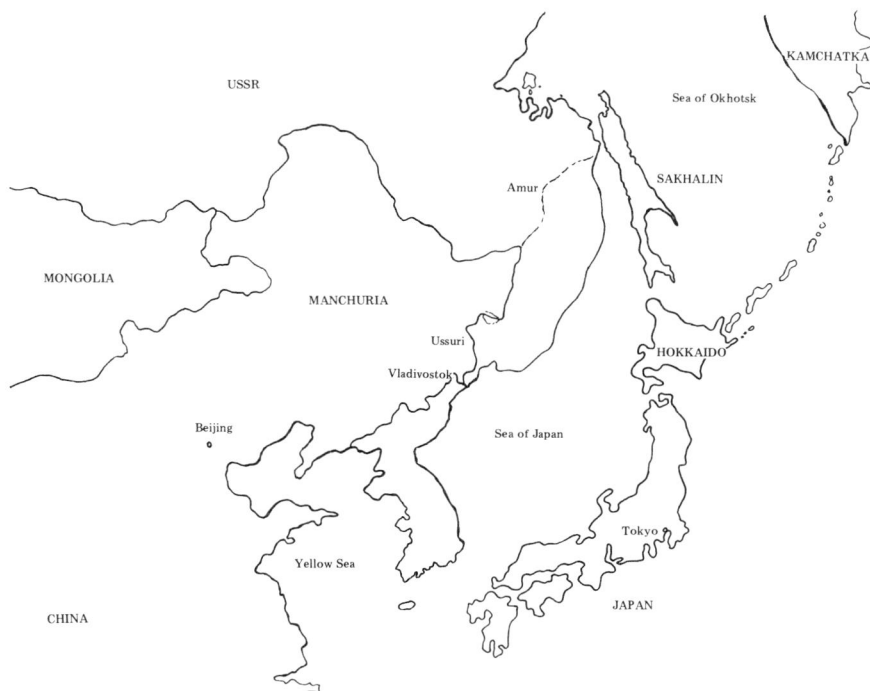

MAP 2.   Soviet Far East—Manchuria—Japan Triangle

1 THE STRATEGIC CONTEXT

Sino-Soviet relations since the death of Mao Zedong, as in the final years of his life, have been characterized by a high degree of surface tension. The tension oscillated, from low simmer through dazzling eruption and back to low heat, but it was never absent. Some of the extremes of public antagonism have been engineered for domestic benefit. The Damansky/Zhen Bao border skirmishes of 1969 provided the patriotic glue to allow Beijing to call a Party Congress long delayed by protracted and intense domestic policy differences. China's early 1979 incursion into northern Vietnam served similar purposes (though this effect may have been a coincidental benefit rather than a causal consideration).[1] Some of the intermittent calls for border negotiations, on the other hand, were clearly bids for temporary, tactical advantage, in that they were accompanied by preconditions and posturing that appeared calculated to preclude or sabotage fruitful bargaining. Nevertheless, although the apparent highs and lows of public tension were often deceptive, the roots of antagonism were real, deep, and complex. The danger of war, while generally not acute, was rarely altogether absent. It therefore appears fitting to begin this analysis of Sino-Soviet relations by setting out the military-strategic parameters within which the war spectre must be judged. The military-strategic balance of power furthermore provides a crude but vital context for the interplay of other considerations.

The evolution of Soviet military prowess since the Second World War will first be sketched,[2] as the backdrop tapestry against which China's more limited capabilities and potential may be gauged. There are marked parallels, though also certain notable anomalies, between the military power of China today and that of the Soviet Union of 1956–57. Against an opponent with an unquestioned capacity to devastate her, China's damage-inflicting ability is limited. The deterrence value of present and foreseeable Chinese capabilities, even when these are maximized through secrecy and propaganda-generated uncertainties, remains far from absolute, and its credibility therefore depends on the degree to which China does not pose an absolute security threat to the Soviet Union. It is the classic stance of the weaker power, that its defeat will be viewed as promising only limited benefit and therefore not as something worthy of disproportionate cost or effort. It is a posture of relative deterrence, espoused by China, by Sweden, by all whose means are less than possessed by others.

The Soviet Union of 1956–57 was a nuclear power with a multimillion standing army honed in the tank and combined-arms operations perfected during World War II's final phase. She has shorter-range missiles and was capable of inflicting severe punishment on Western Europe, on the outer reaches of the U.S. dominated world. But her long-range bomber capacity was poor in quality, scarce in quantity, and its penetration potential against U.S. home defences was highly dubious. Washington could obliterate Soviet society; Moscow could not reciprocate.

The first intercontinental range missiles (ICBMs), deployed through the latter 1950s, were seen to redress the imbalance. But it was soon realized that the missiles, their fuel, and their command and control systems were subject to a plethora of faults and inadequacies, so much so that perhaps only 10 or 15 percent could realistically be expected to reach designated targets (this would have meant two or three by 1959). To make matters worse, it would take one to two weeks to get them ready for firing, and during this time their above-ground deployment made them eminently vulnerable to U.S. bomber attack. Rather than balancing the strategic equation, Soviet ICBMs served to fuel exaggerated U.S. fears (the "missile-gap myth"), fears which led to U.S. ICBM procurement rates that the then Soviet industry could not hope to emulate and which hence ultimately exacerbated Soviet inferiority.

The early 1960s saw a multipronged Soviet effort aimed at securing the invulnerability of the limited forces at their disposal. The navy, originally believed to have become redundant with the advent of missiles, was now seen as necessary to maximum missile dispersal and survivability. Missiles were put to sea. On land, protective silos were constructed and mobile missile launchers experimented with. Missile quality, fuel storability, and command and control efficiency were all upgraded. Work on ballistic missile defences, tentatively begun already by the time of the first ICBM tests, was accelerated, leading to the deployment of a still very primitive proto- type system around Leningrad in 1961. By 1964 the first operational system was ready to be installed, around Moscow.[3] The Soviet Union was acquiring a true second strike force, a force essentially immune from immediate destruction. This eliminated the "temptation syndrome" to strike first, which had been associated with high vulnerability (and which had been made more acute by a state of intelligence that allowed for instances of Canadian geese being "read" by U.S. radar scanners as incoming Soviet bomber squadrons).

Early Soviet missile defence efforts were not emulated by the United States, due to the professed belief that they were cost ineffec- tive and that such effectiveness as they might achieve could be offset at less cost by increasing U.S. offensive capabilities. Nevertheless, the perceived military requirement for "worst case" planning, to counter intelligence deficiencies by a sometimes ludicrous maximizing of enemy potentials, escalated the requirements associated with offensive improvements. While the Soviet Union concentrated on improving its missile defence the United States produced an ever more sophisti- cated array of penetration aids (decoys) designed to confuse target identification and saturate defence capabilities. This process led eventually to the use of multiple warheads, at first free-fall, then individually targetable: Multiple Independently-targeted Reentry Vehicles (MIRVs) and a subsequent variant, Maneuverable Reentry Vehicles (MARVs).

The U.S.'s pioneering of MIRVs entailed a saturation potential that could not be countered by then existing or immediately fore- seeable defence technologies. In acknowledgement of this prospect the Soviet Union began, about 1966–67, to redirect its efforts. Further Ballistic Missile Defence (BMD) deployments were deferred, in favor of concentration on research. Civil defence programs were stepped up in order to perpetuate at least a modicum level of surviv- ability, if not defence. And the offensive Strategic Rocket Troops received increased priority. Moscow initiated a quantitative procure- ment spurt that was to equal and then surpass U.S. missile numbers by the early 1970s (although Soviet missile booster superiority would be balanced by continued U.S. bomber advantages); this was coupled with a drive to catch up in the qualitative realm of multiple warhead abilities. Extensive Soviet MIRV testing in 1974 led to rapid deployment thereafter.

The late 1960s and early 1970s, the years of U.S. MIRV mono- poly and consequent Soviet deemphasis of defence, witnessed the irony of U.S. pursuit of that once maligned goal. Evidence of Soviet improvements, buttressed by indigenous U.S. research results, led to Washington appreciation of changing "cost-exchange" ratios (this measures the relation between the cost of a defence and the cost of the offence needed to negate it). It was realized that available defence technologies held promise against single-warhead missiles, and that limited defence ambitions against such missiles could now be implemented without undue financial penalty. While Soviet BMD had been emasculated by U.S. MIRV potentials, less-developed U.S. defence prospects retained disproportionate promise due to continued Soviet reliance on single-warhead missiles. It was only with U.S. realization of imminent Soviet MIRV mastery that the Strategic Arms Limitation Talks agreement of 1972 (SALT I) could be signed. It placed a "cap" on offensive quantities, a cap largely irrelevant militarily, since both powers clearly now believed that offensive force improvement could best be effected through qualitative avenues, but one that held considerable political significance. It appeared to demonstrate that superpower negotiations could be fruitful and hence cemented the appearance of detente. A similar comment applies to SALT I's other provision: the limiting of BMD deployments to two and then just one site. In the face of MIRV the pro forma abandonment of BMD extension designs caused no discomfort to either side's military establishment; it merely certified the mutually acknowledged consequences of the "state of the art" of the respective technologies.

Having caught up with the United States in offensive delivery vehicle numbers by the early 1970s, and catching up in quality, Moscow focused through the remaining 1970s on two routes to incremental advantage.[4] One lay in a steady upgrading of her general forces' war-fighting abilities and the pursuit of such global power projection capabilities as might offset also the wider panoply of nonstrategic U.S. force advantage. By the end of the decade she had not yet equalled U.S. interventionary potentials, but she had established her own capacity to act and react in distant arenas. A Soviet alliance prospect became credible in areas previously associated with Western military impunity, and this wrought a dramatic change to the international environment in general, to Third World power calculations in particular.

Moscow's second focus stemmed from a determination to guard against the possibility that Western Anti-Submarine Warfare (ASW) breakthroughs might jeopardize the survivability of her Submarine Launched Ballistic Missiles (SLBMs). The short range of early SLBMs had necessitated firing locations close to enemy shores, in waters dominated by hostile ASW concentrations. To some extent Moscow circumvented the danger by developing an ability to operate in and through Arctic waters, by establishing less threatened Arctic transit routes. But the main emphasis was placed on the perfecting of intercontinental range SLBMs that could be fired from secure home waters. By 1972 she was able to begin deploying Delta I class submarines capable of reaching U.S. targets from the Barents Sea.

The late 1970s saw the establishing of the Okhotsk Sea in the Far East as a second area of SLBM concentration, as the second area in which SLBM forces could safely be "withheld" if so desired (for intrawar bargaining and war termination leverage).[5] The 8100–9000 km. range of the "MIRVed" SS–N–18 Delta III missiles now being deployed (as opposed to some 7700 km. for the SS–N–8 Delta I and II missiles) placed the Okhotsk within reach of all major targets. Increasing Delta numbers, the wish not to put all eggs in one basket, and the 1970s' development of a much more formidable Far East land, sea, and air support infrastructure were factors that contributed to the Okhotsk development. It should be noted that while the existence of the infrastructure was in part a heritage of Sino-Soviet tension, the Okhotsk deployment of Delta II vessels was coincidental to that tension, a function only of the U.S.-Soviet context. Shorter-range Yankee class SLBMs capable of covering Chinese targets had been assigned to the Pacific Fleet/Okhotsk already by 1968. On the other hand, the presence of Delta boats obviously increased the area's general importance to Soviet strategic planning. And some of the means assembled to insure Okhotsk inviolability, like the Backfire bombers assigned to naval aviation and the new Minsk Vertical Take-Off and Landing (VTOL) aircraft carrier, did also serve to significantly extend Soviet options for action against China.

In fact, the 1979 arrival of the Minsk exemplified the difficulty of distinguishing between a multiplicity of strategic and other considerations. Thus there can be little doubt that its assignment provided added insurance of Delta survivability. Yet, the date of its dispatch from the Black Sea, scene of its shakedown cruises, startled Western naval analysts accustomed to longer trial periods and obviously mirrored Soviet impatience to secure its presence. That impatience was clearly related to China's early 1979 incursion into northern Vietnam and her subsequent withdrawal. The Minsk symbolized Soviet ability to provide effective support to initiate action from the south and east as well as from northerly and westerly directions. It reconfirmed the implications of the Soviet-Vietnamese alliance that was forged during 1977-79. Chinese planners were forced, for the first time, to face the same spectre that they had long posited to

Moscow, namely, the possibility of two-front war. Furthermore, whereas Soviet options for military pressure on China had previously been restricted to too little (border skirmishes) or what would normally be seen as too much (nuclear war), the alliance with Hanoi provided a range of possibilities for medium-level pressure.[6]

But before delving more specifically into Chinese power realities, and constraints, into the immediate Sino-Soviet military balance, one must first return to the question of Soviet missile defence capabilities.[7] The arresting point about SALT I was that some missile defence was allowed at all, in spite of its impotence against MIRVs. Even more arresting was the evidence that accumulated as the 1970s wore on of increasing levels of Soviet BMD research funding. The answer of course lay in the fact the MIRV technology was likely to remain a U.S.-Soviet preserve for the foreseeable future. While Moscow had been forced to concede Mutual Assured Vulnerability (or Mutual Assured Destruction, MAD) as the unavoidable corollary of current superpower technologies, she did not feel similarly compelled to concede third power penetration capabilities. The defence of the Moscow heartland, already in place (and supplemented by a SALT-condoned "testing" range in Central Asia), was seen as providing a decisive advantage for possible confrontations with China or other nuclear aspirants. The stepped-up research into improved endoatmospheric Anti-Ballistic Missile (ABM) types, new mobile radars, and, increasingly, novel interceptor concepts based on high energy laser and particle beam potentials was fuelled by Moscow's determination to perpetuate this advantage. The ultimate hope of securing an effective defence against the other superpower, so long a Soviet goal, may be presumed to have helped oil the bureaucratic budgetary process. But the more realizable immediate aspiration clearly centered on the emasculation of lesser threats.

Like the Soviet Union of the mid 1950s the China of 1980 was a nuclear power with a multimillion man standing army; yet hers was an army even less equipped for offensive modern warfare.[8] China's economy and her scientific-technological infrastructure in general was less advanced than that of the Soviet Union some two and a half decades earlier. China possessed one advantage not then enjoyed by Moscow, namely, access to Western credits and Western technology. This access was not unrestricted, however. Quite apart from domestic Chinese economic and ideological constraints, the West remained leery of at least certain high-technology exports. Although tempted by profits sorely needed by their recession-plagued industries and lured by the implications of the old adage that your enemy's enemy is your friend, Western governments, nevertheless, remained ambivalent about the wisdom of easing China's road to military superpower status. Thus there appeared to be little prospect that Washington would dispense the kind of information that might allow for crucial Chinese breakthroughs (even presuming the by-no-means-certain ability of Chinese industry to follow through). The high tension aftermath of the December 1979 Soviet intervention in Afghanistan and U.S. Secretary of Defense Brown's (long scheduled) January 1980 visit to Beijing brought U.S. willingness "to sell military support equipment to China." It was, however, stressed that such equipment would be "non-lethal."[9]

China had acquired short and medium-range missiles, and she had a number of medium-range bombers based on older Soviet designs. She could with some confidence expect to be able to inflict punishment on targets in the Soviet Far East, in southern Siberia, and in Central Asian Republics. But her longer range capability had not evolved as originally expected. U.S. Defence Department analysts had thought that limited Chinese ICBM capability was imminent by the late 1960s;[10] by the late 1970s there were conflicting reports that China might be on the verge of deploying a small number of ICBMs, but numbers exceeding a handful remained a prospect for the future rather than a reality of the present.[11]

It appeared questionable whether Chinese ICBM numbers of the early or mid 1980s would exceed the capacities of the 64 Soviet ABM sites established around Moscow since the mid 1960s, or the 100 ABM sites authorized by SALT I (as amended in 1974). Even if a somewhat larger number could be procured, there was the question of how many could be considered effective; there seemed little reason to presume that early-generation Chinese missiles were less prone to faults than those of the Soviet Union of the United States had been.[12] But even if the Chinese prove capable of effecting the numbers–sophistication mix to saturate SALT I designated defences, this might not prove sufficient to offset future Soviet ability and determination to preserve the inviolability of the capital. That would depend on the success of Moscow's ongoing BMD research efforts. As noted above, the funding of that effort testifies to the fact that Moscow does not deem Chinese penetration ability to be inevitable.

The contrast between the early-generational character of Chinese missile and command and control systems and Moscow's far more sophisticated intelligence (satellites), information sifting, and processing and command reaction procedures, is so consequential that a Soviet response might conceivably be capable of aborting the preparation-for-firing process that triggered it. China has attempted to maximize the survival prospects of her limited missile forces through the widest possible dispersal and through optimum utilization of the natural obstacles and camouflage afforded by mountainous terrain. Nevertheless, her ability to surprise, to generate uncertainty of success (viz. above), it may well be that Chinese leaders' denial of superpower ambitions should be taken at face today is immeasurably better than was U.S. intelligence during the late 1950s; modern satellite detection leaves little room for concealment.

The problems associated with a Chinese drive towards true military superpower status are indeed immense. The financial, industrial, and scientific-technological manpower drain would severely strain China's more general socioindustrial aspirations. In view also of the uncertainty of success (viz. above), it may well be that Chinese leaders' denial of superpower ambitions should be taken at face value. There are many analysts who believe that China will remain satisfied with "minimum deterrence." She may continue to rely on her probable ability to strike at adjacent regions coupled with at least a possible potential against targets more crucial to an antagonist's survival, as enough of a threat to offset any benefit that the antagonist might hope to derive from action against her.

This does admittedly echo complacent Western assumptions about Soviet prospects during the early 1960s. Those assumptions, however, rested largely on ignorance of Soviet strategic literature. Acquaintance with that literature would have made it abundantly clear that Soviet leaders were determined not to accept perpetual inferiority. There is no similar volume of Chinese literature in the field of "strategic studies," so similar evidence of China's attitude is not available. But there is evidence of a very considerable difference between China's view of the wider world context at the beginning of the 1980s and Moscow's view of the world context two decades earlier. China's late 1970s' approaches to the United States, Japan, and Western Europe appeared to reflect appreciation of the multipolar nature of world political and economic power, as well as awareness of the potential for manipulation that was inherent in any contact with a military power that could confront her adversary on equal terms. There were opportunities for alliances or suggestions of alliances that might have at least a measure of deterrence value. China was in a position where she could, in the tradition of weaker powers, augment the relative deterrence of her own military means through formal or informal alignment with other nations.

The Soviet Union, on the other hand, had found herself in a zero-sum context. She had no formidable military ally to shield her and guarantee her ultimate survival (as did France and the United Kingdom), and she could find no source of political or economic support of consequence—no source from which she could derive relative succor (of the type available to China). Other potential sources of political-economic power were all tied umbilically to her main military opponent. Thus advantages enjoyed by that opponent were absolute, in the sense that they were direct reflections of Soviet disadvantages. It was a situation that could be tolerated as a temporary phenomenon. But acquiescence in its permanence would make a mockery of her ideological pretensions as godmother to a new socioeconomic, politic reality, and it would torpedo her national aspiration to leadership and protector of a self-contained independent alliance system. If she was not to abrogate her ideological beliefs and her self-perception as a nation, she had to strive for the means necessary to deter perceived threats. To sustain her existing alliance commitments and to make future commitments credible, the Soviet Union had to develop the wherewithall to stand up to possible challenges, and she had to do it herself. That she succeeded was a tribute in part to her industrial and scientific-educational base, in part to the depth of her determination and her consequent ability to divert the required resources, and, finally and ironically, it may be said to owe something to the U.S. involvement in Vietnam. (That the United States for so many years had to divert between a quarter and a third of its military budget to Vietnam-related endeavors, at a time when the overall military expenditures of the "superpowers" was thought to be roughly equivalent, obviously entailed a cushion permitting the Soviet Union to spend more on research and development.)

Before turning to an examination of the particulars of the Sino-Soviet border confrontation, some further comment must be made on the general state of the opposing armed forces. Soviet "nonstrategic" forces, already more mechanized by 1956–57 than Chinese forces entering the 1980s, have gone through at least two notable developmental stages during the intervening years.[13] The first stage was a response to the Soviet belief that the advent of nuclear weaponry would revolutionize the annals of warfare as thoroughly as had gunpowder. The manpower contractions that Soviet armed forces underwent during the later 1950s reflected this belief, as well as the corollary assumption that manpower could now safely be diverted to meet the pressing needs of the civilian economy. The point is that Soviet forces entered a process of "nuclearization" more extensive and more comprehensive than any effected in the West. The Soviet Union chose not to emulate the Western preference for keeping nuclear and non-nuclear forces in clearly separate compartments. Expecting a major conflagration to be nuclear, she chose rather to effect the widest possible distribution of nuclear war-fighting capability. Individual soldiers were provided protective masks and clothing; tanks and other equipment were designed to be able to operate in a nuclear environment.

The second stage, increasingly prominent as the 1970s progressed, saw no dilution of the belief that a major conflagration would be nuclear, but it saw increased emphasis on the possibility of localized non-nuclear wars—conducted under the umbrella of ever-present nuclear potentials. The emphasis was encouraged by the development of ever more potent "conventional" technology: "smart bombs" and the like. New tanks and armored personnel carriers were complemented by helicopter gunships able to sweep forward areas. Motor rifle battalions were trained and equipped with a new range of transport helicopters. Improved fighter-bombers capable of long range interdiction of enemy reserve, supply, and communication lines and able to provide sustained and aggressive ground support were procured. The stress was on combined arms, combined central command, leapfrogging into the enemy rear, air and helicopter sweeping, and disruption of enemy front and rear, followed by the vigorous advance of tank and antitank units for punch and envelopment.

China's forces are less mechanized, less motorized; they are not similarly prepared for the eventuality of nuclear war, and their logistical capabilities are far more suspect. These factors lay at the core of the Maoist preference for large numbers, trained to afflict maximum rates of attrition on invading forces, capable of resorting to guerilla tactics, and sustained by an extensive network of local depots and supplies, but patently unable to project power very far from home territory. The post-Mao trend towards more mobile and modern, if also more traditional, formations represents an ambition, not an actuality. Though of questionable authenticity, the spring 1979 rumour that People's Liberation Army officers had supported the attack on Vietnam in part due to an expectation of heavy losses and the calculation that these might serve as a dramatic stimulus to their budgetary aspirations does reflect on real inadequacies.[14] China could possibly take and hold certain territories immediately adjacent to her border. But longer term occupation of even limited areas would appear to be a dubious proposition,[15] the more so if one conceded the oft-expressed Soviet intent to use nuclear weaponry if and when necessary (nuclear mining of mountain passes and other natural funnels for a Chinese advance would have to be expected).

China long tended to belittle the nuclear option, much as Stalin did during the late 1940s and for much the same reason. To acknowledge its consequences would have meant admission of morale-shattering inferiority; in both cases the public posture screened a level of research funding that bespoke starkly different private appreciations. China's subsequent attempt to assert her immunity through the digging of shelter and evacuation tunnels under her major cities has been equally deprecated by most Western military observers. Here again, as perhaps also with Soviet civil defence efforts, the factors of morale, domestic perception, and societal cohesion may have been more weighty than the pro forma rationales. One may presume that the nuclear eventuality is most unlikely, that it will only be resorted to under perceptions of dire need. But one cannot discuss the Sino-Soviet military balance merely in terms of long-range strategic abilities on the one hand, and local conventional capabilities on the other. Soviet medium-range missiles covering China are not restricted by SALT (the sole concern of SALT I and II negotiations was intercontinental delivery vehicles). Soviet nuclear means in place in the Far East at the end of the 1970s, from the MIRVed and mobile SS-20 missile down through short-range "tactical" nuclear delivery modes, were of a different order than those of China. And the difference was real, not theoretical. The dual-capable delivery systems that China was negotiating to buy from the West (late 1970s' negotiations centered on the British Harrier jet) promised some relief. Yet, few observers thought the imbalance could be fully redressed within a foreseeable future, either through China's efforts alone, or with the additional increment of such foreign purchases as seemed likely (in view both of Chinese payment difficulties and Western reticence, or ambivalence).

Following the buildups occasioned by the border clashes of 1969, the forces facing each other across the Sino-Soviet border remained quantitatively stable through the remainder of the 1970s.[16] China maintained about 55 "main force" divisions plus about 25 "local forces" divisions in the north and northeast (Shenyang and Beijing military regions), with at least 15 main force and eight local forces divisions in northwesterly provinces (Lanzhou and Xinjiang military regions).[17] All in all, about 40 percent of the People's Liberation Army was deployed in areas contiguous to or relevant for the 4160 mile common border with the Soviet Union.[18] Tensions on the Sino-Vietnam border were to cause some diversion from the northern force concentration. The north and northeast lost three main force divisions, while the northwest lost two. But four more local forces divisions were added to each total to make up for the loss.[19]

Opposing Soviet forces (in the Central Asian, Siberian, Trans-baikal, and Far Eastern military districts) rose from 33 in 1970 to 44 by 1972. Soviet division numbers in Mongolia remained at two.

1974 saw 45 divisions along the Sino-Soviet border, still two in Mongolia.[20] By 1978 the first figure stood at 44, including about six tank divisions and with an airborne division in the process of assembly; the Mongolian presence rose to three.[21] Soviet force levels involved in the confrontation with China represented about 25 percent of the Soviet armed forces.[22] It should be noted, however, that the early 1970s' buildup was effected without detriment to her forces facing NATO.[23] The increment was drawn, rather, from interior regions and new formations. It should also be pointed out that less than half of the Soviet divisions deployed along the border were "Category 1" (between three-quarters and full strength, with complete equipment).[24] The rest were "Category 2" (between half and three-quarters manning, all equipment) or "Category 3" (about one-quarter strength, though probably also complete with fighting vehicles).

The relatively modest level of Soviet effort was underlined by considerations of cost. According to U.S. government sources, Soviet forces aimed at China took about 11 percent of the total military budget between 1964 and 1976. The same sources assert that during these 12 years the growth in the Soviets' level of military effort that could be attributed to a buildup in the Far East averaged roughly 15 percent (the remaining 85 percent was said to be allocated to strategic nuclear forces and forces deployed opposite NATO in Europe). On the other hand, there could be no doubt that Soviet leaders viewed their eastern and southeastern security situation with concern. The Far Eastern military district and Pacific Fleet commander positions carried with them automatic elevation to Candidate member status in the select Central Committee of the Communist Party of the Soviet Union (CPSU).

The Chinese navy grew by nearly 50 percent in personnel numbers during the 1970s, yet at the end of the decade her tally of 25 not-overly-sophisticated major surface combat vessels remained greatly outmatched by Soviet Pacific Fleet elements.[25] China's one submarine designed as a missile launch platform still had no missiles. She only had one nuclear-powered submarine. Her general submarine total (91 by 1979), her destroyer complement (11), as well as what she could field of other classes of consequence, all fell short both quantitatively and qualitatively by comparison with the Soviet Pacific Fleet. Even newer Chinese vessels suffered from technological deficiencies and sometime obsolescence. Short range was a general characteristic. In effect, the Chinese navy remained a coastal defence force with limited prospects against more modern naval concentrations.

The Soviet Pacific Fleet saw a slight contraction in total submarine numbers during this period, from 105 to 100, but the decline was offset by rapid nuclearization: by 1974 there were 40 nuclear-powered submarines, by 1978 there were 55. The start of Delta II class submarine construction also at Komsomolsk on the Amur (Delta Is had been built only at Severodvinsk in the north) promised to speed up the nuclear acquisition rate still further. Soviet Pacific Fleet numbers of advanced rocket destroyers rose from four in 1968 through nine in 1975 to 15 in 1978; rocket cruiser figures rose from two in 1968 to three in 1975 to six in 1978. By the end of that year it was clear that these would be joined by the Minsk carrier. It was to be accompanied by the Ivan Rogov, precursor of a new Soviet class of large amphibious assault vessels carrying surface effect landing craft capable of 50 mph.[26] The Pacific Fleet was being assigned both a formidable capacity to protect home waters and a very considerable potential for sustained operations in more distant reaches. By January 1977 General Brown, Chairman of the Joint Chiefs (in Washington), found cause to maintain that the Soviet Union had led all nations in significantly expanding its maritime activities in the South Pacific. The fact that the Soviet Union "moved expeditiously to establish diplomatic relations with the newly independent island states of the Pacific, as it seeks to expand its merchant and fishing activities in the area"[27] in one sense merely reflected Moscow's general expansion of distant-ocean activities and the generally growing importance of such activities for the Soviet economy. Yet the evolving naval cover was not just a part of the complementary expansion of Soviet distant power projection means. It must also be seen more specifically as a function of Moscow's striving for an Asian security system, and, inter alia, containment of China.

The two years leading up to the Sino-Vietnamese War of spring 1979, years of increasing Chinese unease and hostility occasioned by the warming of Soviet-Vietnamese ties, saw a steady shift in deployment and procurement patterns. Northern force numbers were, as mentioned, allowed to contract somewhat, though main forces losses were to be offset by increased local forces. Released main force divisions were diverted to the southeastern theatre. The east and southeast (Jinan, Nanjing, Fuzhou, and Guangzhou military regions) force structure rose from 28 main force divisions, and 18 local force divisions in 1977,[28] to 32 and 28, respectively, just one year later.[29] The Soviet pace of qualitative upgrading of Far East force potentials was quickened.[30] The area was given priority call on new SS-20 missiles and supersonic Backfire bombers (assigned to both naval aviation and the long-range air force). The sixth airborne division, at Khabarovsk, was brought up to full strength. The panoply of measures related to the buildup to and prosecution of the Sino-Vietnamese eruption is detailed elsewhere.[31] Suffice it to note in this context that China's withdrawal did not lead to diminution of Chinese concentrations in the area, to the contrary, and that Soviet-Vietnamese military coordination was to grow, in quality and in quantity. Tension persisted. The "southern front" had been established as an extension of Sino-Soviet border confrontation.

Finally, a 1980s' perspective must also take cognizance of "the Afghanistan crisis," and the impact on the Sino-Soviet balance of the bitter freeze in superpower relations that this crisis symbolized. U.S. Secretary of Defense Brown's post-Afghanistan visit to Beijing fleshed out the Sino-U.S. rapprochement dramatised in early 1979, when Washington chose to send its first ambassador to Beijing while invading Chinese troops still remained on the soil of Moscow's Southeast Asian ally. But in view of the fact that the United States continued to shy away from total commitment (see above), the visit did little more than confirm an already established process of incremental accommodation.[32] The Indian government's reaction to Washington's embrace of China (and Pakistan) appeared rather more startling.[33] Newly-elected Prime Minister Indira Gandhi's January 1980 statement that she accepted Moscow's rationale for intervening in Afghanistan, that it was a response to Chinese and U.S. subversion, lengthened the shadow of Soviet influence along China's southern border. A function of continued Chinese occupation of Indian border lands (a legacy of the Sino-Indian conflict of 1962) and of entrenched distrust of Pakistani ambitions, India's "understanding" attitude to the Soviet presence in Kabul hinted that Moscow and Hanoi were not alone in their endeavor to contain Chinese assertiveness. Asian alliance patterns were clearly in flux. The point should be made that if the Sino-Indian front should become involved in any future crisis scenario, the involvement would not mirror the events of 1962. The Indian armed forces, extensively modernized and retrained since 1962, with a much-improved logistics capability and a not inconsiderable nuclear potential, now looked far more potent.[34]

The tables below are intended for illustrative purposes, to supplement the data provided in the text. The first one, "The Strategic Balance, United States-Soviet Union-China, January 1980," presents some of the main parameters of the interstate balance of power. The figures are from U.S. Secretary of Defence Brown's "Annual Report, Fiscal Year 1981"; the relative paucity of Chinese strategic means is manifest. The second table, "The Emergence of Soviet Naval Power, 1950–79," is a composite prepared by this author. It is presented in part as an indicator of how Soviet military power has evolved, an indicator which when viewed against above descriptions of Chinese capabilities in the naval arena also serves as a measuring stick to judge Chinese prospects. More importantly, perhaps, the table and accompanying comments testify to the nature and extent of Moscow's buildup of Far East and Pacific force structures.

Table 1. The Strategic Balance, United States–Soviet Union–China, January 1980

	United States	Soviet Union	China
Intercontinental Ballistic Missiles (ICBMs)	1,054	1,398	First true ICBM tested in 1980; two limited-capability ICBMs deployed.
Submarine Launched Ballistic Missiles (SLBMs)	656	950	None
Intercontinental-Range Strategic Bombers	573	156	None
Total Warheads	9,200	6,000	Chinese missiles are "early generational" and carry only one warhead each.
Throw-Weight (lbs.)	7.2 million	11.8 million	Not known
Of particular reference to Sino-Soviet Context:		Soviet Union	China
Intermediate- and Medium-Range Ballistic Missiles		About 40 new SS20 (each with three independently targetable warheads) deployed against China	About 100 ("early generational")

Table 1. The Strategic Balance, United States–Soviet Union–China, January 1980 (continued)

	Soviet Union	China
Medium-Range Bombers	About 40 Backfire supersonic bombers (half assigned to naval aviation) plus about 100 bombers of earlier vintage	Somewhat over 100 (older TU16 and TU4 planes)
Ballistic Missile Defence	Soviet antiballistic missiles deployed around Moscow and available at central Asian test site effective against projected Chinese ICBM designs	No capability

Table 2. The Emergence of Soviet Naval Power 1950-79

	Northern Fleet 1950-68-73-75-78-79						Baltic 1950-68-75-78-79					Black Sea 1950-68-75-78-79					Pacific 1950-68-75-78-79				
Strategic SLBM armed subs																					
nuclear	0	14	34	38	48	49	0	0	0	0	0	0	0	0	0	0	0	6	11	20	24
diesel	0	21	16	15	10	8	0	0	0	6	6	0	0	0	0	0	0	14	8	6	6
Attack subms w/ torpedoes & cruise missiles																					
nuclear	0	18	27	28	27	28	0	0	0	0	0	0	0	0	0	0	0	10	12	19	17
diesel	0	13	16	16	14	12	0	6	2	3	2	0	0	1	3	4	0	3	9	6	6
Attack subs w/ torpedoes																					
nuclear	0	10	22	26	25	32	0	0	0	0	1	0	0	0	0	0	0	5	6	16	13
diesel	30	105	72	55	65	20	135	63	74	29	51	40	40	44	27	38	110	62	46	33	44

	1950	1968	1975	1978	1979
Total Attack Subs	315	335	319	267	268
Total Attack and Strategic Subs	315	390	391	357	361

	Northern Fleet 1968-73-75-78-79					Baltic 1968-75-78-79				Black Sea 1968-75-78-79				Pacific 1968-75-78-79			
VTOL aircraft carriers	0	0	0	1	1	0	0	0	0	0	1	1	2 building	0	0	0	1

Table 2. The Emergence of Soviet Naval Power 1950-79 (continued)

	Northern Fleet 1968-73-75-78-79	Baltic 1968-75-78-79	Black Sea 1968-75-78-79	Pacific 1968-75-78-79
Helicopter carrier/cruiser	0 0 0 0	0 0 0 0	2 2 2 2	0 0 0 0
Rocket cruisers	3 6 7 10 9	2 2 2 1	2 5 7 11	2 3 6 7
Conventional cruisers	2 3 1 2	4 5 2 3	5 5 6 2	4 3 3 3
Rocket destroyers	6 13 9 14 8	7 14 11 5	11 15 18 16	4 9 15 10
Conventional destroyers	18 10 13 5 11	15 14 24 13	18 14 16 12	25 18 13 17
Total capital ships	29 31 32 31 31	28 35 39 22	38 42 50 43	35 33 37 38

All Fleets: 1968 total 130; 1975 total 142; 1978 total 157; 1979 total 134.

	Northern	Baltic	Black Sea	Pacific
Large amphibious assault vessels (Ivan Rogov)	0	1 building	0	1
Amphibious assault vessels (other)	2	10	4	9

NOTES

1) The 1979 figures should be treated as provisional, notwithstanding the eminence of the source (*Jane's Fighting Ships, 1979-1980*). Single-year figures can never be absolutely reliable; Jane's cautions: "It must be remembered that at any normal time at least some ten percent of submarines, cruisers, destroyers, frigates, amphibious forces, depot ships and service forces are deployed 'out of area' i.e., in the Mediterranean, Indian Ocean, West Africa etc. or on passage. The figure is normally higher for ballistic missile submarines." As concerns 1979 figures there are furthermore two category changes that appear particularly anomalous and that therefore deserve to be treated with particular caution. One is the apparently sudden deployment of diesel-fuelled, torpedo-armed attack subs away from the Barents (Northern) base area. Redeployment to the Pacific appears a logical consequence of the fact that these subs are especially suited to operations in shallow waters such as the Okhotsk, and the point that this area is not (yet) as advantaged in terms of general antisubmarine warfare capabilities as is the Barents—which of course also is rather shallow. The logic refers to the exclusive status of the Northern and Pacific Fleets, as foci for strategic SLBM deployments and possible "withholding" aspirations. The strengthening of Baltic and Black Sea numbers must derive from different reasoning and invites speculation (if, indeed, the change proves permanent). The second jarring anomaly of 1979 is to be found in the suggested redeployment of conventional destroyers in favor of the Northern and Pacific Fleets. These ships are of older, pre-1962 vintage and had tended to be concentrated in the Baltic and Black Sea Fleets, as their final way-stations. Again, the change invites speculation, if proven not to be temporary or abberational (it might, for example, be a short-term measure with which to strengthen the Northern and Pacific Fleets until the advent of the new nuclear Soius-type "battleships" now being built).

2) It is worth noting that total Soviet fleet numbers have remained remarkably stable since 1968, though quality has of course improved markedly.

3) The Barents Sea clearly stands as the preeminent base area for Soviet SLBM capabilities and indeed Soviet submarine potentials in general. The emergence of the Pacific Fleet as a second focus for consequential SLBM deployment is equally evident (while Delta I construction took place only at Severodvinsk in the North, the post-1975 Delta IIs and IIIs have also been built at Komsomolsk, on the Amur). Its share of the protective shield potential of attack submarines should be seen in this light.

4) The Northern and Pacific Fleets are equally favored as concerns major surface combatants; this is particularly evident if considerations of quality are added to considerations of numbers and if the quixotic impact of 1979 distribution figures are disregarded (on the grounds, for example, that 1979's favoring of the Black Sea responded to unfolding crises in Iran and Afghanistan, that it was time and situation dependent). Older conventional destroyers, already mentioned, as well as conventional cruisers (pre-1957 vintage) have tended to spend their final years in the Baltic and Black Sea Fleets. In the North the percentage of missile-armed cruisers rose from 60 percent (representing 3 vessels)

in 1968 to 70 percent (7) in 1975 and to 91 percent (10) in 1978, before dipping to 82 percent (9) in 1979; in the Pacific the percentage rose from 33 percent (2) in 1968 to 50 percent (3) in 1975, to 67 percent (6) in 1978, and 70 percent (7) in 1979; the Baltic figures went from 33 percent (2) through 29 percent (2) to 50 percent (still only two vessels), and to 25 percent (1) in 1979; while in the Black Sea the respective numbers were 29 percent (2), 50 percent (5), 54 percent (7), and 85 percent (11) in 1979. As concerns missile destroyers the Northern percentage rose from 25 percent (6 vessels) in 1968 to 41 percent (9) in 1975 and 74 percent (14) in 1978, before sliding to 42 percent (8) in 1979; the Pacific share rose from 14 percent (4) in 1968 to 33 percent (9) in 1975 and 54 percent (15) in 1978, then dipped to 37 percent (10) in 1979; Baltic figures were 32 percent (7), 50 percent (14), 32 percent (11), and 28 percent (5), respectively; with the Black Sea coming in at 38 percent (11), 52 percent (15), 53 percent (18), and 57 percent (16).

5) To put it another way (and disregarding 1979): as the tempo of introduction of modern ships increased (18 new vessels during 1975-78, as against 27 in the seven-year period 1968-75), so did Northern and Pacific priority. The Northern and Pacific shares both rose by 9, while the Black Sea received 5, and the Baltic lost 3. As previously noted, the lumping of old and new vessels fudges Black Sea and Baltic weakness.

6) Finally, it should be noted that although increased quality has to a large extent offset quantitative contractions, especially as concerns submarines, newer ships do also age. The dramatic improvement of Soviet naval capabilities dates from the 1960s and early 1970s. Notwithstanding the development of the Pacific Fleet, it could be argued that Soviet procurement rates during the last few years evince basic satisfaction with levels already reached.

NOTES

1. For a review of the war, see C.G. Jacobsen, "Sino-Soviet Crisis in Perspective," *Current History*, (October 1979).

2. For a fuller treatment of the evolution of Soviet capabilities from World War II to the early 1970s, see C.G. Jacobsen, *Soviet Strategy—Soviet Foreign Policy*, (Glasgow: the University Press, 1st ed. 1972, 2nd ed. 1974).

3. See C.G. Jacobsen, "Soviet Strategic Capabilities: The Superpower Balance," *Current History*, (October 1977), and "Ballistic Missile Defence: A Survey of Soviet Concepts, Research and Development," *Soviet Armed Forces Review Annual I*, (SAFRA), Academic International, 1977.

4. C.G. Jacobsen, *Soviet Strategic Initiatives: challenge and response*, (New York: Praeger, 1979); see especially Chapters 2-4.

5. The below is taken in part from J.K. Skogan's excellent "Nordflaaten: utvikling, status, utsikter," *Internasjonal Politikk*, (December 1978); see also this author's "Strategic Considerations Underlying the Development of Soviet Naval Power," *Canadian Defence Quarterly*, (Spring 1980).

6. Jacobsen, "Sino-Soviet Crisis."

7. Jacobsen, "Ballistic Missile Defence."

8. *Senate Hearings, Department of Defence Appropriations for F.Y. 1980*, (Washington, D.C.: GPO, 1979), p. 343: "Offensively, conventional operations outside China's borders are constrained by inadequate logistics, insufficient tactical air support, and limited air and sea lift capability." (General D.C. Jones, USAF, Chairman, Joint Chiefs of Staff).

9. *ABC News* (January 24, 1980). A report that accompanied an interview with National Security Advisor Z. Brzezinsky ("it is not in our interest to give them [China] arms, but we don't mind if our allies do") attributed these quotes to "Pentagon officials." For an interesting background analysis of the various weapon systems sought by China from the West during the latter 1970s and Moscow's reaction thereto, see "Peking Looks for Arms," *International Affairs* (Moscow, March, 1979), pp. 142-3. Note also, e.g., *Aviation Week and Space Technology* report, April 14, 1980.

10. For earlier overestimations of Chinese potency and prospects, see references to China in the U.S. Defence Department's *Posture Statement*, (January 1968), p. 64, and, *Authorization for Military Procurement, Research and Development F.Y. 1970 and Reserve Strength*, (Washington, D.C. GPO, 1969). The factor X attached to Chinese ICBM numbers (projected as between X and 7.5X by the mid 1970s) represents "10" (in other words, projections ranged from 10 to 75). See also H. Gelber, "Nuclear Weapons and Chinese Policy," *Adelphi Papers*, No. 99, London: IISS, 1973) and the *Fourteenth Annual Conference Proceedings* ("East Asia and the World System: China and Japan in the 1970s") of IISS.

11. *Senate Hearings, Department of Defense Appropriations for F.Y. 1980*, (F.Y. 1980 Posture Statement by H. Brown, Secretary of Defence), p. 59. See also this author's *The USSR-China-Japan: Strategic Considerations Affecting the Triangle of the Soviet Far East-Manchuria-Japan*, Columbia University Russian Institute Report, March 1973, published as (Canadian) Department of National Defence DRAE Memorandum, Spring 1974.

12. *The China Youth News*, January 24, 1980 contains a lengthy piece on the nuclear weapons program in general. It throws considerable light on Chinese perceptions of the program's weaknesses.

13. Jacobsen, "Soviet Strategic Initiatives," Chapter 2. See also Jacobsen, "*Soviet Strategy—Soviet Foreign Policy*," Chapter 2.

14. Western embassy sources, Beijing.

15. *Senate Hearings, Department of Defense Appropriations for F.Y. 1980*, p. 310: "...for the foreseeable future the armed forces of the PRC will remain inferior to those of the Soviet Union.... the PLA has limited offensive conventional capabilities against countries on its periphery...." (Jones).

16. The buildup was substantial, from a mid 1960s level of "about 150,000" men in 20 divisions to a 1970s level of "over 450,000," in "well over 40" divisions. *Senate Hearings, Department of Defense Appropriations F.Y. 1980*, p. 309.

17. *The Military Balance, 1978-79*, p. 56.

18. *Statement by George S. Brown, USAF, Chairman, Joint Chiefs of Staff,*

to the Congress on the Defense Posture of the United States for F.Y. 1978, (Washington D.C.: GPO, 1978), p. 25. See also *Senate Hearings, Department of Defense Appropriations F.Y. 1980*, pp. 8 and 378.

19. *The Military Balance, 1979-80*, p. 60.
20. *The Military Balance, 1974-75*, p. 9.
21. *The Military Balance, 1978-79*, p. 9.
22. *Senate Hearings, Department of Defense Appropriation F.Y. 1980*, pp. 8 and 378.
23. Ibid., p. 378.
24. *The Military Balance, 1979-80*, p. 10.
25. Ibid., p. 60.
26. *Aviation Week and Space Technology*, (January 21, 1980).
27. *Statement by George S. Brown, USAF, Chairman, Joint Chiefs of Staff, to the Congress on the Defense Posture of the United States for F.Y. 1978*, (Washington D.C.: GPO, January 20, 1978), p. 47.
28. *The Military Balance, 1977-78*, p. 53.
29. *The Military Balance, 1978-79*, p. 56. A limit appeared to have been reached as concerns main force divisions. 1979 saw local forces divisions increase to 26, but no change in main force numbers. See *The Military Balance, 1979-80*, p. 60.
30. *International Defense Review*, No. 7 (1978): 1009.
31. Jacobsen, "Sino-Soviet Crisis."
32. *The New York Times*, (January 7, 1980) demurred: it did see Brown's call (in Beijing) for "parallel actions" in security affairs as marking a "U.S. policy shift."
33. *The New York Times*, (January 6, 1980).
34. *The Military Balance, 1979-80*, pp. 65-7.

2   THE ROOTS OF FRICTION: CULTURAL, TERRITORIAL, GEOPOLITICAL, AND IDEOLOGICAL

Some of the sources of Sino-Soviet tension can be traced back to Russia's penetration of the Amur river basin during the 1640s and 1650s and beyond. There are deep cultural differences, differences that spawned misunderstanding in 1619 when Russian envoys first reached Beijing (they offered no tribute and received no audience) and that continue to bedevil negotiations today. There are territorial, geopolitical disputes of long standing. Major economic and military issues are involved. By the 1930s there emerged also major differences in ideology between the Stalin-dominated Communist Party of the Soviet Union and the then increasingly Mao-dominated Communist Party of China. This ideological rift persisted until the 1976 death of Mao and the subsequent ouster of the Gang of Four and their followers. The core issues of those years have now been put on a back burner, as a consequence of the very different ideological priorities and perceptions of the successor regime. Other grievances rose to the fore, however. Ideology remained a sphere of contention.

When the two empires met in the seventeenth century, it was a meeting of different worlds. China was the "Middle Kingdom." It saw itself as encompassing the civilized world. Other nations were, per definition, peripheral and were also subsumed under the rubric "barbarian." The Emperor was the "Son of Heaven," with a "Mandate from Heaven" (and revocable only by Heaven). Russia was the bastion of Christianity. The first Rome had fallen, as had the "Second Rome," Constantinople. Moscow was the "Third Rome," the last, the eternal. The Tsar was annointed by Heaven, answerable only to Heaven. No wonder the 1619 negotiations, as with so many later attempts, foundered on shoals of incomprehension.[1] No wonder that early treaties had to rely on the interpretation and advice of Jesuit missionaries, or that their official text had to be written in Latin.

Soviet and Chinese propaganda at the time of the 1969 border skirmishes dramatically illustrates the perseverance of cultural antagonism and distrust. Ironically, the propaganda of both sought to blacken the other through association with their common historical scourge, the Mongol "hordes" that had swept into both during the early thirteenth century. The most prominent Russian folk-poet, Evgenii Yevtoushenko, composed a poem that spoke of the Chinese as the Mongols of today; it was read to acclaim in factories and institutions throughout the Soviet Union. The mirror image permeated China's media. The Soviets were the new barbarians to the north. The intensity of the image was of course manipulated. The point is that it clearly struck a cord in the respective national psyches. In both countries fables and song had kept alive the historical memory of defeat, humiliation, and suppression. Resentment, chauvinism, and racism, though perhaps obfuscated by layers of other experiences and concerns, nevertheless remained latent and sufficiently consequential to invite manipulation.

Differing messianisms and clashing cultural chauvinisms have tended to make practical problems of realpolitik even more intractable than they might otherwise have become.[2] The one such problem with the longest roots is that of territorial differences, the location of the boundary. It is a problem of many dimensions. Some were occasioned by misunderstandings caused by negotiation through intermediaries, some by vague and imprecise knowledge of and reference to geography (epitomized by questions as to just which grazing fence it was that had provided a point of reference for early Central Asian border delineation talks); others concerned mundane but vital issues of economy and security. These dimensions will be dealt with below, but it may be useful to begin with a more narrowly focused sketch of official attitudes.

The main bone of contention is the Far East border. China has pointed to the fact that the present border resulted from the "unequal" treaties of Aigun (1858; it confirmed Russian suzereignty north of the Amur, as well as Russian codominion over the area between the Ussuri River and the Pacific Ocean) and Peking (signed in November of 1860, it formalized sole Russian ownership of the lands east of the Ussuri). The Russian gains at Beijing was the price for purported though, to say the least, rather ineffectual Russian support against the territorial and concessionary demands made by the Western powers that pushed their way to Beijing in October

1860, thus climaxing their successful persecution of the "Opium Wars." Russia obviously exploited Chinese weakness and disarray in order to secure its own slice of the cake. Proceeding from the fact of inequity, modern Chinese leaders invoke the 1919 Karakhan Manifesto, issued by Lenin's Council of People's Commissars. It renounced all rights and interests gained by the Tsarist government at the expense of Beijing and expressed Soviet sympathy for the oppressed Chinese people.

The Soviet Union has dismissed Chinese claims as ridiculous, on the grounds that the disputed area was settled by (at least some) Russians as early as the sixteenth century, before it was even disputed by the Manchurians, far less the Chinese (the "Han" people).[3] Moscow professes shock that China bases her demand for border revisions on the contention that the present borders were imposed through "unequal treaties."[4] The Soviets describe China's quoting of Lenin as out of context, as a perverted attempt to cloak chauvinist aspirations with a veneer of respectability. They have conveyed an image of men who have lost their illusions, retaining only a taste of betrayal. There emerged a "recognition" that Mao's petty bourgeois and nationalist anticedents went back further and had a profounder impact than his Marxist affinities (never mind that the first point at least could be seen as equally applicable to Lenin).[5] Mao's communist mantle was alleged to have been necessary to secure the domestic and foreign (Soviet) support without which, it was claimed, the revolution and subsequent consolidation would have been impossible.[6] The mantle was asserted to have been discarded once power was firmly established.[7] Earlier Soviet expectations that Chinese deviations were abberations and that China might return to the fold were "confessed" to have been naive; it was "recognized" that the advent of true communist ascendancy in China awaited the discrediting of Mao and his supporters.[8] The Maoists were claimed to have adopted adventuristic foreign policy stances in order to divert attention from domestic failings.[9]

Concerning the territorial dispute per se, the Soviet position emerged from a premise diametrically opposed to that of the Chinese. When Russian explorers arrived, in dribbles during the last part of the sixteenth century, in greater numbers during the first half of the seventeenth, the regions were said to have been unpopulated, except for "small tribes, which ... pursued a nomadic existence .... neither the Manchus, nor still less the Chinese, lived on these lands" prior to their annexation by Tsarist Russia in 1649. But the then powerful Ching empire was expanding: "The balance of forces in Russian-Chinese relations was in China's favour. The Ching empire was the

thrusting and aggressive party.... under military pressure the Russians
were compelled to surrender lands in East Siberia and the Far East
... which had already become part of the Russian state. The Treaties
of Nerchinsk (1689) and Kyakhta (1728)... constituted concrete
expressions of these unequal treaties."[10]

Later Chinese concessions were therefore seen to have constituted
the return of Russian territories occupied by the Chinese during the
seventeenth and early eighteenth centuries. Moscow scorned China's
claims that the crucial treaties of Aigun and Peking were unequal.
She asserted to the contrary that these were the only treaties that
could be considered equal, since it was only then that Russian power
became comparable to that of the Chinese empire. The modesty defied 1860 realities. Still, the point emphasized is that even then
"Russia regained (only) part of the territory seized during the 17th
and 18th centuries."[11] China's limited 1860 concessions were, as
indicated above, said to have reflected appreciation that Russian
friendship could only be gained through some restitution of previous
wrongs and the fact that Russian friendship was needed to ward off
the ever-increasing encroachments of more powerful Western nations;
the Treaty of Peking ensured that the Amur region remained outside
their spheres of "concessions." That the restitution of Russian lands
was only partial, in spite of the pressures exerted on the Chinese
empire by the colonialist powers, is invoked as evidence both of the
residual strength of the empire and of the relative restraint of the
Russians. The implication is that Russia could have wrought havoc
through cooperation with Western colonial interests. As a tangential,
but not inconsequential point, Soviet authors harp on and return to
the fact that the Manchu dynasty, which encroached on Russian
territory, was not Chinese; it was one that imposed a "foreign feudal
yoke" on the Chinese people themselves.[12]

The claim that the nineteenth century treaties returned to Russia
only "part of the territory" that had been wrested from her by the
expanding Manchu empire was clear warning that the game of
territorial demands could be played by more than one player. Yet
both held back from foreclosing venues of compromise for the
future. Moscow insisted that Soviet borders were "sacred and inviolable," that the Soviet Union "will not forego the national interests
of the Soviet State."[13] Yet, though she noted that success depended
on "a constructive approach... not only from the Soviet side,"
Moscow did repeatedly declare her willingness "to conduct consul-
tations aimed at clarifying the position of the state border between
the two countries in individual sectors."[14] And while China tended
to insist on obviously unacceptable preconditions for negotiations

(such as Soviet troop withdrawals from border areas), she did allow that the existing border could provide the basis for negotiation.[15]

The sensitivity of the border is, as previously suggested, not only due to its symbolic role as reminder and custodian of past grievances. There are definite security and economic corollaries. The former will be looked at first.

The spectre of China's need for "lebensraum," for expanding living space for her teeming millions, is often mentioned, but is not central. The spectre ignores the fact that China's ratio of population to arable land is considerably more comfortable than that of Holland and a number of other countries in Europe and elsewhere. It also ignores the fact that regions to the north could not sustain a major influx of new population, certainly not an influx of sufficient scale to make much of a dent on China's population density. Areas hospitable to habitation and cultivation—as well as military bases—are severely restricted by geography and climate. Siberia and the Soviet Far East are characterized by daunting mountains and inhospitable permafrost that place heavy penalties on construction endeavors. On land only the Amur and Ussuri river basins, and Sakhalin Island, enjoy the topographic and climatic prerequisites for easy exploitation.[16] They alone enjoy a favorable combination of soft contours, sufficient rain, more than 120 frost-free days a year, and arable soil. They embrace the few Soviet cities of consequence east of Lake Baikal, the areas under cultivation, and the major missile base at Khabarovsk. Indeed, it is to the Soviet presence in central and eastern Siberia that they are vital. Without these areas even a limited Soviet presence in Siberia would be jeopardized. They form the sustaining core of Soviet aspirations for a viable and dynamic Far Eastern industrial center.

As geographically constrained land potentials in the Soviet Far East are vital for prospects of economic-industrial development, so the geographically constrained shores and waters of the area are crucial to the maintenance of a credible force presence. Ice and shallow seas hamper the location and development of naval bases.[17] A survey of the three main bases in the region is indicative.[18] Petropavlovsk, on the Kamchatka peninsula, is primarily a submarine center. It freezes in December and remains subject to freezing for three to four months. The ice can be cleared by icebreakers, and the base area is protected from winds and fog by Kamchatka's mountain ranges. But its isolation poses supply problems. The second naval complex at Sovetskaya Gavan, opposite Sakhalin and about 500 miles northeast of Vladivostok, is also a submarine base first and foremost, although it does possess dock facilities to accommodate other naval vessels. It is icebound from December to March. The ice can be cleared, but the fog is more problematic; up to 22 foggy days have been noted in July alone. The third major base area, and the headquarters of the Soviet Pacific Fleet, is Vladivostok. It has about 85 days of fog and freezes for three months as of December. Icebreakers keep it open. Another of its disadvantages is that all channels of access into the bay, except the shallow and frequently iced Tatar Strait, face Japan. Mobility in and out of Vladivostok is therefore subject to a degree of foreign surveillance. It could be fettered by barrier operations in times of conflict. The danger is minimized through forward deployment patterns and the fact that Japan, from which harassment could be a problem, is not likely to allow herself to become involved, either directly or indirectly. The 1970s saw the development of yet another base complex, at Magadan. Furthest of all from Kurile Island, Tatar Strait, and other "exits," and behind an extensive reach of shallow waters "in which nuclear (attack) submarines cannot develop their full potential"[19] Magadan was eminently suited for "withholding" purposes. But it was also belabored with severe weather constraints and less than ideal inland communication means. One understands Russia's drive for possession of Port Arthur during the late 1890s, and Stalin's refusal to relinquish the facility even after the 1949 establishment of the People's Republic (it was finally returned in 1955).

Soviet military bases on land in the Far East are similarly crimped by the dictates of geography. The proximity to the border of major base areas (such as the aforementioned missile concentration near Khabarovsk), as well as of the major cities, carries with it certain military consequences. The survivability, the defence of equipment and population, demands absolute air superiority over the immediate environment. And it demands the intelligence capability necessary to ensure adequate warning time for maximum defence activation. This demand has been met by the emplacement of extensive satellite surveillance capability, over Chinese territory in particular, plus the routinizing of manned overflights. There is no reason to doubt Chinese charges concerning the latter;[20] though perhaps not a legitimate encroachment on Chinese sovereignty, it is a clear requirement of the geopolitical constraints under which Soviet defence planning must operate.

To sum up, the Amur and Ussuri basins, together with the southern Pacific coast of the Soviet Union, form the area most sensitive to the state of Sino-Soviet relations. Its exposed location in proximity to China poses unusual security problems. But the geographical conditions that have dictated its development also dictate its unique importance. As the only Soviet Far Eastern area hospitable to larger-scale development and population it performs functions essential to the development of the eastern half of Siberia and to the unity of the nation, functions that could not be adequately performed by more distant centers. As a focus of Soviet civilization it stands as a perpetual affirmation of Soviet sovereignty, not only over the immediate environs, but also over the sparsely developed lands to the north. It serves as the motor for the development and exploitation of these lands. And by binding them to itself it binds them also to the more westerly centers of Soviet civilization with which it is intimately connected. Conversely, it provides reasonable linkage facilities for ties between these western centers and Pacific civilizations—most notably Japan. Its processing and harbor facilities encourage not only trade per se, but also a more economically optimal distribution of resource investment and development.

The Amur-Sakhalin region underwent extensive and rapid development during the post-war decades.[21] But its isolation meant that the building of infrastructures and amenities, not to mention more ambitious projects, placed extraordinary demands on scarce finances. The heyday of detente, the early 1970s, witnessed truly gigantic schemes for Siberian investment in return for produce by resource-starved Japan and a United States increasingly conscious of the need to secure foreign energy supplies.[22] The more grandiose plans withered with the disrepair of detente. After Congress torpedoed U.S. participation in 1974, when it refused to ratify the text of the U.S.-Soviet Trade Agreement of 1972, Japan also felt forced to hold back. She was leery of the vulnerability that might ensue from not having an independent partner of consequence. Concern over Chinese displeasure also became more weighty. Japan did not withdraw altogether. But she diverted her investment to more modest and proximate forestry and mining ventures on the Soviet mainland and to oil and gas exploration on Sakhalin and in the Okhotsk Sea, and she coupled these efforts with "equidistant" investments directed to China. As concerns the larger Siberian context Moscow was forced to push ahead on her own. While west Siberian oil and gas development came to be tied to European Russia rather than the Far East, the engineeringly and financially awesome northern BAM railway parallel to the trans-Siberian received top priority during the final years on the 1970s. It promised greater logistical security vis a vis China and better access to more northerly riches. The scale of Soviet investment was testimony equally to the impact of security consideration and to long-term economic expectations.

The Soviet Far East was being developed not only as a natural transshipment center, but also as home to sizeable petrochemical, pulp, and mineral processing industrial complexes. The gradual

establishment of associate industries and the general emergence of
a major industrial conurbation on the Pacific coast furthermore
promised to result in self-generating capacities of consequence. The
easing of developmental pressure will allow for more concessions to
previously neglected areas; Sakhalin, for example, is thought to have
the dairying potential of Denmark. But herein lay another cause for
Chinese unease. The export-oriented industrialization of the Soviet
Far East meant the emergence of a serious rival to Manchuria, the
heartland of Chinese industrialization. And geography provided the
rival with potential access to both raw materials and markets of a
scale that might well leave Manchuria disadvantaged.

But a discussion of border issues—past, present, and, perhaps,
future—cannot be complete without mention of ths issue over which
China purportedly initiated the border skirmishes of 1969,[23] namely
ownership of Damansky (Zhen Bao) Island, in the Ussuri River. It
was perfunctorily occupied by the Soviets, as it had been through the
preceding decades. The Soviet Union allowed for no question of
sovereignty, on the grounds that the 1860 Treaty of Peking (its
version?) unambiguously stipulated that the western bank of the river
was to constitute the border, a stipulation which per definition
conceded Russian/Soviet sovereignty over all islands. China now
professed ignorance concerning this clause (another incidence of
communication difficulties having spawned different appreciations?)
and therefore insisted that the line of delineation follow the path of
greatest river depth. This would be in accordance with the emerging
tradition of international law, for such cases where different principles had not already been agreed upon. To make matters worse, the
Ussuri is a river of shifting sand and silt, and hence shifting deep-water
channels. It was a criterium that would see Damansky (Zhen Bao)
located alternately east, alternately west of the boundary. Then there
is the point that Damansky (Zhen Bao) is itself a silt concentration;
although larger than most, it is but one of the many islands of the
Ussuri that are built up, shaped, reshaped, and eroded by the shifting
currents. The fact that China chose such a point of attack, a locale
of no military and little real estate relevance, and that Moscow
focused most of its (strong) counteraction on the same area, testified
to the preeminence of political rationales. The nature of this particular apple of discord reflected political, primarily domestic imperatives
and a determination that the challenge (and response) not be such as
might get out of hand. Moscow's concessionary offer in March 1973
to apply more recent international law precepts rather than the

1860 Treaty of Peking to the Amur-Ussuri river boundaries (the offer was refused by Beijing)[24] underlined the point that the method of resolution holds primacy over the form of resolution.

Finally, a look at the tension occasioned by the sometimes intertwined themes of ideology and Party to Party and state to state relations. These themes or forums have not been unaffected by the dissonance of chauvinist antipathies and territorial insecurities. And their effect on these antipathies and insecurities have in return often been less than soothing.

Sino-Soviet ideological differences go back to the 1920s and 1930s. Rightly skeptical of the revolutionary potential of the miniscule Chinese "proletariat" of the 1920s, and hence judging that priority must be accorded to the solidifying of Chinese anticolonialism under the nationalist banner of the Kuomintang, Stalin proceeded to direct the small Communist Party of China to continue to operate within and cooperate with that organization. It was a pattern encouraged by the father founder of the Kuomintang, Sun Yatsen. When his successor, Chiang Kaichek, turned on the CPC and other elements of the organization's left wing and crippled them during the later 1920s, Stalin's Russia chose to accommodate itself to the new realities. The remnants of the Soviet trained leadership of the CPC split. Some stayed in the cities, trying to survive and organize as a precariously embattled underground. Others felt forced to join the previously disparaged peasant forces that Mao had heretically assembled, on his own initiative, in the remote borderland provinces of Jiangxi and Hunan. Soviet priorities did not waver. Support for Chiang continued. The chauvinism embodied by the Kuomintang was seen to answer immediate Soviet (and hence by Soviet definition, communist) needs.[25]

The Stalinist apparat had scant faith in the survival prospects and potential of the Maoist forces. They represented an adventurist group that had in effect defied Party directives and Party discipline. Moscow had no control. Distance and obstacles of geography minimized communication. The chances of Mao's scattered and isolated peasant forces ever defeating the armed forces at the disposal of the Kuomintang did indeed appear dim, especially in view of the ease with which the latter had disposed of the established CPC. The pragmatic disparagement was reinforced by ideological prejudices, the dislike occasioned by Mao's espousal of certain particular Leninist and Trotskyite positions now in disfavor in Moscow. This point will be returned to below. In the meantime realpolitik was seen to

require support for Chiang. Moscow adopted a blind eye posture to
the extermination campaigns launched by Chiang against Mao during
the early 1930s (the fifth and largest, in 1934, conducted with the
aid and advice of officers from Nazi Germany, was to force the epic
6000 mile Long March to the caves of Yanan, in the remote northern
province of Shanxi). The posture persisted through Chiang's late 1930s
and Second World War diversion of resources from battle against
the Japanese invader to debilitating harassment of Communist
forces.

Moscow, as did Western capitals, appeared oblivious of the degree
to which the contrast between apparently single-minded Communist
prosecution of struggle against the invader and Chiang's fratricidal
blinders sapped Chiang's greatest strength, namely his supposed
embodiment of Chinese patriotism.[26] At war's end Moscow felt compelled to hand sizeable amounts of captured Japanese war material
over to the Communist forces who had by now extended their
northern sway and who were filling the Manchurian vacuum left by
the departing enemy. But Stalin plainly still did not appreciate the
true potency of the CPC's new patriotic image, or its reputation for
honest, effective, and socially equitable administrative policies; nor
did he appreciate the depth of alienation caused by a burgeoning
Kuomintang reputation for self-seeking profit and corruption. Immediate Soviet interest was seen to legitimize the "war reparation"
extraction of Manchurian industries. Long-term Soviet interest
continued to be identified with amicable relations with Chiang.
Financial support for Chiang continued right up until the 1949
collapse of his house of cards.

Mao arrived in Moscow in December 1949. His emergence, survival, and triumph had been rooted in Chinese realities and owed little
if anything to Soviet support. His was a national movement. But the
country was abysmally underdeveloped; it was a country of little
industry, a country accustomed alternately both to drought-induced
starvation and to the ravages of floods and natural disasters. There
was a desperate need for technical and financial assistance to build
a more viable industrial base, to spread irrigation, and to construct
dams. China's level of industrialization at this time has been compared
to Russia's in 1900. In fact:

> Russia in 1900 already had a higher per capita production of pig iron,
> steel and cotton goods, and more railroad track per square mile than
> China in 1952—and only one quarter the rural population density. By
> 1928 Russia has a much more extensive rail network and her produc-
> tion of coal, iron, steel, power, textile products and the like in per
> capita terms was far greater than China's in 1952.[27]

Revolutionary euphoria notwithstanding, Beijing also realized that the temporarily disorganized Kuomintang armies, now ensconced on Taiwan, remained an opponent of considerable potency. It was, moreover, an opponent that enjoyed the unquestioned support of the dominant superpower of the day. As compared to the struggling Soviets during the period of civil war and foreign interventions following the 1917 revolution China had even less indigeneous power with which to confront an "interventionist" antagonist far more capable and confident than were the war-weary opponents of the Bolsheviks. Mao Zedong and Zhou Enlai, his Premier-to-be, had tried to forge understanding with Washington during and immediately after the Second World War—another indication of their instinctive preference for distance between themselves and Moscow. But Roosevelt's interest was replaced by Truman's more conservative and skeptical ideological stance, a stance that became increasingly rigid and uncompromising with the onset of the Cold War.

China urgently needed a source of economic, scientific, and technical aid, and she urgently needed an ally to help deter against "counterrevolution." There was nowhere to turn but the Soviet Union. The Soviet Union, on the other hand, was increasingly jittery about the consequences of heightened East-West tension at a time when she remained manifestly inferior. (She had a small, crude, just developing nuclear arsenal but as yet no secure means of delivering that arsenal, as against an opponent that possessed the unquestioned capacity to destroy her.) Moscow was highly conscious of the power increment inherent in the propaganda image of a Chinese alliance. It was an alliance that must give pause to the "capitalists." Its psychological effect would inevitably augment the aura of Soviet power and, therefore, the credibility of Soviet deterrence.

Both sides needed the appearance of close alliance, the appearance suggested by their pro forma ideological affinities. Yet, the bargaining was tough and drawn out. It was nine weeks before Mao could return to Beijing. Over the next decade thousands of Soviet technicians were to help with 336 major industrial construction projects. Thousands of Chinese students and trainees were accepted to Soviet schools and institutes. Beginning in 1950 the Soviet Union loaned China 60 million dollars a year for five years, followed by a second five year period of 26 million dollars a year (these were *not* 1980 dollars). Technology, military hardware, and capital equipment flowed in. Soviet air squadrons were dispatched to help guarantee against the threat from Taiwan.[28]

The price was high. Sino-Soviet "joint stock" companies were set up on the East European pattern to pursue mining and other ventures of disproportionate benefit to the Soviet Union. Moscow retained a special position in Manchuria, a position exemplified by joint control of the main railway, and she maintained her control over Port Arthur. These privileges, including the joint stock ventures, were discarded after Stalin's death. But other advantages were maintained. Soviet credits and loans were repaid by Chinese exports of raw materials, thus tying Chinese extraction industries to Soviet processing facilities and Soviet markets.[29]

Perhaps more important was that Soviet aid directives and Soviet repayment demands fostered and shaped a Chinese industrial development program that was modeled on early Soviet experience. Yet, "primitive socialist accumulation" of the Soviet (Stalinist) type, the squeezing of peasant "surplus" for the purpose of industrial investment, was stymied in China by the more backward and more pressingly needy nature of Chinese rural society. It was also stymied by Mao's peasant orientation, his perception of the peasant as the main revolutionary class and force in China, and his consequent aversion to anything that smacked of rural exploitation. With Soviet loans and advisors impressive industrial progress was effected through the 1950s, but the emphasis on technologically-intensive ventures skewered the overall development of society. It also created a command economy that put a premium on engineer-managers, pragmatism, and expertise. It encouraged the development of a manager elite of experts, a phenomenon favored by those trained in and attracted by Stalinist management techniques, but one deeply distrusted by a Mao acutely conscious of the dangers of a "new class."

Mao used his authority to force a reorientation in 1958, towards a Great Leap Forward based rather on labor-intensive, decentralized cottage industries. Each collective was to have its foundry, each rural community was to develop its own industrial infrastructure: the period "was epitomized by the frenzied effort to increase iron and steel production by unskilled use of small, uneconomic backyard smelters."[30] The effort was accompanied by a drive to amalgamate huge cooperative farms (of 20,000 and more people, perhaps 5,000 different households) into self-sufficient communes responsible for their .own agricultural and industrial production and needs. The project was pursued with utopian vigor and determination, and much was achieved. But the pace was too frenzied. Economic dislocation and transportation breakdowns ensued. Some areas were faced with starvation, industrial stagnation, and apathy. It was a situation ripe for exploitation by Mao's ideological antagonists. He had overextended himself and left himself open to the charge of dangerous idealism, subjectivism, and jeopardizing the planning structure necessary for the development of socialism.

Moscow reacted in similar fashion. Soviet unease was furthermore heightened by the implied assertion that there was a quicker and better way to socialism than that developed in the Soviet Union. Mao was flaunting an independent alternate route and was, hence, by definition challenging Soviet hegemony over the world communist movement. It was perhaps the straw that broke the camel's back. In 1960 Soviet aid, technicians and blueprints were abruptly withdrawn.

The precipitate Soviet withdrawal exacerbated the dislocations occasioned by the Great Leap Forward. It was to take China at least two or three years to recover.[31] The end of this period saw a CPC dominated by Liu Shaoqui and Deng Xiaoping—by Soviet-trained proponents of central planning and directives, and Party and labor discipline. Mao's naivete was blamed for past troubles. His aura as father of the revolution was too powerful to allow disgrace, but his influence within decision-making counsels became minimal. Powerful circles in Moscow became persuaded that pragmatic accommodation with Beijing was a realistic prospect. This was dramatically illustrated by one of the charges marshalled against Khrushchev in the fall of 1964; one of the justifications for his ouster was that he remained uncompromisingly hostile to China.[32]

Friction over the Great Leap Forward had of course not been the only reason for the crumbling of the alliance. A large number of issues were involved, some caused by and some merely inflamed by ingrained antipathies, different memories, different perceptions. China's history, culture, world view, its size and population, all served to inculcate the expectation that China could be no less than a partner. She might willingly concede a pioneering status to the Soviet Union. And she might therefore wish, seek, and even expect, as birthright, to be able to draw on the economic and military power of the Soviet Union. But there could be no question of anything less than equal potential. It would appear inevitable that a Soviet Union that defined socialism in terms of its own destiny ("socialism in one country" was one Stalinist theme that was not discarded by his successor), and that was used to allies that acquiesced in her definition of priorities would find Chinese assumptions presumtuous and, indeed, dangerous. It was equally inevitable that Chinese leaders would chafe at what they saw as quasi-colonialist arrogance. Moscow resented the drain on Soviet resources. She resented diverting money and experts needed at home to an unappreciative ally, an ally whose inclinations and aspirations she did not trust. China, on the other hand, resented the "selfish" limits placed on aid, the imposition of conditions, and what she considered to be overly harsh demands for repayment.

Mao viewed Soviet pressure for a "Joint Fleet," in the late 1950s as an arrogant attempt to ensure Soviet control, Soviet dominion.[33] And it probably was an attempt to ensure against Chinese naval "adventurism" against Taiwan. The incidence culminated a period of strong Chinese demand for Soviet military backing for "reunification," as well as for greatly increased Soviet assertiveness on behalf of "socialist" causes in general. Mao clearly thought that the Soviet acquisition of a nuclear arsenal provided sufficient deterrent "umbrella" to pursue such territorial and other grievances as "the socialist bloc" might have. He castigated Soviet caution. Soviet refusal to stand up to the imperialists was scathingly condemned as self-centered timidity, as betrayal of common ideals. Mao went further. It was a sign of softness, indicative of the "goulash" communism of the Soviet elite, of the degree to which they had been seduced by the self-centered values of their pro forma antagonists. This was strong language, and Moscow was obviously appalled. The charges were additional proof, if such was needed, of Mao's "adventurism," his "subjectivism."[34] The Soviet Union had no illusion about the potency of its nuclear capabilities. She knew she had no secure means of delivering them, and she knew that she remained decisively inferior in the strategic realm. One might speculate that Soviet leaders may have been somewhat less candid on this score in communications with Beijing than they were in their own policy counsels. The point was made, but the absolute degree of continuing inferiority may have been fuzzed over—or it may just be that it was not believed. Whatever the role of possible communication problems, whether deliberate or accidental, there is no doubt that Moscow (and Khrushchev in particular) found Mao's charges unjust, demagogic, and hostile.

As if the accumulation of real grievances was not enough, there clearly developed what can only be called personal antipathy between Mao and Khrushchev. Mao had his differences with Stalin. And they were, as indicated, neither few in number nor superficial in character. Yet Stalin was deferred to in public. He was the link to Lenin, and he had succeeded in the building of Soviet power. To a certain extent the deference may have reflected Mao's accommodation with Soviet-trained and Soviet-oriented colleagues; or it could be seen as realpolitik pure and simple. An element of calculation concerning the leadership mantle after Stalin's eventual demise may also be presumed to have been involved. Like Tito prior to 1948, Mao after 1953 saw himself as the elder statesman of the movement that supposedly bonded the "socialist" alliance. To Mao Khrushchev was an upstart

chauvinist Russian peasant. To Krushchev Mao was, yes, like Tito—
a petty-bourgeois nationalist too big for his britches.

But we must concede, with the Marxist, that such "subjective"
matters are peripheral. The main theme around which other grievances revolved was ideological, and it must be addressed specifically
and at some length. It remains important.

The original clash between Mao and Stalin lay, as previously
suggested, in Mao's furthering of Lenin's insistence on the necessary
role and participation of the peasant in the revolution.[35] To Lenin
the enlarging of the "revolutionary" class from Marx' stress on the
proletariat to a trinity of "workers, peasants, and soldiers" was
necessitated by Russia's backwardness, by the presence of a huge
and largely dissatisfied peasant class, and by a mobilized army that
had bled too much and to too little effect. Mao carried Lenin's logic
to the even more extreme ("non-Marxist") conditions of China:
still greater backwardness, a still more miniscule proletariat, and a
numerically more overwhelming peasantry. But the Stalinist apparat
that succeeded Lenin reverted to the narrower Marxist tradition,
ignoring the fact that the realities of Russian underdevelopment
jarred sharply with the conditions for communism that Marx had
postulated. Stalin increasingly used the peasantry as the goose from
which to squeeze the eggs that would fund and feed the industrialization drive.

Mao also pursued and furthered Lenin's and, especially, Trotsky's,
concept of permanent revolution. He insisted on the continuation
of class struggle: on the need never to flag in the pursuit of revolutionary ideals, on the need continuously to guard against the emergence of "a new class." It was a call to arms that struck at the heart
of the Stalinist system, though it was aimed less at Stalin and more
at Mao's opponents at home. It was a line trumpeted with increasing
vigor during the late 1950s, the 1960s, and until Mao's death in
1976. To Mao the emergence of a new ruling class emphasizing
industrial productivity and efficiency at the expense of social goals;
a ruling elite that would, moreover, inevitably prove self-perpetuating,
could mean only the failure of revolution and the success of counterrevolution. Mao's perception that this was occurring or had occurred
in the Soviet Union constituted his most damning indictment. He
became pursuaded that the Trotskyists were right, that Stalinist
Russia had embraced "state capitalism." And this was an aspect of
Stalin's rule that was not repudiated by either Khrushchev or his
successors.

Mao launched the Cultural Revolution in 1965 because he believed that such a new class had taken control of the Party. He
believed that their single-minded focus on cost effectiveness, on

hierarchy and centralism, must inevitably degenerate into the exploitation and class antagonisms of old. Echoing Lenin's "Last Testament"
call to oust the Stalinists from the CPSU for their arrogance, for their
chauvinism, and, above all, for their denial of a democratic hearing
for minorities and other factions,[36] Mao now urged his disciples to
"storm the Party headquarters." But as Stalin had survived through
interception and censorship of Lenin's correspondence, through
suppression of the "Last Testament," and through a concerted propaganda drive to affirm his fidelity to the ideals of Lenin,[37] so the
Chinese Party establishment of 1965 now organized their own "Red
Guards," proclaiming themselves true disciples of Mao and his
"thought." The lines of battle were blurred. With opposing Red
Guards all claiming to be Mao's followers, all claiming to be fighting
the same evil, chaos was guaranteed. The People's Liberation Army
had to step in to prevent anarchy. Mao's stature was too potent to
be fully deflected. Liu Shaoqui, the titular President, was disgraced
and would never recover. Deng Xiaoping was also humiliated. But he
was later to be protected by PLA sympathizers. Most of his supporters retained their positions of influence.

Mao's victory was not complete. His inability to control the
Cultural Revolution and his consequent need to accept PLA media-
tion crimped his subsequent freedom of action.[38] Contrary to the
claims of his detractors, Mao was not a totally naive visionary. He
acknowledged the need for pragmatic expertise. His point was rather
that when pragmatic expertise became an end goal, divorced from
the directing stimulus of ideology's social vision, then what should be
a corrective aid becomes rather a corroding enemy.[39] Hence the "red
versus expert" campaigns. Hence his absolute insistence towards the
end that mini Cultural Revolutions must be launched every seven
years or so. It was because cancerous tendencies had had so long to
imbed themselves that the Cultural Revolution of 1965 had become
such a cataclysmic phenomenon. It was because the bureaucrats, the
"new class," had been given time to take such complete hold of the
Party apparatus that the campaign against them had to go to such
extremes—and that it still did not fully succeed. The call for similar
campaigns to be launched every seven years was precisely so as not
to allow for this kind of entrenchment of particular interests. It was
to ensure that such totality of effort would never again be required,
and that one would therefore never again have to face and brave
debilitating chaos. Mao's death in 1976 came in the midst of such
an attempt. Again the campaign centered on Deng Xiaoping (he had
been brought back to work under Zhou Enlai, Mao's premier, and
appeared poised to reacquire independent status after Zhou's death).

The campaign was aborted after Mao's demise and the arrest of the Gang of Four. It was announced that there would be no more Cultural Revolutions. Mao's fears were borne out. While his vision might have taken roots of future significance, it was now (once more) excused from policy deliberations of the day.[40]

It is salutary to remember that Marx and Lenin had indeed equated communism with greater democratization. The point was of course that in a system that allowed for extremes of economic disparity it did not matter how extensive democratic rights might be in theory; the unemployed or otherwise impoverished would not be able to translate theoretical rights into real privileges to the same extent as would more fortunately endowed members of society. (The extraordinary cost of a modern U.S. Senate campaign, estimated at over a million dollars, might by some be taken to indicate that the point may have continuing relevance.)[41] The concepts of an elitist Party run according to "democratic centralism" (the widest possible "democratic" input to policy discussion; "centralism" once a majority decision emerged) was Lenin's heritage. But he guarded against the potential for perversion, the suppression of the first or base rule of the Party's modus operandi, that was to become so blatant under Stalin.[42] Lenin saw his structure as an unavoidable necessity, dictated first by the need to survive in a society permeated by the Tsar's secret police apparatus and later by the emergency requirements of civil war and foreign interventions. It is symptomatic that he invited into his government L. Kamenev and G. Zinoviev, the colleagues who had betrayed his coup plan to a bourgeois press.[43] There is no question that Lenin, Trotsky, and Mao himself proved they could be ruthless in times of extremity against those they believed to be sabotaging their revolutions, against perceived agents of "capitalist" and foreign interests. Nevertheless, it is crucial to point out that their belief systems (though sometimes belied by actions thought to be dictated by needs of the moment) were founded on a philosophical bias against *dirigisme*. That bias lay at the core of Lenin's "Last Testament" indictment of Stalin, and it provided the justification for Mao's exhortations against the 1965 leadership of the CPC.

Mao's pragmatic successors came to echo rather the organizational and theoretical preferences of Moscow of the 1930s, Stalin's Russia.[44] The need for centralism and discipline was stressed over the ideals of democracy, mass participation, workers' councils, and the like. They prioritized economy and efficiency over social transformation.[45] The Party became an administrative organ first and foremost, not the custodian of theoretical strivings. The administrative role of the military (the PLA) and the security services were enhanced. Command economy prerogatives prevailed over decentralized management. Greater income differentials, profits, and bonuses were seen to be more effective efficiency stimulators than moral and social awards. Mao's successors emphasized industrial production over agricultural needs.[46] They were more willing than their predecessor(s) to seek foreign investment and foreign credit.[47] They felt more comfortable negotiating with "capitalist" interests.[48] While Chinese leaders at the end of the 1970s had not left themselves open to the same charges of paranoia and extremes as had Stalin, their principles of government did appear strikingly similar to his.

Three comments need to be made. One concerns the reactions of independent Western and Third World Marxists. The perception that China was following the Soviet path towards "state capitalism" and "socialism in one country" meant that they now felt divorced from external ties and obligations. This necessarily encouraged the evolution of national movements. It was a development that drew strength from the fact that accusations of foreign dependence would henceforth be less credible. It was equally a development that entailed a final splintering of the spectre or promise of "a world communist movement." To Moscow, long dependent more on the attractions of power than the allure of ideology, it served to remove the dread that China might be able to generate and sustain the ideological following that she herself had once commanded. Finally, it might be worth noting a variant reaction. To some Marxists China's course, as that of the Soviet Union, entailed a selling out of sovereignty as much as ideology. Beijing's and Moscow's willingness to commit future resource development to the repayment of foreign credit, technology, and investment was seen to promise increasing dependence on capitalist benevolence. China and the Soviet Union were thought to be slipping into the status of "neocolonialist" states, hewers of wood and drawers of water, with branch plant economies beholden to foreign interests.[49]

The second line of commentary might cause more pause to Western government analysts. If "socialism in one country" was an apt description of current Chinese policy directions, as appeared to be the case, and if Soviet policy of the 1930s therefore was a proper analogy, then the future might bring as many hazards as it did promises. The Soviet Union of today might again be seeking economic ties with Western interests. But the promise of the 1930s had been cut short; so had expectations generated by later periods of increased contacts. There was also the point that Soviet policy had at times proved pragmatic beyond the imagination of Western pragmatists; the Molotov-Ribbentrop pact of 1939 stood mute testimony.

A final thought concerning "socialism in one country." In China as in the Soviet Union it corresponded both to a degree of nationalism (xenophobia) and to an originational preference that had deep roots in their respective histories. A China on this course could not threaten Soviet ideological pretensions to the extent that Mao could. But that was Moscow's sole solace. Because such a China was no more likely to accept tutelage than Mao had been, it was clear that any resolution of Sino-Soviet differences would be on the basis of pragmatic and leery state-to-state bargaining, i.e., on the basis of traditional great power accommodation. Neither side entertained illusions about the relevance of an ideological bond.

NOTES

1. J.K. Fairbank, E.O. Reischauer, and A.M. Craig, *East Asia: The Modern Transformation*, (Boston: Houghton Mifflin, 1965) (Volume 2 of *A History of East Asian Civilization*), p. 46.

2. See introduction to this author's *The USSR-China-Japan: Strategic Considerations Affecting the Triangle of the Soviet Far East-Manchuria-Japan*, Columbia University Russian Institute Report March 1973, published as a (Canadian) Department of National Defence DRAE Memorandum, Ottawa, Spring 1974.

3. *Mezhdunarodnaya Zhizn*, No. 6 (1972): 14–29.

4. Ibid. It is asserted, to the contrary, that these treaties merely returned to Russia what had been taken from her by the (truly) "unequal treaties" imposed by the aggressive Ching empire in 1689 and 1728.

5. O.B. Borisov and B.T. Koloskov, *Soviet-Chinese Relations 1945-70*, (Moscow: Mysl, 1972), and O. Vladimirov and V. Riasantsev, *Stranitsy Politicheskoi Biografii Mao Tse-duna*, Izdat. Polit. Lit., Moscow, 1969.

6. Borisov and Koloskov, *Soviet-Chinese Relations*. Not only was Soviet aid instrumental during the civil war; it was equally vital during the period of reconstruction. The Soviet air force units lent to Shanghai, the industrial center of east China, and to the industrial areas of the northeast in 1949–50 provided protection during a most vulnerable period; Soviet aid was also of inestimable value in the construction of a viable economic base.

7. Ibid. The "ideas of Mao Tse-tung," which had dominated the Seventh CPC Congress of 1945 but had subsequently been discarded in favor of "the spirit of internationalism," "Marxism-Leninism," "friendship with countries of the camp of peace, democracy and socialism, headed by the Soviet Union," "collective leadership," and so forth, were again (allegedly) imposed on the Chinese people.

8. Ibid. Brezhnev's acknowledgement (on March 20, 1972 at the Trades Union Congress in Moscow) of Chinese suggestions that relations between the two powers be based on "peaceful coexistence" can be seen as recognition of the fundamental nature of their differences. "Peaceful coexistence" regulates relations between states with "different social systems."

9. I. Alexandrov, *Peking's Policy—A Threat to Peace*, (Moscow: Novosti, 1978).

10. *Mezhdunarodnaya Zhizn.* The co-authors of this major exposition were L.G. Beskrovny, Head of Department, Historical Institute of the Academy of Sciences (specialist in pre-1917 Russian history); S.L. Tikhvinskii, Professor, Institute of International Relations (served in China before and after 1949, author of a number of books on 19th and 20th century Chinese history); and V.M. Khostov, Director of the Historical Institute (diplomatic historian). See also Borisov and Koloskov, *Soviet-Chinese Relations*, and *Vneshnaya Politika KNR*, Izdat. Mezhdunarodnie Otnoshenie, Moscow, 1971.

11. *Mezhdunarodnaya Zhizn.*

12. Ibid. The Soviet Union, furthermore, asserts that this had previously been recognized by Mao himself and quotes earlier Mao comments to the effect that the treaties presently in force are indeed "equal"; see, e.g., *Pravda.* (March 30, 1969). The herein quoted speech by Mao was presented to the 1945 Seventh CPC Congress.

13. *Mezhdunarodnaya Zhizn.*

14. Ibid.

15. See, e.g., Lin Biao's *Speech to the Ninth Congress of the CPC.*

16. *Atlas SSSR*, (Moscow: Glavnoe Upravlenie Geodezii i Kartografii, 1955); *The World Atlas*, (Moscow: GUGK, 1967); Kingsbury and Taafe, *An Atlas of Soviet Affairs*, (New York: Praeger, 1965), pp. 88-91, 95. See also J.J. Stephan, "Sakhalin Island: Soviet Outpost in North-East Asia," *Asian Survey*, (December 1970).

17. T.J. Laforest, "The Strategic Significance of the North Sea Route," *U.S. Naval Institute Proceedings*, (December 1967). See also *Relef Dna Tikhovo Okeana*, Carleton University (Ottawa), Geography Map Library, 9200, Acc. 1651.

18. S.A. Swartstrauber, "Alaska and Siberia, A Strategic Analysis," *Naval Review 1965*, U.S. Naval Institute, (1966): 159.

19. See *Jane's Fighting Ships 1979–80*, (London: Jane's, 1979), p. 513 for description of new disel-powered Soviet hunter submarines, the Tangos (in shallow waters "the diesel boat is still the quietest platform"; the Tangos "possess excellent underwater performance and a considerable firepower"). On Magadan's geographical characteristics, see *The New York Times Atlas* (co.op. with *The Times* of London), (London: Times Newspapers Ltd., 1972).

20. An example is provided by *New China News Agency's* report of September 16, 1968. It listed about 40 sorties into Heilungkiang Province between August ninth and twenty-ninth. Far from being restricted to Manchuria's northern and eastern regions, such supervision is supplemented in the west by jointly crewed Soviet-Mongolian helicopter inspection of the Mongolian-Chinese border and other means.

21. Stephan, "Sakalin Insland."

22. C.G. Jacobsen, "Strategic Considerations Affecting Soviet Policy Toward China and Japan," *Orbis*, No. 4, (1974).

23. *Trud*, March 4 and 5, 1969. See also *Pravda*, March 1, 8, 12, and 20 and June 12, 1969; *Izvestia*, March 4, 1979; *Krasnay Zvezda*, March 9, 1969; or, e.g., *Sovetskaya Rossia*, March 19, 1969. For Chinese accounts, see *HSINHUA*,

March 3, 1969; also Beijing *NCNA* domestic service reports of March 3, 5, 7 and 10, 1969.

24. *Asian Analyst*, (February 1975). See also *The Times*, (September 29, 1978) for an account of the same problem as it has affected navigation on the confluence of the Amur and Ussuri Rivers, near Khabarovsk. Deeming the confluence an internal waterway Moscow had from 1967 to 1977 forced Chinese vessels to use the Kozakevicheva channel, or stream, which links the waterways some 25 miles above the confluence—it was a channel with a silting problem even more severe than that affecting the Ussuri. Moscow's quiet 1977 lifting of the de facto blockade might be presumed to have been related to her then very tentative dialogue with the post-Mao leadership.

25. For an excellent overview, see J.W. Strong's "Sino-Soviet Relations in Historical Perspective," in *Communist States at the Crossroads*, A. Bromke, ed. (New York: Praeger, 1965).

26. Ibid. The dichotomy is exemplified by the 1936 incident when "still determined to rid China of Communism, Chiang put into operation plans for a powerful extermination campaign against the Yenan regime. Suddenly, in December, he was kidnapped and held prisoner in Sian, the capital of Shensi, by Chiang Hsueh-liang, the 'young marshal' of Manchuria. Tired of the civil war the Manchurians wanted a united Chinese resistance against the Japanese, who had invaded their homeland. The Communists decided to plead for Chiang Kai-shek's life in return for his effective promise to stop the civil war and take a firm stand against the Japanese ...."

27. Fairbank, Reischauer, and Craig, *East Asia*, p. 872.

28. Ibid. See also this author's *China Notes*, Hudson Institute report, September 1974, for interview with Peking Foreign Affairs Commission spokesman.

29. Fairbank, Reischauer, and Craig, *East Asia*, p. 871. A somewhat different account may be found in O. Borisov's *Soviet-Chinese Friendly Ties, a historical review*, (Moscow: Novosti, 1974).

30. Fairbank, Reischauer, and Craig, *East Asia*, p. 878.

31. Jacobsen, *China Notes*.

32. This was in fact the first of the 29 specific charges levelled against Khrushchev by M.A. Suslov, the Party "theoretician," at the decisive Central Committee meeting of October 14, 1964. See *Keesing's Contemporary Archives 1963–64*, pp. 20361-20368, 20389. See also *Pravda*, editorial of October 17, 1964, and *HSINHUA*'s report of October 16, 1964 (Chinese leaders send "warm greetings" to Mr. Brezhnev and Mr. Kosygin and "sincere wishes" to "the fraternal Soviet people," with the hope that "the unbreakable friendship between the Chinese and Soviet people may continue to develop"). "Der Anklager: Suslow," in *Die Zeit*, (October 32, 1964) is another good analysis.

33. Jacobsen, *China Notes*.

34. See A. Malukhin, *Militarism-Backgone of Maoism*, (Moscow: Novosti, 1970) Also B.A. Krivtsova, ed., *Maoizm Glazami Kommunistov*, (Moscow: Progress, 1969), and V.N. Alekseev, ed., *Antimarxistskaya Sushnost Voennoi Politiki Maoistov*, (Moscow: Voenizdat, 1973).

35. P.M. Sweezy, "Theory and Practice in the Mao Period," *Monthly Review*, (February 1977). Without jeopardy to Sweezy, or to the text of the final section of this chapter, it is incumbent to note that an ideological stance does of

course not automatically reflect ideological commitment. As Bolshevik policy has been said to embody more of "old Russia" than Karl Marx, so Maoism has by this author been described as "at least 80 per cent old China, no more than 20 per cent Marx"; others (such as H. Ticktin, editor of *Critique*, in a December 1979 conversation) have gone further, asserting that there is no evidence that Mao had ever read any of Marx's writings. Still, it is perhaps the thoughts and prejudices that matter, not their genesis.

36. See, e.g., Moshe Lewin's excellent *Lenin's Last Struggle*, reprinted by Monthly Review Press, 1979 (first U.S. publishers: New York: Pantheon, 1968, and New York: Vintage, 1968 and 1970).

37. Ibid.

38. Franz Michael, "Peking and Moscow: The Past, Present and Future of the Sino-Soviet Conflict," *Korean Journal of International Studies*, No. 2, (1976), see especially pp. 27-8. See also *The Guardian*, (April 28, 1977).

39. See this author's "Developments in the Far East," *SAFRA II*, (1978) especially pp. 267-9.

40. See, e.g., "All radicals eliminated from leadership in China's new Politburo," *The Times* (August 22, 1977); "Rightists Back in China," *The Guardian* (May 15, 1978); and "Astonishing reversions to pre-1966 social policies," *Far Eastern Economic Review* (October 5, 1979).

41. This is, in fact, judged to be a "necessary minimum." See *The Economist* (March, 1980).

42. See Lewin's *Lenin's Last Struggle*.

43. N.S. Sukhanov's unique "eyewitness account," *The Russian Revolution*, Oxford University Press, 1955, provides the single most comprehensive independent account of the revolutionaries, their theory and their practice, during the cataclysmic period of their accession to power.

44. Charles Bettelheim, "The Great Leap Backward," *Monthly Review*, (July-August, 1978) for a more "innocent" analysis (according to the *Economist*, April 12, 1980), see J. Bredsdorff, *Revolution: There and Back*, Faber, 1980.

45. See, e.g., *Communique of the Third Plenary Session of the Tenth Central Committee of the Communist Party of China*, Beijing, July 21, 1977.

46. See "China's Fifth National People's Congress," report in *China Record* (March 1978).

47. Ibid. Compare current Chinese programs with Soviet policies as described by *HSINHUA*'s weekly issue 361 (January 8, 1976): "... Especially noteworthy are the cunning tactics (!) of the new Tsars in growingly making use of Western material forces to keep up the arms expansion and war preparations. Since 1966 the Brezhnev clique has obtained from the West several tens of thousands of million US dollars of credits and imported considerable advanced industrial know-how and equipment and nearly 100 million tons of grain ... blood transfusions to the Soviet war economy."

48. Ibid. For a Soviet analysis of the state and import of Sino-U.S. ties, accommodation and "quasi-alliance," see V.P. Lukin's "Vashington-Pekin: Kvazisoiuzniki?", *S.Sh.A.* (December 1979).

49. This theme is evident, for example, in the editorial pages of *Critique*, the Marxist journal of (critical) Soviet studies edited by H. Ticktin, of the Institute of Soviet and East European Studies of Glasgow University.

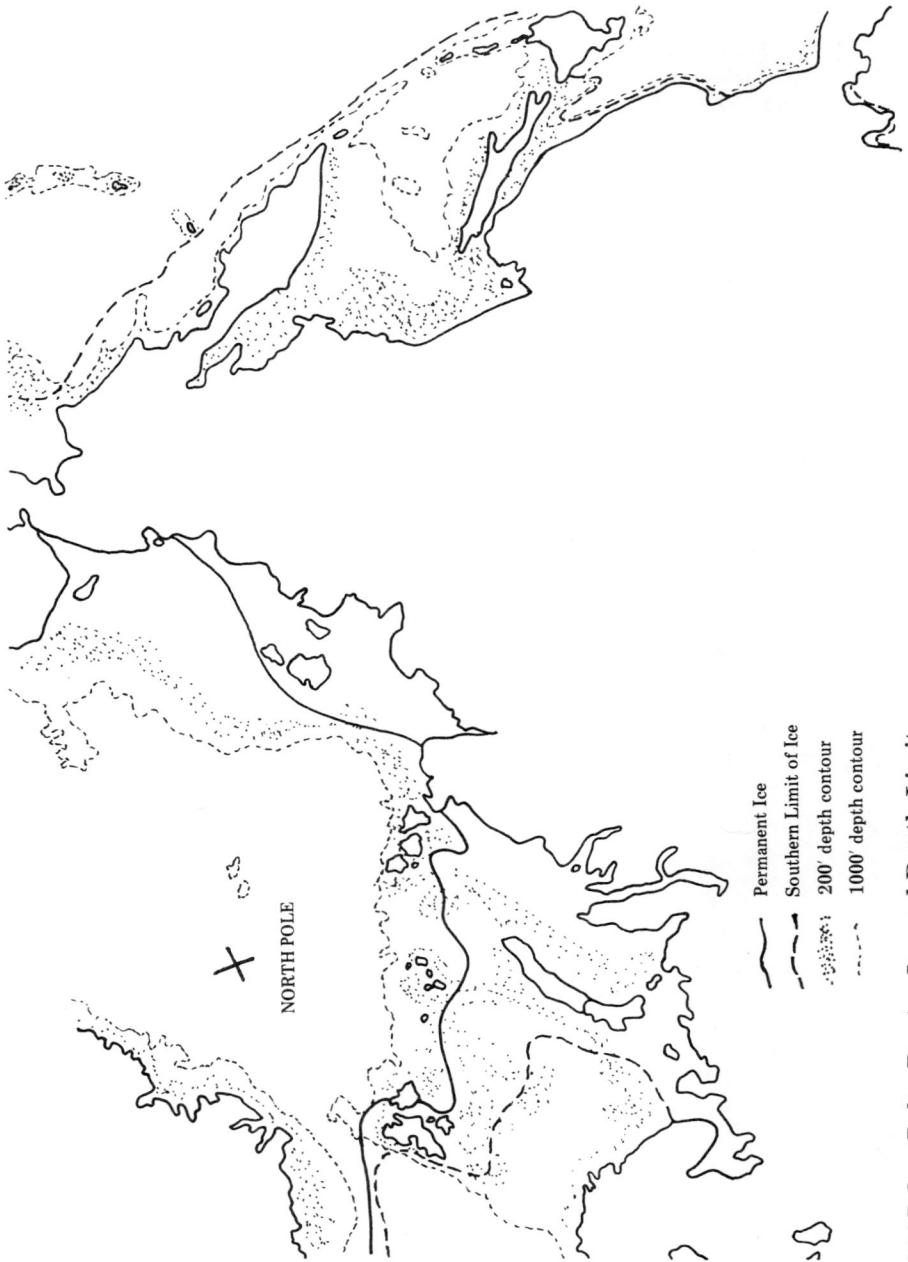

Permanent Ice
Southern Limit of Ice
200' depth contour
1000' depth contour

NORTH POLE

MAP 3.   Polar Route: Ice and Depth Limits

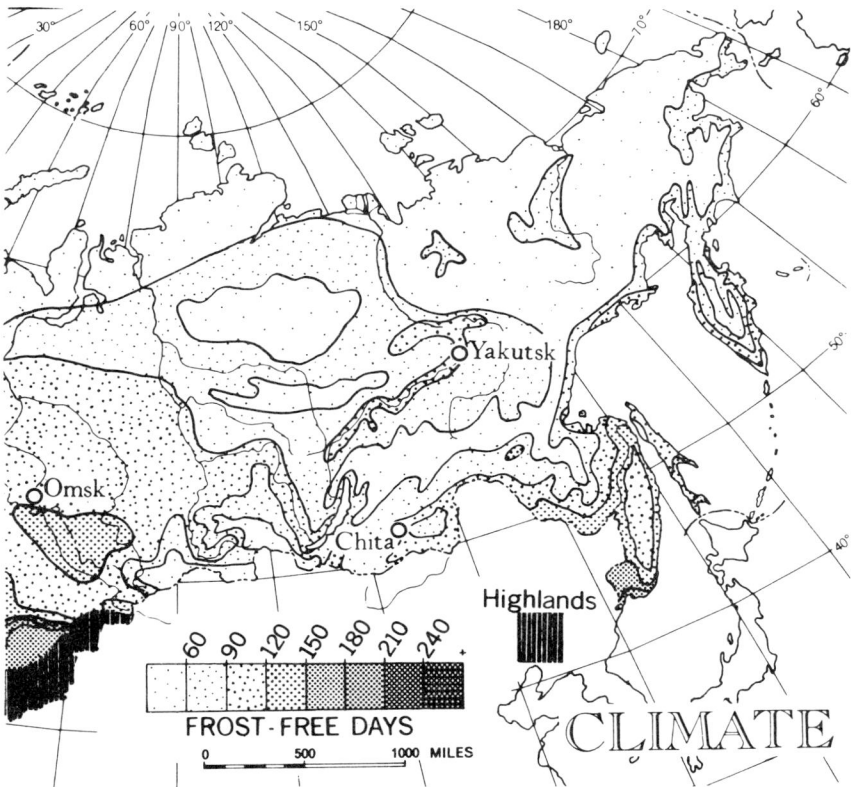

MAP 4.   Siberia and Soviet Far East: Climate

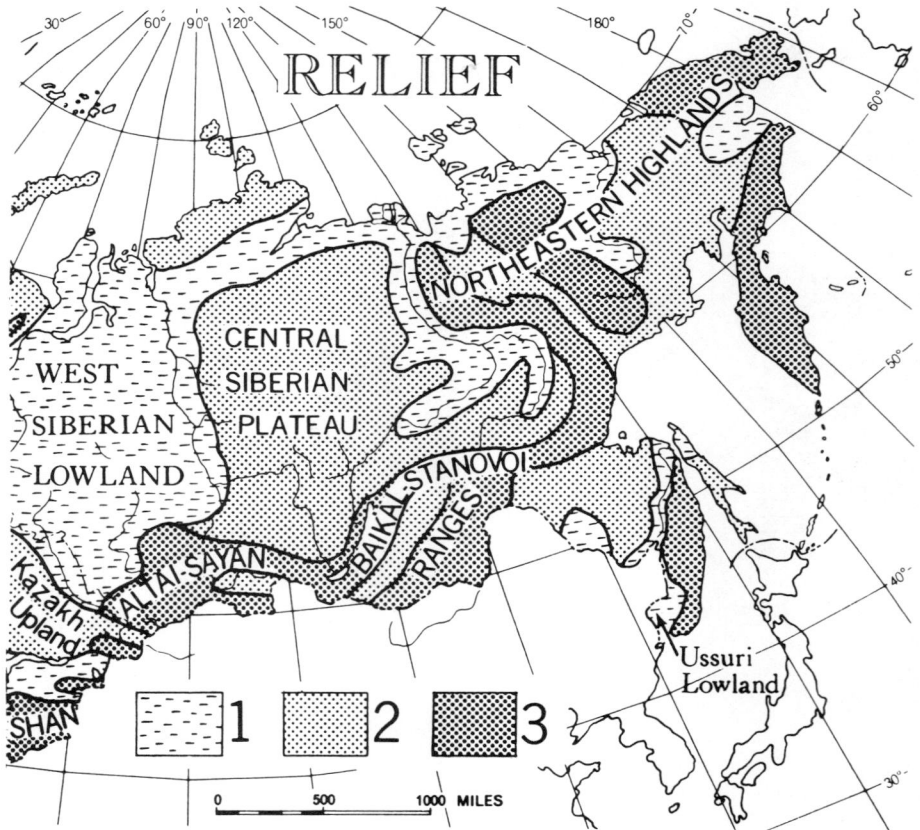

MAP 5.   **Siberia and Soviet Far East: Relief**

NATURAL ZONES

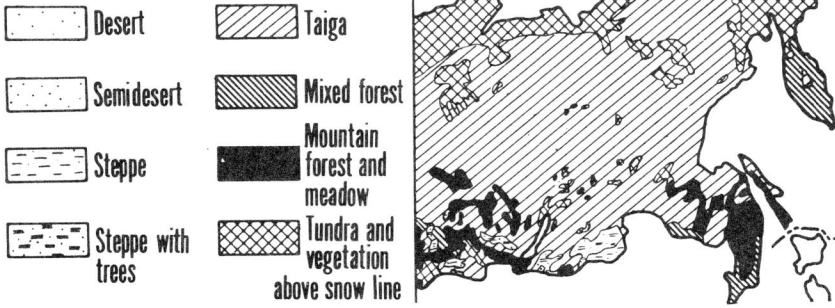

Desert

Semidesert

Steppe

Steppe with trees

Taiga

Mixed forest

Mountain forest and meadow

Tundra and vegetation above snow line

MAP 6.   Siberia and Soviet Far East: Natural Zones

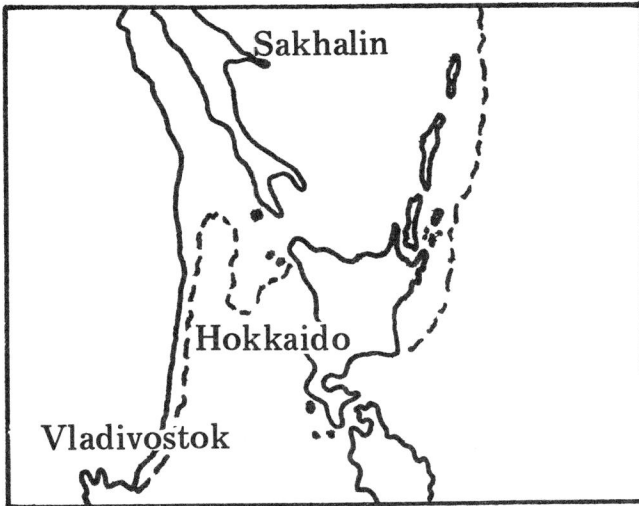

Sakhalin

Hokkaido

Vladivostok

Extreme Limit of Drift Ice

MAP 7.   Extreme Limit of Drift Ice

3 SINO-SOVIET RELATIONS AS A FUNCTION OF DOMESTIC POLITICS, 1965-1980

A nation's foreign policy reflects the needs and perceptions of its governing establishment. Foreign policy may concentrate on finding and securing trade opportunities, in response to the input-output requirements of domestic industry and agriculture; it may concentrate on the acquisition of military-political allies, in response to outside threats to the stability of the domestic policy; or it may seek to artificially generate a spectre of outside threat in order to manipulate a "rallying around the flag" effect and thus undermine support for domestic challenges to the established status quo. In reality, foreign policies are rarely single-issue oriented. They tend rather to be complex amalgams of a wide variety of concerns and aspirations, shaped by the interplay of a multitude of different and not always complementary priorities. The long-term stability of a particular foreign policy depends entirely on the stability of the domestic scene from which it emanates. Where it rests on concensus it becomes the outward reflection of that concensus. Where the socioeconomic or political balance of domestic forces is not in equilibrium, however, foreign policy often becomes hostage to the requirements of home politics; rather than being designed to affect external audiences, it becomes instead a vehicle with which to shore up the internal political fortunes of its protagonists. This "reverse" potential of a foreign policy is of course never altogether absent, and its possible impact will hence never be ignored by the architects of a nation's foreign policy; it will always constitute one of the considerations shaping a country's external posture. It is the relative importance attached to this potential that is crucial, whether it is a secondary consideration, a major determinant of policy, or, indeed, the dominant or even sole concern.

Sino-Soviet relations during the final years of the 1960s and through the 1970s did to a considerable extent fall prey to just such a phenomenon. While the domestic Soviet political scene remained comparatively stable, China's body politic evinced a high degree of flux, veering from periods of tense tactical accommodation to bouts of infighting so uncompromising as to conjure up the spectre of civil war. For much of the period Moscow had to resign herself to the role of impotent bystander, as interstate issues became submerged by the swell of China's domestic convulsion. The Soviet Union could and did react to particular expressions of that convulsion (her forceful ripostes to the 1969 border incidents provide a case in point), but such reactions proved either peripheral or counter productive to the pursuit of her interests. The Soviet Union became a symbol of sometimes vital importance to the resolution of domestic Chinese antagonisms, but the symbol was shaped and manipulated by domestic Chinese factions in response to internal pressures and calculations and owed little if anything to Soviet initiative.

Before attempting an analysis of Sino-Soviet relations during this era it is therefore essential first to look at the domestic factions and forces whose interplay carved the course of events. The particulars of the interstate relationship can only be appreciated on the basis of some understanding of the contending currents that shaped, defined, and used the outward manifestations of that relationship. The analysis below will focus on rival leaders and the perceptions and aspirations that they represent, concentrating on those personal and policy characteristics that can be said to have had an effect on either the reality or the symbolism of Sino-Soviet ties. This analysis will be followed by a discussion of the importance and meaning of the element of symbolism. The final section will look at some of the concrete events of Sino-Soviet relations against the background of domestic policy determinants. It will in effect seek to establish the consequences of the apparent fact that the events were hostage to calculations very different from those suggested by a consideration only of surface issues and tensions.

Mao Zedong occupies center stage. This is not the place for a detailed analysis of his "thought" or his accomplishment, nor for a detailed account of the fractious history of his relations with Moscow and with the more traditionally-oriented "apparatchiks" of his own party.[1] But certain points are pertinent and must be made. The first concerns his ideology. Here the question as to whether he had actually read or absorbed Marxist writings is less relevant. There is little doubt that his yearnings echoed the aspirations of Marx and Lenin, as they echoed also those of the Taipings (the peasant-based rebellion that swept much of south and central China in the 1850s and 1860s) and ealier dynasties.

Mao's vision was peasant-oriented and egalitarian. It was, in a sense, communistic rather than communist. He came increasingly (in his rhetoric if not always in his methods) to espouse antiauthoritarianism, local democracy, workers' control and management, and decentralization of government and economy. He was impatient for progress and had little stomach for bureaucracy. His reading of China's past nurtured deep antagonism towards central elites, which he thought bound to degenerate into self-perpetuating parasites, and towards the phenomena of colonialism, imperialism, and exploitation (whether Western, Japanese, or Soviet).[2]

During the 1950s he recoiled from the effects of the Sino-Soviet ties then shaping Chinese economic progress. He saw the imposition of an alien Soviet model as skewering development in favor of capital-intensive state industry at the expense of an excluded and to some extent exploited peasant majority. He saw the adoption of centralized economic management and command economy precepts by an increasingly centralized, bureaucratic, and hierarchial Party apparat. Propelled by his vision and protected by his stature as father of the revolution he wrenched the ship of state away from this path in 1958 and launched the Great Leap Forward—an all-out drive towards a decentralized emphasis on labor-intensive and self-sufficient local industries.[3] A smelter in every back yard. Relations with Moscow were but one casualty of the frenetic efforts and pace that ensued. The chaos, distribution breakdowns, and in some areas even starvation that resulted from what could only be described as a naive attempt at instant social engineering came back to haunt the visionary. The problems were exacerbated by the Soviet withdrawal of aid, technicians, and blueprints. By the early 1960s Party control had effectively reverted to the apparatchiks. But while his opponents succeeded in effect in retiring Mao from governmental authority, they held back from any attempt to undermine his outward status. His revolutionary aura was retained. It lent legitimacy to Party rule.

It was a decision that came back to haunt his enemies in 1965, when Mao used his mantle to launch and fuel an all-out attack against the Party hierarchy, calling on his followers to "storm the Party headquarters" and oust "China's Khrushchev" (President Liu Shaoqui).[4] Liu Shaoqui and Party General Secretary Deng Xiaoping were reviled as traitors to revolutionary ideals. They were attacked as representatives of a new class, a ruling elite for whom the enhancement and perpetuation of central authority took precedence over social goals. The long catalogue of Mao's very real grievances against past Soviet policy and action was crystalized in the charge that the revisionism of Khrushchev and his "heirs" constituted a betrayal of revolutionary ideals; their "goulash" communism was described as crassly nationalistic and commercial, using the traditional economic tools of profit and cost accounting to buy off sectoral interests at the expense of the longer-term needs of less privileged groups at home and abroad. The accuracy of the charge is of less interest than the fact that Mao felt able to smear domestic opponents with the same brush. Since the venom of his anti-Sovietism found resonance in popular perceptions of injustices wrought by Russian and "foreign" interests, he was able to add the forces of xenophobia to the appeals of his ideology and the glory of his past.

It was a volatile mix that could not be met head on, and the symbols of his enmity, Liu and Deng, were soon forced out of office. But by organizing their own Red Guards in the name of their tormentor, and by unleashing them to fight in the name of his cause and his ideals against forces of anarchy and chaos, they and their allies did succeed in generating confusion and turmoil of a degree that could not be controlled. Mao's victory had to be bought at the cost of People's Liberation Army intervention, PLA inclusion as a privileged member of the Revolutionary Councils established to replace older-style Party committees, and retention of much of the Party bureaucracy upon which Liu's and Deng's prominence had rested. To these concessions were added a final flash of the anti-Sovietism that had served Mao so well in his campaign against his opponents; the physical clashes along the Ussuri in March of 1969[5] provided the final unifying impetus to the April calling together of the long delayed Ninth Congress of the Communist Party of China (the Eight Congress had met in 1958). But while perhaps necessary for the convening of the Congress, the border events also reinforced the preeminence of the PLA. Its Commander, Lin Biao, now Vice-Chairman of the Party, delivered the main report of the Central Committee.

Mao was under no illusion as to the qualified nature of his victory. The prominence of the PLA and the survival of the Party apparat meant that the seeds of future conflict remained. It was for this reason that Mao came to insist that a controlled cleansing of the hierarchies of power, modelled on the Cultural Revolution, must be an intermittent feature of the future. He asserted that miniassaults on bureaucracy's inherent proclivity to entrenchment should occur every seven years or so. These would ensure that events never again force a choice between the turmoil of a full-blown Cultural Revolution, which endangered the revolution, or acceptance of ossifying bureaucracy or soulless pragmatism, in which the revolution was forgotten. Seven years later Mao's final campaign was to sanction just such a minipurge of officialdom. It was once again to be centered on Deng, his old nemesis; once again the theme of anti-Sovietism was to cow those who might have opposed the campaign.

Before proceeding to a discussion of later events, however, it must be noted that Mao was not merely a utopian visionary. Tempered by decades of intra-Party factionalism, war against the Japanese, and civil war against the Kuomintang, his idealistic impatience was also seared by the failure of the Great Leap Forward. His writings are permeated by insistence on the need to "walk on two legs," to straddle two horses; the stress on "unity of opposites" may be seen as the very core of Maoist prescription.[6] The point is that Mao did not give free reign to the "radicals" or "fundamentalists" who rallied to his vision ("fundamentalists" is indeed a more appropriate term, in that the roots of China's past have probably had a profounder impact than the dictas of ideologists). Mao was in fact often instrumental in limiting their influence on the daily affairs of government. Even in his final years it was in the realms of ideology, philosophy, culture, and longer-term strategy that he sought to give them predominance.

Mao demanded that the "radicals" (fundamentalists) be represented in the highest institutions of government. He insisted on the absolute necessity of their inclusion as integral parts of the nation's elite. He saw their presence as essential to the continued pursuit of revolutionary goals and aspirations. Without their presence he felt that revolutionary ideals would inevitably fall victim to bureaucratic expediency and self-serving power manipulators.

At the same time Mao realized that moderates and technocrats had an essential role to play in building a revolutionary society. He recognized the self-destructive potential for chaos in the zealots (and his own?) more utopian designs for precipitous change. Mao's choice of Zhou Enlai as Premier symbolized his acceptance of the need for a restraining hand on the rudder. This would temper the idealists' inclination towards self-defeating excesses and moderate their hasty efforts to transform society. But whenever this cautioning influence threatened to predominate, as during Liu Shaoqui's ascendancy in the mid 1960s or when Deng Xiaoping emerged from his administrative rehabilitation under Zhou to become Zhou's heir presumtive in 1975, Mao threw his weight on the radicals' side of the scale.[7]

There is some evidence that the ebb and flow of post-1969 compromise had shifted quite markedly against Mao's interests by the fall of 1974. There are indications that Mao did not acquiesce in Zhou's decision to bring Deng back as his deputy, and that he may in fact once again have found himself in de facto "honorary retirement" as he had ten years earlier. If that interpretation is correct, and the matter will be returned to below, then Zhou himself may have been scheduled for targeting by the campaign against Deng. But it must be said that with the possible exception of Mao's final years, when even Zhou may have become persuaded that the attempt to institutionalize radical guidance was too disruptive, Zhou's earlier history suggested no personalized ambition. Zhou had appeared the epitomy of the civil servant, the technocrat, the administrator, and had appeared content to leave the realm of theory to Mao.

There is one dichotomy between Mao's theory and Mao's action that needs to be mentioned. He espoused extreme egalitarianism and democracy based on the supremacy of local organs and institutions. Yet neither he nor his followers had the patience (or survival confidence) to wait for the required educational process to unfold and take effect.[8] They felt compelled to force revolutionary change from the top, to dictate and guide the democratization process. Propelled by their aversion to the dangers of a new elite they commanded to the populace that was supposed to command. They left themselves open to the charge that they were using Stalinist methods, resorting to coercion to speed the fruits of persuasion. The pace of their demands was destabilizing, and they confused and alienated their natural constituency at the grass roots. The constituency had been their safety net against the wrath of the apparat. The demise of Mao was to indicate that grass roots loyalty may have owed more to the power of his aura than to the appeal of his ideas. In fact that very aura, the Cult of Mao, could be seen to epitomize the gulf between theory and practice. It was justified as a unifying force to weld a disparate country of family loyalties but no state loyalty, a country with no tradition of nationalism of the Western type. The Cult of Mao was to be a substitute for nationalism, a vehicle with which to generate the unity of purpose that rapid progress required. And there is little doubt that it did serve such a function, as evidenced by the fact of Liu and Deng's fatal hesitancy to undermine it during the early 1960s, and Deng's still lingering reluctance to do so during the later 1970s. But it was also open to manipulation, by its embodiment and by his disciples.

The first challenge to Mao after the Cultural Revolution, however, had not come from the then humiliated Party leadership. It came from Lin Biao. Lin's view lay at "the opposite extreme from the former Chief of State, Liu Shaoqui, who favored economic development as the first priority and put social transformation and an egalitarian society in the second place (or lower)."[9] But Lin also recoiled from Mao's Trotskyite call for permanent revolution, from the insistence that social transformation required ever increasing vigilance and effort. To Lin the essential goals of communist society, of the revolution, had been achieved. The perversion and inequities of the ancient regime had been eradicated. China had achieved self-sufficiency in the socioeconomic realm, and her People's War potential (supplemented by a *tous azimuths* "force de frappe" of ICBMs)[10] was thought to promise protection against foreign encroachment. Lin was not driven forward as was Mao, or Liu and Deng; rather, he looked back to an older, agrarian, more harmonious, isolationist China, a China that could afford to disdain both Eastern and Western "barbarians."[11] He called for the Cultural Revolution to be followed up by struggle which might "continue for years," but the struggle was to preserve the great victory already achieved and to ensure that still scheming class enemies would not be able to effect a comeback; the struggle was not to be aimed at new victories or future visions of communism. He called for vigilance against counterrevolution and imperialism, but apparently saw less need for further struggle for social or internationalist causes. He called for "peaceful coexistence with countries having different social systems" and "respect for territorial integrity and sovereignty," but the stress was on arms-length accommodation, not empathy.[12]

But in the end Lin Biao's concepts appear to have found little resonance, either within the armed forces or in other elements of society. His purported coup attempt in 1971 and his subsequent fatal crash in Mongolia (the suggestion is that he was attempting to flee to the Soviet Union) remain shrouded in mystery and dubious assertions. Air force elements are supposed to have been temporarily grounded due to their alleged complicity, but otherwise the coup attempt appears to have occasioned few social ripples. In the end Lin's aspirations provided only a temporary diversion from the main focus of contention. His most important contribution may have been inadvertant, in that the methods and consequences of his ouster strengthened the Party and its functionaries. As Mao had needed PLA support to overcome his Party rivals, he now needed the support of the apparat built by those rivals to overcome the challenge from Lin.

The main gauntlet remained that thrown by Liu and Deng. It was epitomised by Deng's legendary statement that it mattered not what color a cat was as long as it caught mice. It was a theme of cost effectiveness for the sake of cost effectiveness. The core principle of traditional capitalism, it had been borrowed by the Stalinist managers of "state capitalism" in the Soviet Union and remained central to the analagous aspirations of the Chinese Party apparat that had evolved under Deng.

It was a credo abhorred by Mao and the radicals. They saw it as the same credo that had occasioned the social wrongs and inequities against which the revolution had been fought. The prioritizing of cost effectiveness over social justice meant that profitability became more important than protection for the disadvantaged. Mao had synthesized the two goals into his dictum "red and expert."[13] But history may record that the compromise union of the superficially divergent goals of efficiency and justice may be one that can only be afforded by the affluent (viz. Scandinavian and German social democracy), and that it can otherwise only be sustained by the extraordinary (Mao, or President Nyerere of Tanzania). In situations of developmental shortage or scarcity the norm may be that the differing priorities are not reconciled, that they instead diverge into mutually exclusive extremes—of perception, if not reality.

Whatever the inevitability of the phenomenon, it is clear that the heirs to China's revolution did tend increasingly to associate themselves with one or the other extreme. The history of purges, humiliation, and revenge ensured that Deng's policy differences with the Maoists became subsumed by the passion of personalized vindictiveness (the same phenomenon that had made Mao-Khrushchev differences irreconcilable). The radicals caricatured Deng as the embodiment of the ancient regime. They in turn were caricatured by Deng as hopelessly naive utopians whose inevitable failure would pave the way for the return of that regime. The radicals sought to guarantee rural employment and self-sufficiency and equated progress with self-sustaining decentralization. Deng sought state economic power and equated progress with increased state output and productivity. The radicals espoused the Marxist priorities of right to work, right to equal opportunity, and right to social security. Without these rights the right to freedom of choice would have meaning only for the affluent few. Deng, on the other hand, placed his emphasis on a more elitist human rights code. Contrary to some Western interpretations, he did not espouse general freedom of choice. He also saw this as a Western charade that portrayed reality for the privileged and illusion for the less fortunate. He encouraged and manipulated the appearance of wider choice. Yet, he equated its reality with deception at best, chaos at worst.[14]

Deng's focus was on managerial and technocratic freedom from pressure. He sought to free the intelligentsia from ideological strait-jackets and ideological belief. Brusque in the extreme, he was intolerant of opposition and tended to tar all opposition with the brush of dreamers. He wanted freedom to manage and get on with the job. His was a pragmatic state. Cultural freedom could be permitted, but only so long as it did not spill over into criticism of state structures and state prerogatives.[15] The post-Mao assertion that there would be no more Cultural Revolution was not just a negation of one of Mao's most central dictums, it was the quintessence of Deng prescription.

Deng's views of cultural freedom paralleled those of Khrushchev and his successors. They also owed a debt to early Stalinist practice, as did his definition of state economic requirements. Deng followed the early Stalinist pattern of industrial development. Basic state control was unquestioned. But foreign technological and other aid was sought with ardor; ideologically dubious foreign investments and joint management schemes were tolerated and indeed encouraged. Rather than fearing that such foreign contacts might ultimately undermine the sovereignty of the revolutionary state, Deng (as Stalin before him) saw them as necessary to speed the pace of industrialization and close the developmental gap to more advanced societies. Deng was not ideologically adverse to tapping the advantages that could be obtained from accommodation with Washington or Moscow. To the contrary, he saw the developmental constraints of isolation as unnecessarily constricting—and perhaps dangerous.

It may be appropriate at this juncture to look more specifically at the symbolism of Sino-Soviet ties, or rather the use to which symbols of that relationship were put. One aspect arises from the fact that challengers, real or imagined, to Mao's predominance were always ousted to the tune of allegations that they had enjoyed or sought Soviet support. It was a pattern repeated through the 1950s (Peng Dehuai was the most prominent victim of this era), the 1960s, and the 1970s. Where the charge was not direct it was implicit, in that the ouster or demotion was engineered to coincide with a stepping up of anti-Soviet rhetoric.

Liu Shaoqui had been explicitly categorized as "China's Khrushchev." The Cultural Revolution campaign against him and Deng in 1965 was accompanied by the renaming of the Soviet Embassy address and of the hospital reserved for Soviet and East European diplomats. The former became "Combat Revisionism" street, the latter "Combat Revisionism" hospital. (This campaign did, of course, also take on a more general antiforeign hue: the hospital for Westerners, built with Rockefeller money before the revolution, became "Combat Imperialism" hospital.)[16] Lin Biao, when his turn came, was grandly accused of "seeking a Soviet nuclear shield";[17] the purported location of his death was apparently thought to prove the allegation. Deng's second ouster in early 1976 was accompanied by this diatribe:

> The rise of power of revisionism means the rise to power of the bourgeoisie ... The Soviet Union today is under the dictatorship of the Bourgeoisie ... a dictatorship of the German fascist type ....

> This scientific thesis of Chairman Mao's has profoundly exposed the class nature of Soviet social-imperialism and its reactionary character. The Soviet bureaucrat-monopoly bourgeoisie represented by the Khrushchev-Brezhnev clique which is utterly reactionary, inveterately hostile to and morbidly afraid of the people can only rely on the most barberous fascist dictatorship to buttress its reactionary rule.[18]

A second aspect of Sino-Soviet symbolism as a weathervane for and of domestic politics is provided by the question of the border. Soviet propaganda following on the Ussuri border skirmishes had to dig back to 1945 to find a Mao statement to the effect that present borders might be just.[19] At the Seventh Congress of the Chinese Communist Party in 1945, in the flush of victory against the Japanese and on the threshhold of a final effort against the Kuomintang for which Soviet aid might prove decisive, Mao apparently opined that the treaties in force were "equal."

Moscow had no similar difficulties as concerns more "pragmatic" Chinese leaders. Lin Biao's speech to the Ninth Congress of the CPC in 1971 has already been referred to. During Liu and Deng's dominance of Chinese leadership councils prior to the Cultural Revolution it was announced that China "is willing to respect them (present borders) and take them as the basis for a reasonable settlement of the Sino-Soviet border question."[20] And Zhou Enlai evinced equal flexibility: the unestablished sectors of the frontier were "insignificant discrepancies in the maps, easy to solve peacefully."[21]

The post-Khrushchev leadership in Moscow apparently recognized that the real grievances dividing the nations had been aggravated and perhaps made insoluble by the implacable personalized hostility of Mao, a hostility reciprocated with like intensity by Khrushchev towards the end of his tenure. This had provided a major justification for their move against Khrushchev in the fall of 1964. They clearly felt they could negotiate with the then leadership in Beijing. The demise of that leadership and the resurgent Maoist influence that ran rampant with the onset of the Cultural Revolution forced resigned acceptance of the fact that substantial negotiations would have to await a swing back of the pendulum in Beijing. The next decade and a half would see tentative Soviet initiatives whenever that reversal of the pendulum appeared to be taking place, such as in 1969 after the flash of the first Ussuri border incidents,[22] in 1971 prior to the fall of Lin Biao,[23] in 1974 when an enfeebled Mao appeared (once again) to be losing control, this time to Zhou,[24] and in 1977 when Deng Xiaoping looked set to dominate the successor regime (see below). With early approaches repeatedly floundering in the face of renewed bouts of fundamentalism, Moscow's posture became ever more cautious, hesitant, and cynical.

The third aspect of symbolism lay in the deliberate selectivity of Soviet propaganda towards Beijing. The most uncompromisingly hostile verbiage was always directed at Mao, at the radicals/fundamentalists, and, after the ouster of the latter, at the one Mao-appointed official who retained prominence in the leadership that coalesced in the late 1970s, namely Hua Guofeng.[25] Attacks on Peng Tehuai, Liu Shaoqui, Lin Biao, Zhou Enlai, or Deng Xiaoping did occur through the 1960s and 1970s, but they were invariably muted in comparison. The 1979 crisis occasioned by Soviet-Vietnamese alliance and Sino-Vietnamese hostilities brought different factors to the fore. But the above-described dichotomy remained startlingly evident at least until 1978.

There is indeed little doubt that Mao's opponents wished to exorcize his personalization of Sino-Soviet differences. They clearly saw his personal phobia as harmful in that it entailed an unnecessary constricting of China's options and freedom of maneuver. They appear to have feared the danger of undue provocation. Some of them furthermore considered it to impede economic progress and prospects. There is considerable evidence that Zhou and Deng in particular were pragmatic believers in the benefice of normalized relations with both Moscow and Washington and that they were fully conscious of the bargaining advantage vis a vis either that could be gained from ties with the other. But the course of events was to show that it was easier to overcome Mao's ideological antipathy to ties with Washington. The 1970s were to witness considerable vacillation in China's attitudes to the outside world, vacillations which to a large extent mirrored the ebb and flow of Mao's influence. Whenever that influence appeared strongest Beijing veered towards a pox on both your houses attitude; whenever it waned Beijing tended to focus on improving relations with the United States while at the same time, on a less public level, also sounding out the possibility of accommodation with Moscow. The low key nature and ultimate failure of these latter endeavors reflected residual Maoist influence and potency. Yet, they were too substantial to be dismissed as tactical maneuverings occasioned by the approach to Washington. Certainly there is no convincing evidence that Mao ever favored a benign posture towards Moscow either as a basis for talks of substance or as a temporary tactic to facilitate gains elsewhere.

Before proceeding with a chronology of actual events it is necessary finally to comment somewhat further on the political balance of forces in Moscow, to the extent that it appears to have affected or been of relevance to the state of Sino-Soviet ties. The 1964 ouster of Khrushchev removed the one leader of prominence whose views on China were most vividly colored by personal antipathy.[26] The successor regime remained basically stable through the remainder of that decade and the 1970s. Policy towards China remained relatively constant. They did not concede past Soviet wrongs. But they did repeatedly stress their willingness to negotiate without preconditions. And they adopted a flexible posture on at least some of the outstanding issues (once the immediate emotionalism of the 1969 clashed died down, for example, they proved willing to depart from their earlier stand on border demarcation principles).[27] Their posture was pragmatic. Kosygin and government agencies took the lead in approaches to Zhou and other presumed moderates in Beijing. They were supported by Brezhnev, who diluted possible Party rancor by conceding that China had evolved a different social system and that relations with China must therefore be based on "peaceful coexistence."[28] This meant that priority be accorded to state to state relations, an area that fell within the purview of government, rather than to inter-Party relations as was the wont between "socialist" nations.

Party considerations of morale and propaganda obviously encouraged a harder nosed stand during periods of Maoist ascendancy and "provocation." Yet, the Party always proved willing subsequently again to sanction limited concessions, though it sometimes chose not to bathe them in the glare of publicity. There is evidence that what may have been the one most serious challenge to the Brezhnev-Kosygin leadership, that of A.N. Shelepin,[29] sought to enlist the forces of anti-Chinese chauvinism and enmity. If so, it is a moot point whether the effort represented personal antipathy on the part of Shelepin (an old Khrushchev protege) or whether it reflected merely on calculations of political impact and expediency. There is no question that Shelepin, who was associated with moderate inclinations as regards many other spheres of foreign policy, such as relations with West Germany, did adopt or sponsor harder line attitudes on China. By the end of the 1960s, however, his influence appeared to

have been checked. After what some observers saw as a near successful final effort to prevail in the early 1970s Shelepin was dismissed.[30]
The rest of the 1970s saw no evidence of substantive challenge to the
prevailing leadership and its established policy preferences, either in
the domestic sphere or on the question of China.

The following chronology of some of the major events and turning
points of Sino-Soviet relations during the period from 1964 to the
1977–80 establishment of the perhaps uneasy tandem of Hua Guo-
geng and Deng Xiaoping in Beijing is presented for illustrative purposes only. It is not intended to be comprehensive. The purpose
will be to demonstrate the relationship between interstate events
and domestic politics, the degree to which particular events may be
said to have been determined by the fluctuating fortunes of domestic
interest groups.

The positive atmosphere occasioned by the 1964 ouster of
Khrushchev, at a time when Maoist influence in Beijing policy councils was at its nadir, was, as mentioned, short lived. Negotiation
prospects were crippled by the onset of the Cultural Revolution,
and they remained fallow while its vitriolic anti-Sovietism (and more
general xenophobia) ran its course—until it ended in 1969 with the
final spasm of border incidents, the calling of the Ninth CPC Congress, and the formalizing of PLA prominence and Mao compromise.
A Kosygin approach immediately after the first Ussuri clash in March
of 1969[31] was unsuccessful. After the April Congress, however, (and
spurred, perhaps, by the politically telling military overkill employed
by Soviet forces in a final August border clash in Xinjiang, Chinese
policy began to change.[32]

On the one hand, Premier Zhou Enlai began to initiate or reciprocate higher level contacts with the Washington administration, contacts
that were to lead to Secretary of State Kissinger's July 1971 visit to
Beijing and the subsequent invitation to President Nixon. On the
other hand, there was also quiet movement on the Sino-Soviet front.
On July 1, 1971 Moscow offered to negotiate all outstanding border
issues.[33] One may presume that the accommodating Soviet stance
was prompted in part by the very fact and potential of Sino-U.S.
talks. But it also appears to have been solicited or encouraged by Lin
Biao. He is thought to have opposed rapprochement with Washington,
and the suggestion that Sino-Soviet differences could be negotiated
amicably may have been designed to undermine advocates of that
course. Whatever the truth of the matter, the "official" version of
Lin's alleged coup attempt and his supposed death while fleeing
towards the Soviet Union torpedoed the idea of Sino-Soviet talks.
1972 saw Nixon in Beijing and the signing of the Shanghai communique, to guide the process of normalization of relations. China had

adopted a definite tilt towards Washington: pro United States, anti-Soviet.

The situation changed, again, in 1973. The proceedings of the Tenth Congress of the CPC suggested that traditional Maoism was succeeding in reasserting itself, at least to a limited degree. The success of Mao and his radical allies may in part have been due to their ability to manipulate the backlash occasioned by Lin Biao's denouement, as well as to the unease caused by the presence in Beijing of the so recently vilified leader of the capitalist world. It is quite likely that other unknown factors were also at work. The exact interplay of forces cannot be ascertained. Yet, there can be little doubt that Mao had gained an advantage. The Standing Committee of the Party elected by the Congress continued to be dominated by older Zhou-aligned bureaucrats and civil servants. But this continued dominance of state and Party councils by the apparat was bought at the cost of accepting a radical/fundamentalist on the third rung of the leadership ladder, behind only Mao and Zhou, and the jettisoning of ties with Washington.

The tone was set before the Congress opened by Wang Hongwen,[34] the radical brought to prominence during the Cultural Revolution and now due to be installed as apparent heir to the aging duomvirate of Mao and Zhou. He issued a declaration that quoted and reiterated Mao's dictum that the country would need many more Cultural Revolutions before it could hope to have finally purged itself of the bourgeois and reactionary tendencies that still threatened to subvert the revolution from within. The theme was soon confirmed as Party policy. In his report to the Congress Zhou himself was brought to insist that struggles against the incorrect "line" must go on: "such struggles will occur," he said, "10, 20, or 30 times."[35]

Zhou's report also smeared the United States with the same vigor with which it attacked the Soviet Union. Both superpowers were now said to want to "devour China": the West was accused of trying to "urge the Soviet revisionists eastward," while Soviet anti-Chinese propaganda was said to be motivated by the desire to please Western monopoly capitalists, "in the hope of getting more money in reward for services in opposing China and communism." While Moscow might still be considered a more immediate threat than Washington, Zhou acknowledged little difference in the perfidy of their respective anti-Chinese designs. The Soviet Union was no longer described as "more deceptive and therefore more dangerous" than the United States.[36]

The next year or so was to see increased radical prominence. One cause celebre that was itself to become a weathervane of domestic Chinese power alignments was provided by the downing of a Soviet

helicopter and the capturing of its crew.[37] Beijing announced that
the helicopter contained electronic spying equipment and vowed
that the crew would be tried as spies. Moscow declared itself outraged,
asserting that the helicopter had strayed across the border inadver-
tently and that it was in fact on a medical mercy mission. The Soviets
demanded that the crew be released and followed this, a few days
later, with the emotional news that tragedy had resulted from the
helicopter's diversion as the man it was to have saved had died.
Beijing never exhibited any of the spying equipment that had purportedly been on board, an omission that lent weight to the Soviet
case. That case was of course further reinforced indirectly by the
fact that Moscow's established means of intelligence—satellites and
high altitude flights—were sufficiently extensive that the employment
of vulnerable helicopters in hazardous environments appeared anomalous indeed. But while Beijing refused to furnish evidence to buttress
the Chinese contention, it nevertheless held to its interpretation and
insisted that China would proceed to try the crew. There is no
conclusive evidence as to what followed. But Chinese officials
acknowledged that Soviet protests had not been restricted to verbal
varieties; they hinted that Moscow had also applied physical pressure
in the border areas.[38] By early June 1974, however, Soviet reaction
had dried up (at least as concerned its public manifestations).

Moscow's decision to gag its protestations of outrage coincided
with the final mushrooming of the Anti-Lin Biao, Anti-Confucius
Movement that swept China during the summer of 1974. Moscow
clearly did not wish to add fuel to the fire. The frenzy of the Movement climaxed the radicals' campaign. Lin Biao had become the
(probably unjust) symbol for past grievances, real and imagined,
against Russian and Soviet policies. Confucius became synonymous
with class distinction and elitism, a ruling "scholar" hierarchy that
regenerated itself through a carefully controlled system of strictly
traditional and pragmatic exams that weeded out candidates whose
views were at variance with the established social order. In other
words, Confucius became (again unjustly) the catchword for Mao's
opponents within the Party and government structure. As had been
the case with the Cultural Revolution, this campaign was also, at
least in some areas, fuelled by the fanning of the antiforeign phobia.
The industrial (and radical) center of Wuhan, for example, saw the
stoning of trains carrying German and other tourists. Wuhan was also
the scene of a confirmed instance of a poster that named Zhou Enlai
as one target of the campaign.[39] In view of the fact that similar
posters were not reported from other areas this one may have been
an aberration, reflecting on the excessive zeal either of an individual

or of the radical "Revolutionary Council" of the locale. In hindsight, however, it may also have reflected a judgment on the part of Mao and/or some of his allies that Zhou was moving uncomfortably close to an alliance with Deng-associated Party factions. The fact that Zhou had sponsored the partial rehabilitation of Deng (in 1973) by bringing him to Beijing to act as one of his Deputy Premiers may be relevant—the more so since reports of Zhou's ill health suggested that he might be preparing the groundwork for his succession. But then the public convulsion of the Movement fizzled out.

The end of the campaign may or may not have been caused by Mao's deteriorating health.[40] October saw reports that he had suffered a severe stroke and that his "active role" in Chinese politics was therefore at an end. The fact that he had continued to receive foreign leaders through September and into October led some observers to speculate that his physical health had not deteriorated as much as his political health, and that the medical "information" was being propagated by his opponents. This inference was reinforced by the leakage to Western correspondents of some rather emotional attacks on Jiang Qing, Mao's wife and long a standard bearer of radical aspirations. She was said to have succeeded in limiting Zhou's access to her husband and to have bypassed Zhou in issuing instructions to the Party. The allegations were clearly designed to disassociate the radicals' cause from the protective cocoon of Mao's personal authority and mystique. At the same time *Hungqi*,[41] the theoretical journal of the Party and a publication considered to be sympathetic to and possibly controlled by radical spokesmen, published an elliptical article that noted: "Revolution is always developing along the road of twists and turns and is advancing after constantly overcoming all kinds of resistance.... The new things will invariably replace the old." The article insisted that any setback to a revolutionary movement can only be temporary. The implication was that "the old" had succeeded, for the time being, in checking the Movement.

That check was to be formalized when China's long deferred National People's Congress met for the first time in a decade in January of 1975.[42] Zhou prepared the main report and was reelected Premier. The Congress gave ritualistic homage to the benefice of both the Cultural Revolution and the Anti-Lin Biao, Anti-Confucius Movement. It then proceeded to confirm Deng Xiaoping as First Deputy Premier and also elevated him to a deputy chairmanship of the Party. Wang Hongwen, still officially third ranking Party leader, Jiang Qing, and Yao Wenyuan (another radical from Shanghai whose prominence dated from the Cultural Revolution and who was closely associated with Jiang Qing) all sat in the front row, but none received

posts in the government. The one radical figure to be given a substantive government assignment was Zhang Chunqiao, but at the cost
of (or in response to) a muting of his public stance. The governmental
lineup confirmed by the Congress consisted overwhelmingly of
members of the old guard who had been targeted by the Cultural
Revolution and by the Movement of the past summer. The one new
face of interest was that of Hua Guofeng, from Mao's home district
in Hunan. A provincial official with ties to some of the victims of
the Cultural Revolution, he himself had never been targeted; he was
now appointed Deputy Premier and Minister of Public Security.

Mao was ostentatious by his absence from the Congress. By
arranging to meet with Franz-Josef Strauss, visiting leader of the
Bavarian CSU, and with Dom Mintoff, Prime Minister of Malta, while
the Congress was still in session, he advertised the fact that his absence
was not due (only) to physical enfeeblement. That left one logical
conclusion, that he did not wish to associate himself with the proceedings.[43]

The following months were, as suggested, to echo the period
prior to the Cultural Revolution, both in the fact that Mao appeared
removed from effective leadership or influence and in the fact that
he was apparently trying to rally non-Party and nongovernment
support for an attempt to reverse that state of affairs. In the meantime events seemed once more to favor a degree of Sino-Soviet
rapprochement.[44] In stark contrast to his 1973 choice of words,
Zhou's 1975 report asserted that Moscow was only "feinting" to
the East while in reality threatening the West. By conjuring up
NATO's need for accommodation with China, the line was in accord
with the desire for closer contacts with the West. But by suggesting
that Beijing no longer saw the Soviet Union as a threat to herself,
it was also condusive to discussions with Moscow.[45] Towards the
end of the year Deng, now clearly substituting for an ailing Zhou,
followed up on that suggestion, as well as other conciliatory gestures
by Zhou towards Moscow, by authorizing the release of the captive
helicopter crew. As if to emphasize the importance of the move Deng
furthermore bathed it in a measure of publicity, stating publicly that
the crew's profession of innocence was "credible."[46] Having had
their fingers burnt all too often in the past and acutely aware of past
occasions when Maoist influence had arisen like a phoenix from
supposed ashes, Moscow hesitated. Ironically, the very reasons that
appeared to cause Moscow to pause may also have been responsible
for the sense of urgency suggested by Deng's statement.

The opportunity was lost. Zhou Enlai died in early January. The
hiatus in anti-Soviet diatribes survived for only a few days.[47] A re-

newed radical offensive saw the (second) purging of Deng and the resumption of bitter anti-Soviet propaganda. Perhaps Moscow had appreciated the correlation of forces better than Deng, judging that Zhou's terminal illness left Deng dangerously exposed and that a favorable response to Deng could be counterproductive grist to the mill of his enemies.

The first signal of changing winds came a week after Zhou's death when the *People's Daily* published an attack on those who would attempt to restore any part of the pre-Cultural Revolution educational system.[48] The article called on the proletariat to seize back the leadership role in education. A fortnight later the same organ escalated by claiming that recent educational and scientific reforms had constituted an undisguised attack on the entire Cultural Revolution, that they represented an attempt to "reverse verdicts," and that they had been engineered by "capitalist roaders within the Party who were criticized and exposed during the Cultural Revolution but have refused to show repentence."[49] On February seventh the promotion of Hua Guofeng to Premier confirmed the eclipse of Deng. Attacks on Deng continued. Described as China's "new Khrushchev," he was accused of overemphasizing production and ignoring class struggle, of supporting overcentralization of industry and overreliance on foreign technology. Mao was quoted to say: "This person does not grasp class struggle; he has never referred to this key link. There is just his theme of "white cat, black cat," making no distinction between imperialism and Marxism."[50]

But the second banishing of Deng, confirmed on April seventh,[51] was to prove a pyrrhic victory for Mao and the radicals. They won the battle, not the war. They succeeded in forcing out their nemesis. They did not succeed in forcing out his (and Zhou's) old associates. The following months saw an attempt to use the anti-Deng focus as the vehicle for a further-reaching campaign. But the physical weakening and subsequent death of Mao (September 9, 1976) stunted the effort. The immediate aftermath of his death witnessed a radical attempt to rally forces around Mao's declared final instruction, "adjuring" the Chinese people to "act according to the principles laid down: study Mao Tse-tung thought, carry out Chairman Mao's behest."[52] But the extent to which Mao's sponsorship had been crucial to the radical cause was soon to be demonstrated. On the seventh of October the Central Committee appointed Hua Guofeng the new Chairman of the Party. Within a week Jiang Qing, Wang Hongwen, Zhang Chunqiao, and Yao Wenyuan had been arrested.[53] The Gang of Four was accused of having plotted a coup and of having purportedly subverted Mao's purpose and will. Mao's final instruction was said to have been a fabrication. The insistence that radical aspiration be disassociated from Mao's memory constituted a rather blatant rewriting of history; what is more important is the fact that such disassociation was evidently thought to be necessary.

The ouster of the Gang of Four occasioned immediate speculation that Deng would return, to be installed as successor to the presumed transition era figurehead—the compromise stewardship of Hua. Past events led Moscow to view the prospect with as much satisfaction as did Washington. Soviet expressions of respect for Zhou, upon his death, and Deng, upon his dismissal, stood in sharp relief to their evident satisfaction at the news of Mao's death and the ouster of the radicals.[54] The sigh of relief was almost audible. Yet their expectations, or hopes, were to be thwarted.

Deng was duly rehabilitated and given back his old positions in July 1977, and his policies soon appeared to sweep the board.[55] Industry saw renewed emphasis on bonus payments, financial incentives, and greater wage differentiation, coupled with strict calls for labor discipline. Intellectuals were defined as members of the proletariat (Mao had stated that only 10 percent of an estimated 5 million intellectuals took "the stand of the próletariat") and excused from the need to "study a lot of political and theoretical books" and from the need to attend "many meetings not related to their work."[56] Most of those previously disgraced "pragmatists" not yet rehabilitated had their names cleared and honored. A vengeful purge of radical followers or sympathisers was pressed.[57] Mao quotations became a rare (and very selectively chosen) staple. The themes that had permeated Maoist aspirations during his last decades all withered or disappeared.[58] Carefully orchestrated poster campaigns called for Deng's formal assumption of the Premiership.[59] The months following his return to his old posts saw conciliatory Soviet gestures[60] and some reciprocation from Beijing.

But although Deng policies were to predominate,[61] it soon became evident that his personal and political supremacy was not immune to challenge.[62] Hua would on occasion echo one of Mao's main differences with Deng. The following assertion is typical: "We hope our scientists and technicians will keep raising their political consciousness.... Politics is the commander, the soul in everything, and it won't do not to grasp political and ideological work."[63] While most of the remaining victims of Mao's ire were soon rehabilitated, it was not until early 1980 that former Chief of State Liu was even referred to as "comrade."[64] Hua also took a leading role in a renewed ideological offensive against Moscow, epitomized by his 1978 visits to Romania, Yugoslavia, and, in 1979, to NATO capitals.[65] There was some evidence that Hua was finding it opportune, for reasons of self-preservation, to soft-pedal the antiradical campaign now that its leadership had been emasculated. The Gang of Four remained under house arrest but were not put on trial. It appeared that Hua might be maneuvering to swing residual radical strength behind himself in a pact for mutual survival to offset Deng dominance. Anti-Sovietism served as a common denominator binding those leery of total Deng power.

There were no further Deng overtures to Moscow, though he long refrained from the rhetorically extreme anti-Sovietism espoused by Hua (he was also spared being targeted by the harsher bursts of Soviet counter-propaganda).[66] By early 1979, however, that situation changed. Suddenly, in conjunction with the buildup preceding China's February invasion of northern Vietnam, it was Deng who took center stage as the source of the most visious diatribes against Moscow. His new stance stood in marked contrast to his own past. Some observers thought the conversion could be ascribed to the cumulative effect of preceding events, the gradual development of a Soviet-Vietnamese alliance in particular; others suspected that Deng's "born again" uncompromising posture towards both Hanoi and Moscow may have owed something also to tactical calculations of domestic political advantage.

The uncertainty really revolved around the question as to how stable the Hua-Deng "partnership" was. Some observers thought a modus vivendi had been arrived at and that the era of domestic turmoil and quasi civil war was truly at an end; others were far less certain.[67] In the absence of any definitive evidence answers could only be speculative. They therefore tended to reflect more on the biases and prejudices of the observer than on the realities—whatever they might be—of Beijing politics.

NOTES

1. For more comprehensive accounts, see, e.g., Jerome Chen, ed. *Mao Tsetung* (Mao papers, anthology, and bibliography), Oxford University Press, 1970; and *Mao Tsetung in the Scales of History*, Cambridge University Press, 1979. See also sources cited in subsequent footnotes and Chapter 2.

2. P. Sweezy, "Theory and Practice in the Mao Period," *Monthly Review* (February 1977).

3. J.K. Fairbank, E.O. Reischauer, and A.M. Craig, *East Asia: The Modern Transformation*, (Boston: Houghton Mifflin, 1965) p. 878.

4. See J. Gray and P. Cavendish, *Chinese Communism in Crisis: Maoism and the Cultural Revolution*, (New York: Praeger, 1968) for a fine analysis of the background to and early events of the Cultural Revolution.

5. See, e.g., *Pravda* (March 1, 8, 12, and 30, 1969), *HSINHUA* (March 3, 1969), and *NCNA* reports (March 3, 5, 7, and 10, 1969).

6. See C.G. Jacobsen, "Developments in the Far East," in *Soviet Armed Forces Review Annual 2*, ed. Jones, Academic International, 1978, especially, pp. 265-271.

7. Ibid.

8. See C. Bettleheim's excellent analysis of the background to and reasons for subsequent developments, "The Great Leap Backward," *Monthly Review*, (July-August, 1978).

9. C.P. Fitzgerald, "The Emergence of China: Internal Dynamics," *Presentation, International Institute for Strategic Studies Fourteenth Annual Conference*, September 15, 1972.

10. Bill Whitson, "The Present State of the Chinese Military," in *Summary Report: China Workshop*, ed., Jacobsen, PSIA, Harvard University, March 1973. On Mao's similar espousal of "force de frappe," minimum deterrence bolstered by "calculated strategic ambiguity," see H. Gelber, *Nuclear Weapons and Chinese Policy*, Adelphi Paper, No. 99, (London: IISS, 1973) pp. 19 and 27.

11. Fitzgerald, "The Emergence of China."

12. For transcript of Lin's speech see *Keesing's Contemporary Archives*, 1969, pp. 23375-77.

13. C.G. Jacobsen, *China Notes*, Hudson Institute report, September, 1974 (see especially: section "Red and Expert"): also guest editorial analyses "China's Great Debate" in *Washington Post* (August 1, 1974) and "Chou caught in Chinese Power Play," *Boston Globe* (July 7, 1974).

14. See "Democracy movement faltering," AP, in Halifax *Chronicle-Herald* (February 21, 1980). And note followup article in *Beijing Daily* (February 22, 1980)—it castigated Party members who insisted on their right to decide whether the Central Committee's policies are correct or not—and to disobey them if they are incorrect; such members were said to have been brainwashed by "poisons" spread by the radicals, the Gang of Four (!). The article demands "political unity" and "strenghtening" of the "Party leadership."

15. *Beijing Daily*.

16. C.G. Jacobsen, "(1971), Letter from Peking," reprinted in *The USSR-China-Japan: Strategic Considerations Affecting the Triangle of the Soviet Far East-Manchuria-Japan*, Columbia University Russian Institute Report, March 1973, published as (Canadian) Department of Defence DRAE Memorandum, Spring, 1974.

17. A. Whiting, in *Summary Report: China Workshop*.

18. *HSINHUA*, Special Issue News (February 2, 1976). See also Alexandrov article in *Pravda* (January 16, 1976), which noted that "in the first half of January alone more than 100 articles with content hostile to the Soviet Union" were published in Beijing. Peter Osnos, *International Herald Tribune* (January 17, 1976) commented: "(There was a lull in anti-Soviet propaganda following the December release of the helicopter crew) ... But when China quickly re-

newed anti-Moscow statements—particularly in important New Year's messages—the Russians also resumed attacks. The death of Chou En-lai again brought a brief respite, but now that too is apparently over." See also, e.g., "Soviet Social-Imperialism—Most Dangerous Source of War," in *Beijing (Peking) Review* (January 30, 1976).

19. *Pravda*, March 30, 1969.

20. *Beijing Review*, May 8, 1964.

21. According to the Soviet government note to China's leadership of March 29, 1969. See *Keesing's Contemporary Archives*, 1969, p. 23314.

22. Ibid. The Note made it clear that Moscow would be willing to resume economic and diplomatic support for Peking in the event of a change in Chinese policy.

23. See *Summary Report: China Workshop.*

24. See Soviet Government Notes of October 1, 1974 and (following a Chinese Government Note of November 7, 1974) November 26, 1974. For Chinese interest, see e.g., *Historical Research* (Beijing), December, 1974: it "reaffirmed" that China did not reclaim territories ceded in 1858 and 1860, only such additional territories as had purportedly been occupied since the Treaty of Peking—nevertheless, China was said to be prepared to accept (only) "adjustments."

25. See, e.g., Alexandrov article in *Pravda* (May 15, 1977), also *Pravda* (December 30, 1976) which refers to Hua "diatribes" and (February 11, 1977).

26. See *Pravda*, October 17, 1964; *Keesing's Contemporary Archives*, 1964, p. 20389; and "Cool Line in Moscow," *The Sunday Times* (London), May 23, 1965.

27. See e.g., "Sino-Soviet Borderlands," *Asian Analysis* (February 1975). It covers the "Soviet offer in March 1973, to apply international law rather than the 1860 Treaty of Peking to the north-eastern river boundary—a step which would have moved the frontier in places from the Chinese bank to midstream and conceded several hundred small islands to China."

28. From Brezhnev's Speech to the *Trade Union Congress*, Moscow, 1972. See *Soviet News* (March 28, 1972).

29. The first challenge, and first check, was by some observers thought to have occurred already in 1965. See "Shelepin too strong for rivals' comfort," *The Guardian*, (December 10, 1965).

30. Tass (April 16, 1975 and May 22, 1975) notes, respectively, Shelepin's retirement "at his own request" from the Politburo and from his Trade Union leadership.

31. Revealed by Lin Biao in his *Speech to the Ninth Congress of the CPC* in 1969.

32. The August clash (note the Soviet Government statement of August thirteenth and the Chinese governmental response of August nineteenth) was followed by Prime Minister Kosygin's September eleventh meeting with Zhou Enlai in Beijing (the meeting drew up guidelines for future negotiations) and the October resumption of border talks. See *Keesing's Contemporary Archives*, 1969, pp. 23641-5.

33. See *Summary Report: China Workshop.*

34. See, e.g., John Burns' analysis from Beijing, "The lineup to inherit Mao's mantle," in (Toronto) *Globe and Mail* (September 6, 1973).

35. See John Gittings' report "Peking's policy shifts against Washington," in *The Guardian* (September 3, 1973).

36. Ibid. See also *Beijing (Peking) Review*, Nos. 35 and 36, 1973. Still, Moscow was not mollified; see, e.g., *International Affairs* (Moscow), No. 1 (1978).

37. C.G. Jacobsen, "Military Developments in the Far East," in *Soviet Armed Forces Review Annual I*, ed., Jones, Academic International, 1977, pp. 89-93.

38. Ibid. See also *Izvestia* (May 31, 1974 and June 6, 1974), *Pravda* (June 6, 1974), *Novoe Vremia*, (June 7, 1974), and *Mezhdunarodnaya Zhizn* (June 1974).

39. Jacobsen, *China Notes*.

40. "China Watchers Ponder Basis of Report on Mao," *The New York Times* (October 21, 1974).

41. *Hung Chi*, Beijing, October, 1974.

42. "Peking Meetings: Transition Leadership Set," *The New York Times*, (January 22, 1975). See also "China's Congress Meets and Backs Chou Leadership," *The New York Times*, (January 19, 1975), and, e.g., AP and Times-Post News Service reports in the Ottawa *Citizen*, (January 21, and February 22, 1975, respectively).

43. *Ibid*, *The New York Times* reports.

44. *HSINHUA*, (November 7, 1974) reported that Beijing was willing to sign a non-aggression pact and settle border disputes with Moscow (presumably a response to two such proposals put forward by General Secretary Brezhnev). While still tied to Soviet disengagement of border forces, the positive tone of the Chinese message may be seen to have reflected on the failure of the summer's radical campaign, and as an augury of later events.

45. *The New York Times*, (January 19, and January 22, 1975). See also sources cited in the footnote below. For a report on increased 1975 Sino-Soviet trade, see Radio Moscow statistics quoted in *The* (London) *Financial Times*, (June 16, 1976).

46. See "Moscow-Peking Pact in the Making," *International Herald Tribune*, (January 2, 1976), "China Goes Courting," *The Guardian*, (January 3, 1976), and, e.g., "Jetzt Pingpong mit dem Kreml?", in *Frankfurter Allgemeine Zeitlund*, (January 7, 1976).

47. HSINHUA, (February 2, 1976). And see note #18, and e.g., *HSINHUA* reports of February 24, 1976 and March 4, 1976.

48. *The People's Daily*, (January 15, 1976). (Beijing)

49. *The People's Daily*, (February 6, 1976).

50. *The People's Daily*, (March 28, 1976).

51. *Resolution of the Central Committee of the CPC* April 7, 1976.

52. "Chairman Mao will live forever in our hearts," joint editorial in *The People's Daily*, *Red Flag*, and *Liberation Army Daily*, (September 16, 1976).

53. Rumors to that effect began circulating in Beijing already on the twelfth of September; it was confirmed on the twenty-first. See, e.g., *NCNA's* report of that date (the same report also confirmed Hua's appointment as Chairman).

54. Soviet journalist Viktor Louis (a frequent "conduit" for unofficial Soviet government pronouncements) declared to the *London Evening News* (October 13, 1976), that "the majority of the leaders hostile to the Soviet Union have

now been removed from power." General Secretary Brezhnev followed up a fortnight later (Speech to the Central Committee, October, 15, 1976; see *Pravda*, (October 26, 1976) asserting that "there are (now) no problems in relations between the USSR and the People's Republic of China which cannot be solved."

55. For a report on continuing opposition to Deng's rehabilitation, see R.H. Munro's dispatch from Beijing in the *International Herald Tribune.* (February 11, 1977). See also C. MacDougall's report from Shanghai, in *The Financial Times* (London) (April 16, 1977). Deng's restoration was announced in *Communique of the Third Plenary Session of the Tenth Central Committee of the CPC*, July 21, 1977.

56. See Nigel Wade's report from Beijing in the *Daily Telegraph* (London). (May 5, 1978). See also *Far Eastern Economic Review*, (October 5, 1979).

57. See, e.g., D. Bloodworth, "Teng the Executioner Shapes a new China," *Sunday Observer*, (November 6, 1977); or report in *The Times* (London) (August 22, 1977).

58. The course of events was confirmed by official judgments that while Mao may have been 70 percent successful, he was also 30 percent "mistaken." See Reuter report from Beijing in *The Guardian*, (April 28, 1977). See also D. Bonavia, *The Sunday Times* (London) (June 19, 1977), and *The Times*, (March 8, 1978).

59. See *The Economist*, (March 31, 1979); *The Observer*, (March 25, 1979), and *The Times* (London) (January 10, 1977), for report on early posters.

60. See lengthy analysis in *Pravda* (April 1, 1978), also *The Times* (London) (September 29, 1978) for report on Moscow's lifting of the ten year blockade of Chinese traffic through the Amur-Ussuri confluence adjacent to Khabarovsk; and "China: Maoist Line" and "Peking: Balancing on a Dangerous Brink," in *International Affairs* (Moscow), June and September, 1977, respectively.

61. To what extent was perhaps best illustrated by *HSINHUA*'s January 25, 1979 report that China's old capitalists were to have returned to them money and property seized during the Cultural Revolution.

62. See *International Herald Tribune* (May 30, 1979) for report on Hunan radio broadcasts calling for continued class struggle and for reversal of recent policies favoring peasant private plots and increased wage differentials.

63. Address to National Science Conference in Beijing, quoted in the *Daily Telegraph* (London) (May 5, 1978).

64. See report in *The Times* (London) (January 11, 1980).

65. See, e.g., *The Financial Times* (London) (October 27, 1979). Also see *Pravda* article by I. Alexandrov, "Peking's Policy—A Threat to Peace," reprinted in *Soviet News*, (June 27, 1978) and *Pravda* reports of April 1, 1978.

66. For a somewhat different but interesting view (the divergence with the present analysis relates not to Deng's stand, but to a perceived change in the posture adopted by Hua and more radical "Maoist" elements), see "Secrets Behind China's Smile," *The Guardian* (January 27, 1979).

67. "Peking Admits Leaders, People Split on Policy Shifts," *International Herald Tribune*, (June 9, 1979).

4 THE SINO-VIETNAMESE WAR: CRISIS IN SINO-SOVIET RELATIONS

The Sino-Soviet crisis that erupted with China's February 1979 war against Vietnam will be addressed at length below. This was one of the unique wars of history where each belligerent—China, Vietnam, and Vietnam's ally, the Soviet Union—could be argued to have emerged victorious. Ironically, this state of affairs was to prove destabilizing rather than stabilizing. Before delving into the battle-field details and the subsequent course of events, however, it is necessary to place them in a longer-term perspective. A summary review of past Sino-Soviet relations sets the stage.

The years since 1972 have seen Soviet Eastern policy in transition. Evidence presented in earlier chapters might be seen to argue for an earlier cutoff point. But it seems appropriate, in this context, to focus on Mao's final years and the subsequent era of succession uncertainties. They reopened the question of a possible normalizing of Sino-Soviet relations. It must be remembered that the Gang of Four had espoused Mao's anti-Sovietism at its most vitriolic. Deng Xiaoping's past administrative record, on the other hand, clearly encouraged cautious optimism in Moscow (as it did in Washington). Yet the Hua Guofeng-Deng Xiaoping compromise regime[1] was to retain assertively nationalistic anti-Sovietism as one of its prime public policy planks.[2] By late 1978/early 1979, though still focusing most of its anti-Chinese propaganda on the person of Hua, Moscow had clearly resigned herself to a period of high tension gamesmanship.

China continued to insist on obviously unacceptable preconditions for negotiations;[3] an increasingly brusque Soviet stance mirrored growing scepticism in Moscow about prospects for accommodation and renewed interest in containment and other damage-limiting options.[4] When China rejected a Soviet offer to discuss improved relations in March of 1978 (due to Moscow's refusal to consider the suggested goodwill gesture of a border pullback), there followed highly publicized Far Eastern "inspection" trips by Secretary General Brezhnev and Minister of Defence Ustinov.[5] Then, within a fortnight of the late April resumption of border negotiations, Beijing found cause to accuse Moscow of a border violation involving the purported abduction of Chinese citizens. Moscow merely said the violation had been a "mistake," resulting from the "pursuit of a dangerous criminal."[6] When Beijing declared the explanation incongruous and unacceptable,[7] she was ignored.

Soviet policy had focused on the perceived need to contain China. One prong of this policy was provided by the ideological rivalry for leadership of Third World revolutionary movements.[8] Until the mid 1970s Soviet verbal and physical caution had given the advantage to the vigorous rhetoric of Maoism. The Soviet demonstration of newfound distant power projection means, in Angola in 1975 and in Ethiopia in early 1978, changed the situation. The new Soviet ability and willingness to intervene in distant arenas highlighted China's (logistical) inability to compete. China's frantic scrambling to counter the impression of impotence merely added to the damage, by suggesting that her ideological commitment might be as hollow as her military capability. Certainly China's alliance with the U.S.-supported and rather reactionary FNL movement in Angola began the process of disillusionment that was to split many Western Maoist parties and groupings.

The de facto anti-Mao campaign of the Hua-Deng leadership further alienated many Western Maoists.[9] More importantly, in the Third World it seriously undermined the "idealistic" memory and connotation of Mao and Mao's China. Once Moscow had shown off ability and willingness to more actively promote distant interests, Beijing's one remaining advantage lay in the fact that her ideological stance appeared purer, less self-serving. That advantage was being lost, with gleeful help from a Moscow that appeared oblivious of the irony involved. Beijing's staunchest African allies prior to 1975, Mozambique and Tanzania, became pragmatic supporters of Soviet (and Cuban) African policies.[10] China's only European ally, Albania, denounced her new policies as betrayal.

The other element to Soviet containment efforts was more direct. She strove to undermine any movement to formalize the complementarity between China's new policy stance and NATO interests.[11] Moscow reacted with outrage when prominent Western security representatives (such as U.K. Air Marshal Neil Cameron or U.S.

Presidential Advisor "Zbig" Brzezinsky) suggested the commonality of anti-Sovietism, and she warned repeatedly against the sale of Western arms to China (proposed British Harrier jet sales drew the most ire through 1978). A purported hardening of Moscow's arms control negotiating stance was said to be at least partly due to Western receptivity to Chinese courting. Conversely, China's one attempt to supplement her NATO contacts with an undermining of the Soviet Union's position in Eastern Europe, an attempt symbolized by Chairman Hua's visits to Bucharest and Belgrade,[12] was countered by hints that Moscow and Tirana might once again find a communion of interests.

Moscow strove to ward off the prospect of a Sino-Japanese Freindship Treaty. Soviet concern about this Treaty was heightened by the upsurge of nationalistic pro-military sentiment in Japan.[13] Nevertheless, there was little indication of the kind of willingness to compromise that one might have thought would have been induced by this spectre. Moscow proved unwilling to countenance the sacrifices, on the disputed islands' issue, that her purpose would have required (see below). Similarly, the late 1978 normalizing of Sino-U.S. relations did at least to a degree reflect Moscow's refusal to contemplate such strategic arms (SALT) and other concessions as might have stayed Washington's decision to "play the China card."

Moscow's preferred policy options lay elsewhere. On the northern flank, along the Chinese border, Moscow still appeared content with the basic force size that had emerged from the buildup that followed the border skirmishes of 1969. But the pace of her qualitative upgrading efforts was stepped up. The Far Eastern region was accorded priority in the early delivery of mobile SS-20 intermediate-range ballistic missiles. It also received the latest generation combat aircraft, including the newest MIG 23 and 27 variants (the Soviet air force inventory facing China was numbered at 1,800 by mid 1978). The Sixth Airborne Division, stationed at Khabarovsk, was brought up to full strength, 7,200 men. Although clearly targeted primarily against Manchuria/Beijing, the Division made the politically telling point of parachute maneuvers on one of the Japanese-claimed islands opposite Hokkaido (Japanese sources furthermore asserted that 5,000 troops were now stationed on these islands and that permanent bases were being constructed on two of them). A fourth major naval port was also reportedly being constructed, at Korsakov, on southern Sakhalin Island.[14]

But the most noteworthy news of 1978 came late in the fall, with Japanese reports that Moscow was assigning modern Delta-class strategic submarines to the Pacific Fleet (they had previously only been assigned to the Northern Fleet), and that she was also intending to transfer at least one of her new VTOL aircraft carriers.[15] The latter in particular would obviously substantially enhance her interventionary potential off China's coast.

1978 furthermore saw a number of Soviet initiatives on the potential southern flank of a direct conflict. One presumes that China was at least one (if possibly a minor) factor in Moscow's Afghan policy at the time of the April coup that first installed a regime friendly to the Soviet Union. And there is some evidence of a "China consideration" at the time of the June coup in South Yemen, which installed a pro-Moscow faction of the National Liberation Front of that country. But whatever the relevance of the "China consideration" on these events, or of the events themselves, there can be no doubt that Beijing provided the glue of the crucial Soviet-Vietnamese alliance that was cemented during 1978.

The warming of Moscow-Hanoi ties had been heralded in 1977 when the Soviet Union encouraged and supported strong Vietnamese reaffirmations of its sovereignty claim over the Spratly and Paracel Islands (China occupied two of the latter just prior to the U.S. disengagement from Vietnam and remained entrenched).[16] Through 1978 Moscow steadfastly supported Hanoi in its growing military-political-economic confrontation with China.[17] Leery of too great a reliance on Moscow, Hanoi long strove to settle its differences with Beijing. But, as *Newsweek* put it,[18] all Hanoi "olive branches" were "utterly rejected: the Chinese Politburo's line does appear intransigent." Beijing's ostentatious championing of the Chinese minority in Vietnam stirred xenophobic memories of earlier Chinese regimes' attempts to vassalize the peninsula. The ghost of past centuries' battles against encroachment from the north enlivened Vietnam's fears of fifth column potentials.[19] The response, stepped-up expulsion of Vietnam's Chinese business community, served in classic fashion to defuse these fears while simultaneously satisfying demands of chauvinist resentment and ambition. The oldest dictum of realpolitik, seek out your enemy's enemy, made Hanoi increasingly receptive to the blandishments of Moscow.[20]

China's punitive cutting off of all aid to Hanoi, on the third of July, was followed on the twenty-ninth by Vietnam's formal accession to Comecon.[21] China's throttling of aid to Hanoi had been heralded by the withdrawal of most of China's nearly 20,000 man construction corps in Laos.[22] An additional spur to Vietnam's Comecon move, the withdrawal had the immediate effect of conceding Hanoi's dominance in the area. Subsequent Thai reports that a missile tracking and intelligence gathering Soviet radar facility had been established in the Laotian border town of Suvannakhet served to spotlight the reason for Beijing's displeasure and discomfort.[23]

The unravelling of China's southern flank position continued. Public Chinese commitments to the anti-Vietnamese Pol Pot regime of "Democratic Kampuchea" (Cambodia) were followed by the November signing of the Soviet-Vietnamese Friendship Treaty.[24] The announcement of Beijing-Washington ties in December was followed within a fortnight by the Vietnam-sponsored "uprising" (cum invasion) that swept Cambodia in January 1979.

The latter coincidence of timing was of course just that, coincidental. The organizing and planning of Pol Pot's overthrow clearly dated back at least to that regime's suicidally provocative incursions into southern Vietnam in January of 1978 (the southern Vietnamese province had once been controlled by the Khmers/Cambodians).[25] Yet the appearance of sequence was arresting. With the media still in full stride eulogizing the mutual benefit of China's rapprochement with Washington, Beijing suddenly found herself more penned in by Soviet initiatives than ever before. Amidst speculation that the nebulous Chinese-U.S. alliance might give both leverage against Moscow, Beijing found she had to swallow the abject humiliation of a neighboring Soviet ally overturning the one South Asian regime to which she had committed herself and doing so in utter defiance of a Chinese military buildup on their border.[26]

By her encouragement to an alliance with Vietnam Moscow changed East Asian power calculations. Earlier, China could rest relatively secure that Soviet options for pressure were limited to border incidents, which could be tolerated, or else all-out nuclear assault, an eventuality that few analysts thought Moscow would contemplate except as a last resort. Since few if any could conceive of a Moscow thus persuaded, at least not within a limited time frame, the military disequilibrium remained of scant value as a political deterrent. The fact that Soviet opprobrium could only be expressed physically by too little or too much entailed considerable license for defiant action on China's part. Now, however Moscow was acquiring a range of options for a medium-level power response. She was in a position where she could one day, to take just one example, give decisive support for a yet more assertive Vietnamese presence on or around the Spratlies and Paracels (especially in the event that seismic data on oil abundance is confirmed). Moscow might even herself under certain circumstances acquire "facilities" on one of the islands. Her superior naval .capabilities would be eminently suitable should she decide to extend her protection of the Vietnamese homeland seaward. Or one might speculate on Soviet/Vietnamese initiatives vis a vis the hitherto Beijing-oriented rebels of Thailand's hinterland. The power increment that the shadow of Moscow's presence gives Hanoi is of course complemented by the very real military advantage to Moscow of a large, tough, and well-equipped ally on China's southern border.

One of China's greatest advantages has derived from her geographical location, and its implicit positing to Soviet planners of the dread of two-front war. The mutually advantageous realpolitik alliance of Moscow and Hanoi meant that a similar threat for the first time became a fact of life for Chinese planners. And there was little chance that Beijing could finesse the finesse, for example, by perpetuating anti-Vietnamese Khmer guerilla activities. Geography and other power determinants (the state of logistics, power projection means, etc.) favored Hanoi—and Moscow—at least in the longer term.

China's new predicament was placed in sharp relief during and immediately after Deng Xiaoping's historic early 1979 visit to the United States. Again and again the point was made that China could not accept Vietnam's "brazen interference" in Cambodia. Japanese sources described a further influx of Chinese land and air units to staging areas near Vietnam's border. Washington shied away from explicit support. And Thailand ducked repeated Chinese requests to allow arms transits to forces opposed to the new masters of Phnom Penh. But Vietnam's navy appeared finally to have succeeded in choking off Chinese gunrunning to Cambodia's coast and islands.[27] This meant that action that was to have a chance of success could not long be postponed. Moscow tried to ward it off. A Soviet naval squadron sailed into the Gulf on Tonkin.[28] In Moscow Prime Minister Kosygin described China's "outrageous charges" against Vietnam and the Soviet Union as being akin to "a declaration of war," and Kremlin leaders (in the established guise of an "Alexandrov" commentary in Pravda) warned that China must end its "unconcealed military pressure" on Hanoi. More intensive air patrols and fighter sorties along the border underlined the Soviet stance.[29] Yet the momentum of China's commitment and buildup, said to have reached between 330,000 and 360,000 men[30] (probably somewhat exaggerated), was not immediately deflected.

On the morning of February seventeenth tank-led assaults crossed along the length of the border. Beijing claimed the intent was to "punish" Vietnam, not to permanently occupy or annex territory. But her forces soon funneled into what looked like two Hanoi-directed prongs, aiming through Lang Son and Lao Cai. Hanoi's defences, down to about 50,000 men (many of the best divisions remained in the south, supporting the new Cambodian regime's pacification efforts), deployed in an arc north of the capital.[31] On day one the Chinese forces reportedly gained ten kilometers. Although claiming limited success (200–250 Chinese troops killed, an undisclosed number of tanks disabled), Hanoi lost no time calling for Soviet and world support. Moscow reacted with a sharp initial condemnation of the invasion. By day two, with Chinese forces 16 kilometers into Vietnamese territory, Moscow followed up with a sharper warning: to withdraw while there was yet time. Moscow said categorically that she would if necessary live up to the mutual defence obligations implied by the Soviet-Vietnamese Friendship Treaty (she asserted considerable faith in Vietnam's own ability to repel the aggressors), and she orchestrated a national outpouring of expectant outrage.[32] The same day saw more confident assertions from Hanoi (a considerable number of Chinese units were declared to have been destroyed, or to be surrounded) and the first reports of Vietnamese bombing inside China. The third day saw Hanoi claims that 3,500 Chinese troops had been killed and over 80 tanks destroyed.[33] Chinese forces were now said to be only ten kilometers from the border. There was speculation that the strength of resistance and outside pressure might be forcing reevaluation and withdrawal. Vietnam signed a defiant concordat with its Phnom Penh allies, as Washington "intelligence" told of evidence that Moscow was considering its own mini-invasion of China; in Beijing Deng Xiaoping hastened to stress the limited (though still ill-defined) nature of China's intent. The question of Chinese withdrawal then became uncertain; Washington sources talked of lack of clear evidence. Soviet spokesmen announced that their forces had been put on alert.[34]

The next day brought news of increased fighting, some new Chinese advances (especially around Lao Cai), and further Chinese troop reinforcements. Hanoi countered by recalling some of its Cambodian-based forces. Soviet Foreign Minister Gromyko repeated Moscow's blunt warnings. Chinese evacuation of Manchurian and Xinjiang border regions was announced, as was an alert of troops in these areas. The following day, the fifth, saw China pressing an attack against Lang Son. But Hanoi asserted that this attack had been beaten back, thus offsetting the psychological effect of apparent Chinese success against Lao Cai.[35] Hanoi took time out to celebrate its new treaty-defined status in Cambodia (the Treaty specified that Vietnam had the right to station "advisors" in Cambodia to "preserve the territorial integrity" of that nation—the same language as had earlier formalized the Vietnamese presence in Laos).[36] Soviet planes repeated earlier overflights over the battlezone and, according to Japanese evidence, began overflights over sectors of China's Pacific coast; the Soviet naval detachments in the South China Sea and off Vietnam were beefed up.

Beijing appeared to be battling for the kind of symbolic field victory that would allow withdrawal to be accompanied by a "mission accomplished" claim, gambling that this could be effected before and without precipitating major Soviet initiatives.[37] Moscow, on the other hand, clearly hoped that their force demonstrations would suffice, or that Hanoi would succeed in repelling the invaders by itself. The fact that Hanoi had not yet committed its premier battle-hardened divisions encouraged at least some optimism on this score.[38] The optimism was buttressed by Vietnamese statements that while conducting "a very close exchange of views" with Moscow, "we are prepared [at present] to cope with the worst situation."[39] Such an outcome would leave uncluttered a Soviet public relations advantage of major proportions. India had issued a cautious condemnation of China's action. The PLO had terminated its 14 year relationship with Beijing.[40] Others were following suit. The suggestion of Chinese aggressive tendencies doused the prospect of Western arms sales (posing acute embarrassment for British Industry Minister Varley, en route to Beijing to complete a major deal centering on the Harrier fighter).[41] The tarring-by-association of the United States (Tass noted that the *New York Times* found grounds "to state that the United States was informed about China's forthcoming attack against Vietnam") suggested U.S. complicity, but also served to reinforce allegations that Beijing was now a conscious tool of "imperialist" ambition.[42] China was said to be acting as a proxy for U.S. interests bent on revenging their own humiliation at the hands of Hanoi. It was a propaganda theme that found receptive ears. However, appreciation of this fact also acted as a goad to Beijing, making it more difficult to withdraw without some achievement of substance.

The sixth day began with a Chinese advance beyond Lao Cai, to about 25 km. from the border, and a major Chinese buildup against Lang Son.[43] Hanoi reinforcements were said for the first time to include some regular front-line troops.[44] Lang Son seemed set for a confrontation of some significance. At this time it was reported that a Soviet troop concentration was in progress along the Sino-Soviet frontier and that troops in Outer Mongolia had mobilized (it is not clear whether this referred to Mongolian forces or only Soviet forces stationed in Mongolia). China was meanwhile said to have extended its mobilization to Nei Monggol (Inner Mongolia). Moscow also sent a "command destroyer," with "a senior Admiral" aboard, to join its southern flotilla.[45] This was followed on day seven by still-increasing Chinese pressure against Lang Son, coupled with a new prong to the southeast, which was presumed to be aimed at cutting highway four and encircling Lang Son defenders.[46] Vietnamese forces answered with artillery shelling into China's Guangxi Zhuang autonomous region.

The second week of fighting opened with a large scale Soviet sealift of missiles and material beginning to unload at Haiphong.[47] China was said to have launched limited airstrikes against inland warehouses supposed to have received some of the supplies, but damage was acknowledged to be limited, and Hanoi apparently did not engage its interceptors.[48] A major Soviet airlift was reported also to be underway.[49] By the next day a three-front Chinese artillery barrage was said to have become more intense than anything seen during the United States engagement in Vietnam. Yet, while Moscow was coordinating steadily mounting pressure and support in aid of its ally,[50] it still apparently had not felt compelled to call up the reserves needed to provide a full complement for all its Far Eastern border divisions.

In fact, Moscow appeared increasingly confident that Vietnam would succeed in thwarting Beijing intentions. The Chinese statement later that day, that she (now?) would "not move into the flatlands of the Red River Delta"[51] —a de facto concession that Hanoi was immune—might merely have been a belated defining of original modesty; but it would be logical to presume that it also bore a relation to problems on the ground and around the periphery. Still, while Beijing apparently found it necessary to specify that she would not (or could not) defy the presumed limit to relative Soviet restraint, she did need that one victory of seeming substance. Japanese officials announced their understanding that "the mauling of at least one Vietnamese division" was the current aim, and that a final concerted Chinese buildup and drive to this end was in progress. The massive artillery shelling continued. Hanoi serenely (if perhaps deceptively so) repeated claims of mounting Chinese casualties. And if her figure of over 16,000 Chinese killed[52] was thought to be exaggerated, many analysts nevertheless gave credence to assertions that China had suffered disproportionately higher casualty rates. The crawling and indeed halting pace of China's advance, against less than Hanoi's best, gave heart to her antagonist(s). A Chinese hint that her eventual pullback would be to the border as drawn in Beijing, and not necessarily as drawn on international maps, reinforced scepticism.[53] It suggested a limited-area border occupation as a final fallback aim, in the event that regular Hanoi divisions proved too hard-shelled to crack. But Beijing had not yet resigned herself to that proposition.

By the tenth day of conflict the deepest thrust of Chinese advance, in the northwestern sector of the front, reached 40 kilometers into Vietnam. Hanoi announced that engaged Chinese forces now stood at 25 divisions, divided into five army corps. The number of Chinese combat troops (as distinct from support and logistics personnel) was said to exceed the highest total assembled by the United States during its involvement in Vietnam. Deng Xiaoping pointedly welcomed a U.S. call for Chinese withdrawal from Vietnam to be coupled with Vietnamese withdrawal from Cambodia. Moscow warned of Chinese designs against Laos.[54]

But the original invasion plans had clearly gone astray. Fighting continued at an intense level through the following day. No further Chinese advances were reported, however. In fact, Beijing had to acknowledge the galling news that Vietnam had made two substantial counter thrusts into China itself.[55] One roving battalion had struck towards Nanning at the end of the first week of fighting and had succeeded in operating inside China for at least three days. Furthermore, it now appeared that reports of Chinese "strategic" bombing inside Vietnam had been exaggerated and possibly fictitious and that China continued to shy away from confronting Hanoi's sophisticated air defences. Chinese media calls for negotiations to end the war were effectively rebuffed. Hanoi said it would not talk with Chinese troops on its soil.[56]

Still-increasing Chinese pressure focused on Lang Son. Six divisions and over 100 artillery pieces had reportedly been assembled for the assault. The town had been evacuated, but Vietnamese defenders were dug in on heights overlooking the town from the south. Amid constant artillery barrages between the defenders and Chinese concentrations to the north, east, and west, Chinese infantry evidently launched a number of "human wave" assaults on the town below. But while many of the town's facilities, including the hospital, were destroyed by the incessant shelling, physical occupation was thwarted again and again.[57] Vietnam claimed to be inflicting "heavy losses," putting total Chinese dead at 27,000. The Lang Son battle became psychologically important because it saw the involvement of one of Hanoi's finer infantry divisions, the first Vietnamese front-line division to be thrown into the fray.

In the fighting to date Vietnam had employed only militia and regional forces, not main force army units.[58] The rather astonishing success of the "irregular" forces not only reflected on their mettle; their tenacity had flaunted and hence acutely embarrassed China's hopes of at least braking some of Hanoi's vaunted front-line troops. The presence of regular Vietnamese troops by Lang Son appeared to act as a magnet for Chinese reinforcements. But although Hanoi evidently felt forced to call back more of her Cambodia-based units (though not enough to seriously undermine her Phnom Penh ally), the next days saw no Chinese breakthrough. The first Chinese claim that she had taken Lang Son came on the final day of the second week of fighting. Even then, Hanoi refuted the claim. And it appeared that the most that China might have achieved was that her flanking pressure had caused a limited and ordered withdrawal by the defenders. Subsequently, "Thai intelligence sources" indicated that the town of Lang Son had not actually been occupied, that Chinese forces had extended their hold on the surrounding highlands, but that Vietnamese defenders remained entrenched on some of the hills to the south and southeast.[59] A U.S. analyst commented that a Chinese platoon might have managed to scurry in and out under cover of darkness; certainly there was no evidence to corroborate further claims. The fact that a new formal Chinese request for negotiations no longer made any reference to the earlier demand that Vietnam end its role in Cambodia also buttressed Hanoi's credibility.[60]

China's battle field problems were compounded by an intensification of Soviet pressure. Planted rumors that Moscow would send "volunteers" to the Vietnamese front, a *Pravda* warning that the war "can" expand if China did not withdraw "immediately," a Kosygin affirmation that Vietnam "will not be abandoned in a time of trial" (he also warned against a Chinese invasion of Laos and declared that "the changes which have taken place in Cambodia are irreversible"),[61] and a Brezhnev threat that a Laotian incursion would bring "harsh retribution," together with another notching up of Soviet naval strength and activity in the South China Sea, were squeezing estimates of the time still at China's disposal.[62] At the same time Japanese Foreign Minister Sonoda's statement that China's actions were "unjust" brought home international image ramifications. The Chinese claim at the end of the week that "two or three" Vietnamese divisions had been destroyed was clearly false, since Vietnam had not engaged that many of her regulars. But it was a claim demanded by considerations of "face" and propaganda, in the event of PRC disengagement. It therefore appeared to augur a Chinese desire to effect withdrawal.

As the third week began Chinese officials did indeed talk of imminent withdrawal; by day 16 Japanese sources claimed that some withdrawal had in fact begun. But the same day saw Hanoi exhibiting

Chinese prisoners, the first airlift speeding Vietnamese reinforcements northward, and a declaration of general Vietnamese mobilization for a "war of resistance."[63] The day also brought "informed" speculation that Moscow would feel impelled sooner or later to administer "punishment" of her own, even if China now extricated herself. Hanoi asserted that the battle for Lang Son was in fact continuing. This was followed by a Chinese statement that she was beginning to withdraw her forces and by a call for future friendship. Hanoi, however, declared the statement to be a sham, a smokescreen for continued assault, and said that she was pressing the fight.[64] The rationale for the conflict had already been overtaken by the morass of the battlefield; it appeared that its termination might be equally confounding to the assumptions of planners—one of history's oldest lessons.

On March sixth, with three front-line divisions reportedly readied for attack, Hanoi (again) said that she would negotiate peace if China withdrew immediately, totally, and unconditionally.[65] The next day brought a Hanoi claim of "splendid victory"[66] (contrasting with Beijing assertions that her "aims" had been achieved), a statement that Chinese troops would be allowed to withdraw unmolested, and a caution that any further Chinese combat activity would be "severely punished." Specifically, Hanoi asserted that the molesting of civilians and looting of homes, purportedly engaged in by retreating Chinese, had to stop or she would rescind her promise to allow unharrassed withdrawal. China claimed 10,000 Vietnamese killed or wounded and 1,000 prisoners; Hanoi said it had "put out of action 45,000 enemy soldiers, 273 tanks and armoured personnel carriers, and hit hundreds of artillery pieces and mortars." Japan began to act as intermediary. As the third week ended Hanoi expressed scepticism, suggesting once more that China's withdrawal was a ruse to gain respite and time to reinforce. Clashes were said to be continuing north of Lang Son and in other frontier areas. But the general ferocity of the fighting seemed to have abated; the war appeared to be winding down.

Still, the military and political problems of Chinese withdrawal defied easy management. More Hanoi charges of atrocities were followed by reports of intensified battle.[67] Hanoi accused China of burning and plundering. Beijing accused Vietnam of stepped-up harrassment and attack, including renewed shelling into Chinese territory. New reports of Chinese pressure on the Laotian border heightened the uncertainty generated by the fighting on the main front.[68] Attempts to hurry withdrawal grated against attempts to ensure its orderliness.[69] The contradiction kept alive fears of further conflagration(s). There clearly remained a danger that the apparent end to the conflict might yet prove to be merely the end of its first phase.[70]

At this juncture the immediate scoresheet looked as follows. China had not succeeded in changing the course of events in Laos or Cambodia.[71] In spite of reports that she had not expected to succeed, that PLA officers had in fact supported the action on the premise that the expected defeat would be the surest guarantee of future funding commitments of substance, a consideration of Beijing's initial propaganda stance nevertheless indicates that there must have been some hope of greater achievement. There may not have been any intention to attack Hanoi itself, although Vietnam had to prepare for the eventuality. The odds on Moscow intervening if required for the defence of Hanoi/Haiphong were too great. On the other hand, it would appear logical to presume that China might have hoped to be able to take and hold a 15-25 km. strip south of the border. If such a strip could have been secured, then she might indeed have been able to bargain for "mutual withdrawal." It clearly could not be secured. Still, while one must conclude that China was not able to demonstrate the capabilities that she would have liked, she did demonstrate "will"—and this may in fact have been the sum total of her expectation and motive. Beijing had scorned Washington for not backing up its acknowledged means with the requisite will. She had now demonstrated that while she might fall short as concerns the former, she did not fall short on the latter point. Beijing also succeeded in seriously souring Moscow-Washington relations at little cost. (The tilt inherent in Washington's "evenhandedness" and the fact that the scheduled exchange of ambassadors went ahead in the midst of the conflict reflected more favorably on China's diplomacy than it did on that of the Potomac.)[72]

Vietnam, on the other hand, seemed once again to have taught a larger nation not to presume on apparent power discrepancies.[73] The conflict had also diverted attention from admittedly serious economic reconstruction problems. It provided the pretext for the reestablishment of a war economy, the type of mobilized command economy to which their experience was suited. The war served as a valuable patriotic unifier and reinforcer.

Finally, through her carefully calibrated escalation of pressure and commitment, Moscow appeared to have succeeded in "proving" that she would not desert an ally in need. She had done enough to retain her own credibility, yet not enough to sully the memory of Chinese "aggression."

There remained, however, many uncertainties. For the longer-term future, there was little doubt that Moscow remained desirous of accommodation—if too arrogantly so—and that the aspiration found at least limited echo in Beijing. But for the immediate future power politics remained the name of the game. In view of scepticism as to the ultimate character and steadfastness of U.S. aid to China there was surprising but compelling reason to suggest that it was Moscow that emerged from 1978 and early 1979 with the better hand. Certainly China's action against Vietnam indicated that she feared this to be true and, furthermore, that she considered the consequences to be so detrimental to her interests that a major gamble was required.

The very fact that this balancing of accounts can be suggested with a semblance of logic is important. It is particularly important if juxtaposed to evidence that the "China consideration" acted as a spur also to assertive Soviet policies in other regions.[74] Washington and other NATO capitals professed to think of the political effect of their China policies as the handicapping of Moscow. If it led instead to a greater Soviet willingness to pursue particular interests elsewhere, as indeed appeared to be the case, then the weighting of benefits would become a murkier affair altogether.

NOTES

1. R.H. Monro, reports in the (Toronto) *Globe and Mail* (January 10 and 17, and May 10, 1977).

2. *The New York Times* (February 25, 1977), *Pravda* (May 14 and June 7, 1977), and see *HSINHUA* weekly issue 440 (July 14, 1977).

3. L.I. Brezhnev, *Pravda* (June 7, 1977), *The Guardian* (February 8, 1978) report on a speech by Hua Guofeng; and see *International Herald Tribune* (March 23, for Tass statement and April 3, 1978).

4. *Pravda* (March 24, April 1, 19, and 21, 1978).

5. *The Times* (April 3 and 4, 1978).

6. Tass (May 12, 1978).

7. *International Herald Tribune* (May 15, 1978) quotes the Chinese response.

8. See C.G. Jacobsen, *Soviet Strategic Initiatives: Challenge and Response*, (New York: Praeger, 1979), especially Chapters 3 and 8.

9. Note, e.g., Charles Bettleheim's "Letter of Resignation to Franco-Chinese Friendship Association" and his analysis: "The Great Leap Backward," *Monthly Review* (July-August, 1978).

10. Jacobsen, *Soviet Strategic Initiatives*, Chapter 8.

11. John Fraser, "Anti-Soviet Alliances key to China's foreign policy," *Globe and Mail* (August 14, 1978).

12. Ibid.

13. "Japan's New Nationalism," see reports in *Atlas* (November 1978) and "Japan Rearms" report in *Atlas* (October 1978) from the *Economist.*

14. "Soviet Far East Expansion," *International Defence Review*, No. 7, (1978): 1009–1010.

15. *The New York Times* (July 29, 1978).

16. *Keesings Contemporary Archives*, 1979, p. 28913.

17. Ibid., p. 29473 quotes a Vietnamese government note of November 3, 1978.

18. *Newsweek* (July 3, 1978).

19. *Tap Chi Cong San,* (monthly), Hanoi (August 1978). See also *Le Monde* (July 6, 1978), *The Financial Times* (August 4, 1978), and *Atlas*, (January 1979).

20. See *Le Monde* analysis, in *Keesings Contemporary Archives*, 1979, p. 29471, for Soviet response.

21. Reuter in *Globe and Mail* (June 30, 1978).

22. *Atlas* (January 1979): 36.

23. For earlier reports concerning Soviet radars in Viet Nahm (from South China) see *Globe and Mail* (June 30, 1978).

24. *Atlas* (January 1979): 37.

25. See R.-P. Paringaux, "How Pol Pot demolished the Indochinese Alliance," Special report, *The Guardian* (April 16, 1978) and *Atlas* (January 1979).

26. NYT report, in *Globe and Mail* (February 14, 1979).

27. *The New York Times* (February 21, 1979).

28. NYT report, in the *Globe and Mail* (February 14, 1979).

29. Ibid.

30. Drew Middleton (of NYT) in *Montreal Star* (February 19, 1979). Of these, about 120,000 were apparently "amassed" immediately "along the border," Reuter, AP, and NYT composite report, *Globe and Mail* (February 19, 1979).

31. Reuter, AP, and NYT composite report, *Globe and Mail* (February 19, 1979). See also NYT Service "Analysis" by Drew Middleton, in same.

32. *Moscow Radio* (February 18, 1979).

33. *Chicago Tribune* (February 20, 1979).

34. Ibid. *Izvestia* (February 19, 1979).

35. *Chicago Sun Times* (February 21, 1979).

36. *The New York Times* (February 21, 1979).

37. Staff, NYT, AP, and Reuter composite report, *Globe and Mail* (February 27, 1979).

38. *The New York Times* (February 21, 1979).

39. Viet Nahm United Nations Ambassador, Ha Van Lou, UPI, in *Toronto Sun* (February 21, 1979).

40. *The New York Times* (February 21, 1979).

41. John Fraser, *Globe and Mail* (February 26, 1979).

42. See *Pravda* (February 20, 1979).

43. AP, Reuter, and NYT composite report, *Globe and Mail* (February 22, 1979).

44. Ibid.

45. Ibid.

46. NYT and AP composite report, *Globe and Mail* (February 24, 1979).

47. NYT and AP composite report, *Globe and Mail* (February 23, 1979).

48. NYT and AP, *Globe and Mail* (February 24, 1979) and *Boston Globe* (February 24, 1979).

49. *Globe and Mail* (February 23, 1979). See also *Halifax Chronicle-Herald* (February 24, 1979).

50. *Pravda* (February 23, 1979). See also Drew Middleton (NYT) in *Globe and Mail* (February 25, 1979).

51. PRC Vice Premier Wang Zhen quotes by CP, in *Globe and Mail* (February 26, 1979).

52. *Radio Hanoi* (February 25, 1979).

53. On the border question, see *Le Monde* (July 6, 1978).

54. *The New York Times* (February 27, 1979).

55. Reuter, AP, and NYT composite report, *Globe and Mail* (February 28, 1979).

56. Ibid.

57. AP, NYT, Reuter, and Staff, *Globe and Mail* (March 2, 1979).

58. *Boston Globe* (February 24, 1979).

59. AP and Reuter, *Globe and Mail*, (March 3, 1979).

60. Ibid. See also PRC Foreign Minister Huang Huo, as quoted by Reuter in *Globe and Mail* (March 17, 1979).

61. AP, NYT, and Reuter, *Globe and Mail* (March 2, 1979).

62. AP and Reuter, *Globe and Mail* (March 3, 1979). See also "Alexandrov" commentary, *Pravda* (February 28, 1979).

63. Reuter and NYT, in *Globe and Mail* (March 5, 1979). See also AP and Reuter, in *Globe and Mail* (March 13, 1979).

64. NYT, Reuter, and Staff, *Globe and Mail* (March 6, 1979).

65. AP and Reuter, *Globe and Mail* (March 7, 1979).

66. *Voice of Vietnam* (Radio) (March 6, 1979). PRC forces to withdraw "because of Vietnam's military strength, the Soviet Union's support of Vietnam, and objections to the war among the Chinese people."

67. Reuter, in *Globe and Mail* (March 12, 1979).

68. Reuter and AP, in *Globe and Mail* (March 14, 1979). See also Reuter, in *Globe and Mail* (March 17, 1979).

69. See Reuter reports, in *Globe and Mail* (March 16 and 19, 1979).

70. Reuter report, *Globe and Mail* (March 19, 1979). See also Reuter reports in *Globe and Mail* (March 21, 22, and 24, 1979).

71. On "War aims" see John Fraser's report from Beijing in *Globe and Mail* (February 27, 1979). Deng quotes in Reuter, AP, NYT composite report, *Globe and Mail* (February 28, 1979). And see "Chinese halt aid to regime in Laos," *Globe and Mail* (March 12, 1979).

72. John Fraser from Beijing, *Globe and Mail* (March 2 and 5, 1979).

73. "Suck Them in and Outflank Them," *Time* (March 12, 1979).

74. *Le Monde* quoted in *Keesings Contemporary Archives* 1979, p. 29471.

5 SINO-SOVIET RELATIONS: PHONY WAR

The crisis in Sino-Soviet relations that was occasioned by China's attack on Vietnam in early 1979 was the subject of analysis in Chapter 4, as was the fact that although unsuccessful as concerns her presumed primary war aims, China was nevertheless able to withdraw with a certain amount of "face." The remarkable fact that apparent victors and apparent vanquished could all claim success was not, however, to prove a recipe for stability. Subsequent weeks and months saw the ensconcement of a "phoney war" state of high tension, suspicion, and jitteriness, accompanying determined preparations for a possible resumption of military hostilities.[1] The extreme tension was later to be suspended, temporarily. Sino-Soviet relations took on the form of "talks about talks" that degenerated into surreal jousting or shadowboxing. The substance appeared to lie in continued discord within China's leadership and the consequent fact that policies towards Moscow remained hostage to the resolution of domestic Chinese factional struggles (see Chapter 3). Towards the end of the year the Afghanistan crisis and the world polarization which it triggered was to complicate matters even further. Early 1980 saw Sino-Soviet relations also become hostage to the international situation at large.

But the aftermath to the Sino-Vietnamese war must first be dealt with. After formal Chinese assertions that a full withdrawal had been effected, in mid March, Chinese officials were invited to an abortive first "peace talks" session in Hanoi. A Hanoi suggestion of a demilitarized zone along the border was not followed up. Mutual recriminations made further talks impractical. Hanoi returned to its charges that Chinese withdrawal had not been complete.[2] China insisted it had and countered with repeated claims of Vietnamese shelling and incursions north of the border. Hanoi, Laos, and Moscow all made new charges of Chinese force demonstrations and intent along the Sino-Laotian border. Laos expelled the final remnants of the Chinese construction corps on its soil, reaffirming its allegiance to Hanoi.

Vietnam remained mobilized. Some of the front-line troops thus released were thrown into a concerted campaign to break remaining Khmer Rouge guerilla concentrations before the onset of the rainy season.[3] By mid April came reports that some of the last rebel redoubts, against the Thai border, were being overrun (although full control of border regions would remain an elusive goal through 1979, due to unofficial Thai support to rebel remnants). In the meantime Hanoi had continued its more rapid movement of premier divisions to the northern border regions of both Vietnam and Laos. The scale of the buildup was thought by a number of Western analysts to exceed defensive requirements.

Soviet air force units were provided to facilitate Vietnamese troop and equipment transport in Vietnam, Cambodia, and Laos. The Soviet navy began to call on Cam Ranh Bay. Vietnam denied that Moscow had received or would receive permanent base rights. Nevertheless, the extension of limited repair and provisioning facilities was evidently seen to answer mutual interests and this was continued. April also saw the movement of the Soviet Union's new VTOL aircraft carrier, the Minsk, around Africa and into the Indian Ocean, evidently on its way to join the Pacific Fleet. The timing of the cruise astounded Western naval analysts who had presumed that the Minsk was scheduled for a much longer testing period in her launch area in the Black Sea. The obvious inference was to highlight the premium Moscow attached to the Minsk's presence in the Far East. The military-political impact of its appearance off African and Indian Ocean rim countries, while considerable, was clearly not alone sufficiently compelling to hazard extraordinary procedures. The possibility of the Minsk "observing" a Vietnamese "visit" to the two Chinese-occupied Paracel Islands suggested itself as a more plausible rationale, especially in view of Chinese April claims that Soviet and Vietnamese naval demonstrations had already taken place in the area.

The Minsk did not immediately proceed to this theatre of tension. It was deployed in a holding pattern off the Red Sea. The fact that it found a useful detour did of course not lessen its impact further east. Beijing knew it was available. A potential can be as powerful a leverage of policy as an actuality—and sometimes more useful.

By the time the Minsk (accompanied by the impressive Ivan Rogov amphibious assault ship, with its surface effect landing craft)[4] reached the Far East, China had announced that she was withdrawing from the obviously moribund mutual aid and assistance treaty that had previously bound her to Moscow. But she coupled this April announcement with an offer to begin talks with the Soviet Union on the issues that separated the two countries.[5] This time there was no mention of preconditions, a clear departure from the pattern of past Chinese offers. The dramatic absence of a priori demands may have been a purely tactical response to the threat implied by the Minsk, yet it led some analysts to speculate on the prospects of reconciliation. To others it suggested that China was seeking through parallel but separate negotiations with Moscow and Hanoi to make both suspicious that the other might compromise its interests; the spectre of separate accomodation might fray the loyalties of a new alliance. Yet others associated China's offer with a period of Deng Xiaoping prominence, after weeks of rumors that final Chinese evaluations of the war against Vietnam were far from unanimous. That suggestion might appear to jar with the anti-Soviet stance affected by Deng during the late months of 1978 and early months of 1979, but it followed from the openness towards Sino-Soviet talks that had been a hallmark of Deng attitudes during the preceding three decades.

The mid June convening of China's National Peoples Congress, however, saw Hua Guofeng in the limelight, with the assertion that the government had "eliminated the root cause of unending political turmoil and splits."[6] Hua claimed that talks with the Soviet Union would only be successful if there was a substantive change in Soviet global policy.[7] It appeared that preconditions might not be a thing of the past after all.

Mid summer saw continued uncertainty about the cohesion of the Beijing leadership. The imminence of Soviet succession, attendant upon Brezhnev's failing health, added to the uncertainty. Moscow-Beijing talks proceeded haltingly, at best, while Hanoi-Beijing talks remained mired in suspicion.[8] Moscow and Hanoi continued to strengthen their ties.[9] Vietnam allowed the Soviet Union to establish an electronic listening post near Cam Ranh Bay; Tu-95 Bear reconnaissance planes were allowed to operate from Vietnamese airfields.

In fact, the above paragraph appears equally applicable as a description of Sino-Soviet relations through the remainder of 1979. The tone of the relations was exemplified by the rancor surrounding the start of formal negotiations in September. There was to be no honeymoon type suspension of propaganda. The very day negotiations began Chinese media printed a harsh attack on Soviet policies, past and present. Moscow struck back at Hua Guofeng's "slanderous insinuations and inventions" and warned that a revivial of preconditions would "derail the talks...or protract them into infinity."[10] The slanging match evoked memories of earlier periods of Mao and radical dominance of China's leadership councils.[11] To observers who believed that China's current leadership tandem of Hua and Deng was somewhat less than harmonious, and that Hua had rallied erstwhile followers of the ousted radical leadership (Gang of Four) to his cause, the state of affairs suggested that Hua had indeed secured a temporary advantage.

The fall of 1979 was to bring evidence of continued leadership uncertainties.[12] It appeared that Hua's summer assertion might have been a mite too hasty. Embassy and press reports spoke of a new poster campaign reminiscent of that which had called for Deng's rehabilitation two years earlier. Demands that Deng be given the Premiership and perhaps the Party Chairmanship were prominent. The (very) occasional criticism of Deng and sometime calls for more general "human rights" led some Western reporters to speak of a new "Democracy Movement." But that was quite evidently not the intent of what in hindsight came to appear as a carefully orchestrated campaign of far greater singlemindedness. In fact, the appearance of contrary or wider-ranging demands soon led to the demise of the "Democracy Wall," the prominent locale where most of the posters appeared. First a more obscure locale was designated for the display of "spontaneous" posters; then at least some of those who had ventured to take the lead in advocating individual rights were arrested, one to be tried and convicted, others apparently to languish in (formally illegal) judicial limbo.[13]

By early 1980 Deng remained highly visible, but still without the titles that might cement his supremacy. January and February brought Chinese government "leaks" to the effect that wall posters were a pernicious tool of the Cultural Revolution and the radical Gang of Four.[14] Then came an article attacking Party members who insisted on the right to decide whether Central Committee policies were correct or not and to disobey them if they were incorrect. This view was blamed on deep "poisons" left by the ousted Gang of Four.[15]

The media offensive fitted in nicely with Deng's general reversion of Mao's policies and aspirations. (The Maoist doctrines that intermittent assaults on bureaucracy were essential to keep revolutionary goals alive and ensure against ossification or elitism, that the intelligentsia and managerial personnel must continue to receive "political" education, that decentralization and labor-intensive industries were required in order to ensure against the development of a "new class" of mandarins and the distortions of an overly centralized economic infrastructure had all been discarded.) But this time it was Deng himself who had resorted to poster politics. It is impossible to know whether the denouement was decreed by Deng because uncontrolled elements were diffusing the original purpose of the campaign. That interpretation would accord with Deng's character. On the other hand, the campaign's demise might with equal logic be attributed to the success of his presumed opponents. They may well have encouraged the profusion of "spontaneous" posters that so effectively derailed the course of the campaign. If so, then the victory (however partial or ephemeral it might prove in the long run) must have been as sweet as it was ironic. Because such, precisely, were the tactics that Liu Shaoqui and Deng had employed so successfully to stunt Mao's Cultural Revolution during the mid 1960s. By organizing their own Red Guards in the name of their tormentor (Mao) they had not managed to avert their own dismissal (temporary, in Deng's case), but they had managed to generate sufficient chaos to save their followers and force Mao to compromise. Deng's opponents may of course have prevailed for other reasons, a possibility less pleasing to connoisseurs of the whims of Fortuna, but not implausible. That Deng's strategem could be smeared by association with "poisons" spread by the radicals is perhaps sufficient irony.

The point here is not just that Deng's recourse to Maoist methods might have impressed Machiavelli, or that the same comment may be applicable to his opponents' response. The important thing to note is that the evidence suggested continued struggle within China's highest leadership echelons. In this contest Sino-Soviet differences could not be resolved, or indeed negotiated. Sino-Soviet relations remained hostage to domestic Chinese politics.

With movement on the Sino-Soviet front stymied by domestic Chinese discord, Chinese foreign policy continued to concentrate on the less contentious task of limited rapprochement with Washington and Tokyo. China's aims in this regard and the relative strength of her bargaining position benefitted from the steady worsening of Soviet-U.S. (and to a lesser extent Soviet-Japanese) relations that occurred during 1979. U.S. eagerness may be traced through Washington's agreement to exchange ambassadors in early 1979 while invading Chinese troops still remained on Vietnamese soil, to Defense Secretary Brown's January 1980 visit to Beijing, and talks of "nonlethal" military sales and defence policy coordination. China responded with gestures that imparted dramatic political effect. Verbal castigation of Moscow's intervention in Afghanistan was followed by Foreign Minister Huang Hua's visit to Afghan refugee camps in Pakistan (where he promised unspecified military and economic aid), the termination of the in any case floundering Sino-Soviet talks, and the announcement that China would join President Carter's boycott of the 1980 Summer Olympics in Moscow. Yet it should perhaps be noted that Beijing's stand was not as committing as it was politically telling. Bridges might have been scorched somewhat, but they had not been burnt.

China's relations with Tokyo were, as mentioned, also well served by Moscow-Tokyo estrangement, though to a different degree.[16] Tokyo was clearly uneasy about the Soviet buildup of forces on the disputed islands off Hokkaido. The buildup was in a sense merely a reflection of Moscow's more general dual purpose efforts: to guarantee the inviolability of the Okhotsk Sea (and hence the invulnerability of SSBN forces deployed in that sea) and to build and secure the qualitative-quantitative force mix required for the pursuit of further ranging interests—whether in the South China Sea or elsewhere. Jitteriness in Tokyo was inevitable. As might have been predicted, Tokyo pressed opportunities for closer economic ties with China. And she, too, announced that she would participate in Carter's Olympic boycott. Yet she did not follow Carter's post-Afganistan lead in cutting economic investment, trade, and cultural links with the Soviet Union. Perhaps because her investment stake and resource dependence was of a greater order, perhaps because her continued ability to fish disputed waters was more vital, Japan chose to be careful not to circumscribe her options. Sino-Japanese accommodations were furthered. But in this case both partners chose to limit collateral commitments.

But the Afghanistan crisis must be looked at more closely.[17] Although it was the superpowers that took center stage, the drama that unfolded would also have a major impact on Sino-Soviet relations, indeed on international affairs in general. The crisis appeared to transform international atmospherics. The 1970s had been ushered in on the crest of ostpolitik, detente, perceptions of domestic prosperity, and relative world harmony (the still lingering Vietnam War and other lesser conflagrations of the moment were seen as warts, persistent irritants, but of no lasting import). The 1980s, however, opened with Soviet troops entrenched in Afghanistan, talk of Sino-U.S. support to anti-Soviet guerillas, a world energy crisis, recession, increased arms budgets, and international frigidity.

The change was all the more dramatic for being sudden, or, rather, for being seen as sudden. After all, the spring of 1979 had seen the signing of the second Soviet-U.S. SALT agreement and renewed talk of Soviet-U.S. cooperation—leading some observers to speculate that China's subsequent willingness to enter negotiations with Moscow must be motivated by a new desire not to be left out in the cold. The change in climate did not just appear sudden, it also appeared incongruous. One might well argue that the Soviet resort to force in Afghanistan was, at least in one sense, but a reflection of the nasty but persistent tendency of great powers to ignore the niceties of law whenever required by "national interests." China's invasion of Vietnam in early 1979 might have been less successful, but it had of course seen the deployment of a larger force, and perhaps greater brutality (if one accepts reports that chemical-biological weapons were used).[18] French and Moroccan paratroopers had toppled two African governments during the summer and fall of 1979 and "stabilized" others. The United States had desisted from the use of large-scale military force since President Nixon's invasion of Cambodia, but it was open to charges that it had built a rich tradition prior to that event.

The Afghan events were also discouragingly typical in that they mirrored an outside power's decision that further commitment was required to protect established interests from perceived jeopardy (Moscow's "presence" in northern Afghanistan had long roots; Britain's first invasion of the country in 1838 was designed precisely to check Russian influence).[19] Although proclaiming himself a Soviet ally and a "Marxist," Afghan President Amin had ousted Soviet-supported Party members with ties to the clergy and other traditional sectors of Afghan society; he had ousted Soviet advisors of caution and remained incompromising in spite of alienation that generated rebel support in 80 percent of the country. In view of allegations of Chinese and U.S. support for rebel aspirations[20] (and potentially for Amin) the brutal realpolitik of traditional Russian perception left little leeway to opponents of action—especially once attempts at a more "discreet" coup failed. To the Russian psyche one China and one Ayatollah facing Moslem Central Asia was quite enough.

But as the Strategic Arms Limitation Treaty of 1972 came to symbolize the gradual flowering of detente that had preceded it, so the Afghanistan crisis took on symbolic meaning far beyond what might have been warranted by its content alone. It capped and symbolized the unravelling of detente aspirations. The fact that the unravelling preceded the Soviet intervention ironically served to bolster advocates of intervention. The possible disincentives to intervention had already fallen prey to the anti-Soviet mood of U.S. domestic politics. NATO arms budgets had already been increased. Senate ratification of a second SALT treaty looked less and less likely. Hopes that Congress might yet ratify the trade agreement signed by Nixon in 1972 were dashed by the announcement that China's application for "Most Favored Nation" treatment would be decoupled from that of Moscow and that China's would be granted (never mind that Beijing's human rights record appeared even more suspect than Moscow's). American high technology sales were increasingly subject to Administration embargoes. Soviet dissidents continued to find disproportionate fame on U.S. lecture podiums and in the U.S. media. Andy Young, the Administration's most prominent proponent of the thesis that all the world's ills might not be caused by Moscow but might sometimes owe something to local antagonisms, under-development, or different forms of exploitation, resigned his ambassadorship to the United Nations. As already mentioned, early 1979 saw Washington send its first ambassador to Beijing while invading Chinese troops remained on the soil of Moscow's Southeast Asian ally; the end of the year saw preparation for the first visit to China of a U.S. Secretary of Defense amid "leaks" of military-technological aid and defence policy coordination. The President seemed increasingly disinclined to accept the advice of the State Department and its Soviet specialists, choosing to rely more on his National Security Advisor, Zbig Brzezinsky, a man whose views on occasion echoed the anti-Russian antipathies of his Polish ancestors.[21]

Of course, Washington did not cause the Afghan crisis. The Soviet "need" to invade Afghanistan was a function of their rather paranoid concept of security and of internal Afghan events (these probably would have "dictated" a similar denouement even had the Shah remained on his neighboring "Peacock Throne"). Likewise, Western condemnation did not deter further Soviet advance. The last thing Moscow would want is to send the Red Army into Pakistan; her aim was much better served by U.S. support for Pakistani President Zia's unrepresentative dictatorship. It ensured that political and ethnic opposition to his regime would acquire an anti-U.S. hue. A future Pakistan, whether united or splintered into ethnic regions, held definite promise from Moscow's vantage point. And even if such promise should be dashed, Moscow would be more likely to choose to encourage Indian intervention.

The most disturbing fact about this crisis was that U.S. anti-Sovietism had been built on a solid foundation of perceived Soviet perfidy, while Soviet anti-U.S. phobia rested on an equally convincing accumulation of perceived U.S. villainy. The role played by misperception, real or feigned, is illustrated by the debate over the mobile multi-warhead intermediate range SS20 missiles that Moscow began deploying in the European sector of the Soviet Union (as also in the Far East) during the latter 1970s. To Moscow the SS20 finally redressed the imbalance long caused by the potency of U.S.'s "Forward Based Systems" (FBS) of carrier and land-based aircraft with the range and sophistication to reach Soviet targets. Previous Soviet intermediate range missiles targeted on Western Europe had been both less accurate and more vulnerable (to hostile "take-out") than U.S. systems. In an atmosphere of mutual suspicion, however, it was perhaps inevitable that NATO would ignore the fact that the SS–20 did not negate continued FBS efficacy and focus instead on the indisputable point that SS20 accuracy and survivability entailed a greater threat to NATO territory than had previously existed; hence the phenomenon of NATO defence budget increases amid Soviet protestations that these (and not the SS20) constituted the beginnings of a new arms race. Paranoia breeds paranoia; distrust finds its own motivating and indeed reinforcing rationale. As a Zhdanov (Stalin's right-hand man during the late 1940s) justifies and necessitates a Joseph McCarthy (of "Committee for UnAmerican Activities" fame), so a McCarthy justifies and necessitates Soviet demagoguery. As Soviet intervention in Afghanistan provided the clinching argument for U.S. hardliners to rally majority support, so events preceding it had allowed Soviet hardliners to gain dominance in their policy councils. "Moderates" like Carter and Brezhnev embraced the rhetoric of inflexibility.

President Carter announced an extensive wheat, high technology, and trade embargo, cancelled scientific and cultural exchange, called for a boycott of the 1980 Summer Olympics in Moscow, and set forth a "Carter Doctrine" that committed Washington to use military force if necessary to protect its "vital interests" in the Persian Gulf.[22] The "doctrine" epitomized the assertiveness of Washington's new posture. It was not, like NATO, a response to friendly governments who perceived a threat, offered bases, and asked for alliance. It was a unilateral promulgation assuming a right. No country in the region had extended base rights, no country had requested formal alliance (though in at least some cases this reflected less on empathy for Moscow and more on the corrosive effect of continued U.S. support for Israel's occupation of conquered Arab lands).[23] The doctrine's vagueness as to the exact extent of its applicability and the military specifics of its commitment may have been due to this fact. Of NATO governments only those of Margaret Thatcher (Britain) and soon to be defeated Joe Clark (Canada) embraced the U.S. stand unreservedly. Other NATO and West European governments limited their support.[24] They were clearly ambivalent, leery of losing the economic benefice of detente, and nervous about the possibility of military confrontation in a distant arena. Attachment to detente was not the only cause of unease. British General Hackett, author of *The Third World War*, noted that an enemy cornered with no escape route is likely to see attack as the only alternative. U.S. Secretary of Defense Brown touched upon yet another concern shared by many when he acknowledged that U.S. non-nuclear means in the area might not suffice to meet likely contingencies; until new means were procured, effective followup might have to resort to nuclear weaponry.[25]

President Brezhnev's response gave no hint of compromise.[26] Washington was castigated for sabre rattling and war mongering. The Soviet presence in Afghanistan was reinforced. Carter's breaking of past agreements was declared to make him an unreliable and therefore unfit partner for any and all negotiations. Brezhnev asserted continued Soviet commitment to detente but gave no concessions. East European governments such as those of Poland, the GDR, Czechoslovakia, Hungary, and Bulgaria supported Moscow's stand. Yet their support for Soviet policies appeared as reluctant as Western Europe's support for Washington. They also had come to depend rather heavily on the economic (and to a lesser extent cultural) fallout from detente.

The frosty curtain did not just descend along Europe's old divide. It also made itself felt in the Far East and in South Asia. The reactions of China and Japan have already been referred to. In South Asia the emergence of a Sino-U.S. quasi alliance in general, and its focus on arms to President Zia in particular, stirred India's old security phobia. After all, China continued to occupy territories in the northwest that were wrested from India during the 1962 border war, most of Pakistan's armed forces continued to face India rather than Afghanistan, and arms intended to secure against incursions from Afghanistan appeared equally suited to actions against India, or domestic opponents.[27] The Delhi government called for Soviet withdrawal from Afghanistan but accepted the Soviet argument that the intervention had been provoked by the activities of other powers. India's "understanding" attitude toward Moscow undermined the viability of the Carter Docrtine, at least as concerned Pakistan, and extended the ripple effects (and the potential for miscalculation) of the process of polarization.

It was to be expected that the Soviet emergence through the 1970s as a truly global superpower would lead to a difficult period of adjustment. The emergence of the Soviet Union as a power able to intervene effectively in distant arenas altered established "rules of the game." As throughout history when a new power has thus emerged and asserted itself, new limits, new rules evolve. Never an easy process, for either the old established actors or the new aspirant, it is a process that became encapsulated in the Afghanistan crisis. That the flashpoint should be provided by an area not on the fringes, but in the challenger's back yard, provides an ironic footnote to the vagaries of politics. The danger lay in the fact that this was a more dangerous world than that of earlier eras. In a world teetering on the edge of rapid nuclear proliferation, north–south tension, and tattered developmental prospects, a return to Cold War antagonisms was not likely to be conducive to amicable settlement of disputes.

The course of Sino-Soviet relations had clearly become more complex. It still hinged to an extent on the question of domestic Chinese politics, its flux and its uncertainties. But it now appeared to hinge also on the question of the long-term impact of the quasi Cold War polarization process (firestorm?) of the Afghanistan crisis. The logic of polarization must inherently crimp the range of options available to those that it affected.

Through the 1960s and 1970s China had consistently castigated detente as subterfuge for superpower "condominium," with the sometime variation that it must mean Soviet kowtowing to imperialist interests (Mao's charge against Khrushchev), or else U.S. appease-ment of Soviet "social-imperalism" (the more recent preference). Yet detente could, of course, also be seen as the necessary precondi-tion for pursuit of either of the options debated so vociferously in Beijing during these years, namely autarchic isolation, or a policy of drawing the maximum benefits from relations with both by playing the susceptibilities of the one against those of the other—the classic policy of the early nonaligned club of Tito, Nehru, Nasser, and Sukarno. Either alternative is easier pursued in conditions of relaxed international tensions. Polarization encourages a zero-sum type of perspective that equates one actor's gain with another's loss. Kissin-ger-type concepts of multiple and varied linkages allowing advantages in one arena to be offset by disadvantages elsewhere depend on a more fluid environment.

The short-term consequences of the frost of early 1980 were clearly detrimental to advocates of Sino-Soviet accommodation. Opponents of Deng and others who had in the past espoused the desirability of negotiations with Moscow and who might be similarly disposed in the future now found additional arguments for intran-sigence towards "the polar bear." One obvious line of argument was that a bird in the hand was better than a bird in the bush, that protection of established investments must take precedence over the un-certain search for new possibilities. There was also the point that China was in any case hostage to existing realities. The policies pursued during the last few years were already perceived in Moscow to have had the effect of making China a semi ally of the United States. In view of current hard-line attitudes in Moscow (caused in large part by the train of events that culminated in the Afghanistan crisis but exacerbated also by the natural proclivity to chauvinism that seems inherent in any period of succession maneuvering such as Moscow was now in the throes of), Soviet leaders were unlikely to evince the flexibility that substantive negotiations would call for. In the short term Moscow was bound to concentrate on immediate security concerns, and that meant that alliance with Hanoi and accommoda-tion with New Delhi would continue to serve as the lynchpins of Soviet Asian policy.

A longer-term perspective appeared more conductive to limited Sino-Soviet understanding, at least if one assumed that the extremes of current tensions would dissipate with time.[28] Sino-Soviet trade had continued to grow through the preceding years of uncertainty, though it was from a low base, and the total remained but a faint reflection of levels considered optimal by economic planners. And although Deng was still having to forego the distinction (if perhaps not the perquisites) of highest office—indeed, in February of 1980, he gave up his titular command of the People's Liberation Army— Deng nevertheless appeared able to move associates into positions from which they might be expected to be able to dominate Chinese policies after his passing. [29] Some observers even believed that Deng was deliberately shying away from supreme titles, calculating that residual Hua strength and the ghost of past decades held too great a promise of disruption; at 76 Deng was presumed to be more con-cerned with the longevity of his policies than with the accoutrements of office.

The last day of February 1980 saw dramatic furthering of this trend, with the promotion to the Standing Committee of the Polit-buro of two of Deng's most closely identified proteges.[30] Hu Yaobang, initiated into the larger Politburo a little over a year earlier, was also confirmed as new Secretary General of the Party, and hence head of its vital Secretariat (Deng's own position prior to the Cultural Revolution). The other rising star was Zhao Ziyang, provincial leader of Deng's home province, Sichuan. At the same time the last pre-sumed "Maoists" (except for Hua Guofeng) were purged from the Politburo: Wang Dongxing, a Party Vice-Chairman and former Mao bodyguard whose role in the purge of the Gang of Four remains a matter of mystery; Wu De, Mayor of Peking during Deng's "second ouster" in early 1976; Chen Xilian, Vice-Premier and, until January, Commander of the Peking Military District; and Ji Dengkui, Vice-Premier and former Political Commissar of Beijing military units. Former President Liu Shaoqui was formally rehabilitated (a move presaged by the January media decision to accord him the honorific "comrade"). The disgrace of the man formerly reviled as "renegade, traitor, and scab" was "completely overturned" and declared to have been "the biggest frameup our Party has ever known." As if to further emphasize the turn of events the same Central Committee meeting also cancelled the Four Freedoms: the rights to "speak out freely, air views fully, hold great debates, and write big character posters"; the Freedoms were said to have "hampered the people in the normal expression of their democratic rights"! The purges, in conjunction also with the fact that it was General Yang Dezhi (Deng-associated commander of the attack on Vietnam), who had replaced Deng as Chief of Staff of the PLA, made it apparent that critics of that less than glorious venture had been outmaneuvered. The so long anticipated establishment of true Deng prominence appeared at hand. Maoism appeared truly to have been relegated to the dustbin of history, though the operative words was, indeed, "appeared."

The prospect that Deng proteges might come to chart the course of future Chinese policies was one that Moscow could only welcome. The Soviet Union had always felt more comfortable with Deng associates than with any other groupings within the Chinese leadership (see Chapter 3). Yet, the prospect remained uncertain and by no means preordained. The one preeminent lesson of Chinese politics during the 1960s and 1970s was that factional victories had tended to be short-lived and ephemeral. Chinese leadership aspirants themselves would probably be the last to assume that zigzags were a phenomenon of the past. There was also the point that proteges do not always follow as closely in the footsteps of their protector after he (or she) is removed from the scene as they once did. The Khrushchev who launched the de-Stalinization campaign in 1956 had been a Stalin protege; the Brezhnev who reversed so many of Khrushchev's domestic and foreign policy schemes had been a Khrushchev protege, and so on.

NOTES

1. Harrsion Salisbury, "Soviet-Chinese War," *The New York Times* (February 27, 1979) and see Reuter reports in the *Globe and Mail* (February 27 and February 28, 1980).

2. Note also reports that the PRC may have used poison gas, *Time*, (April 9, 1979).

3. NYT and Reuter, in *Globe and Mail*, (April 7, 1979).

4. *Aviation Week and Space Technology* (January 21, 1980).

5. See John Fraser from Beijing, *Globe and Mail*, (May 11, 1979), also *International Herald Tribune* (April 19, 1979), *Le Monde* (April 18, 1979), and *The Observer* (London) (April 22, 1979).

6. John Fraser from Beijing, *Globe and Mail*, (June 19, 1979).

7. *Ibid.* And see *International Affairs* (Moscow), No. 9, 1979, p. 9; and *Pravda* (July 11, 1979).

8. Note, e.g., Bryan Johnson reports from Beijing in *Globe and Mail* (November 21 and November 23, 1979) Also Chinese Vice Foreign Minister Han Nianlong's October 19, 1979 announcement declaring "danger zones" (and banning international flights) around Hainan Island and the Paracels. On PRC-VN border "episodes" see *International Herald Tribune* (July 20, 1979) and *NRK* (July 27, 1979). On Soviet-PRC border events see (Oslo) *Aftenposten* (July 24, 1979). Finally, see, e.g., *Pravda* (July 27, 1979) and *Pravda* (October 3, 1979).

9. *Pravda* (November 24, 1979). See also, e.g., *Izveztia* (August 22, 1979).

10. *Pravda*, (July 11, 1979), Alexandrov article. See also *The Guardian* (July 12, 1979).

11. See *Tass* statement September 26, 1979; and see *Izvestia* (October 17, 1979) "About a certain HSINHUA commentary."

12. November 20, 1979 saw a wallposter accusing Politburo member (and former Beijing Mayor) Wu De of plotting to restore the radical Gang of Four to power. See Reuter report in *Globe and Mail*, (November 21, 1979).

13. "Freedom is all right but only in the abstract," Bryan Johnson report from Beijing, *Globe and Mail* (December 15, 1979). See also AP dispatch in same paper (November 8, 1979).

14. AP dispatch, in (Halifax) *Chronicle Herald* (February 21, 1980).

15. *Beijing Dialy* (February 22, 1980).

16. *International Affairs* (Moscow) No. 8 (1979):70. And see *Pravda* (September 19, 1979).

17. See this author's "Afghanistan: Ice and Fire," *The Bulletin of the Atomic Scientists* (March 1980).

18. *Time* (April 9, 1979).

19. *The New York Times* (January 2, 1980), and same paper (December 28, 1979).

20. *The Manchester Guardian, Washington Post, Le Monde Weekly* (February 24, 1980) quotes U.S. Senate Select Committee on Intelligence Sources (its Chairman, Senator Birch Bayh of Indiana) as indicating that U.S. military sup-

port for Afghan rebels predated the Soviet intervention. "CIA Said to Supply Arms to Afghan Rebels," *Time* (February 25, 1980) further suggests that "Chinese arms aid to the Muslim rebels significantly increased after Vice-Premier Deng Xiaoping's visit to Washington in January 1979." Note also, e.g., *Pravda* (August 26, 1979).

21. See George Kennan's "Was This Really Mature Statesmanship?", *The New York Times* (February 1, 1980). See also commentary in *The Bulletin of the Atomic Scientists*, April 1980.

22. *The New York Times* (January 5, 1980).

23. *Ibid.*

24. *The New York Times* (January 8, 1980).

25. Note Drew Middleton's analysis in *The New York Times* (January 7, 1980).

26. See, e.g. *Tass* statements of January 3 and 5, 1980. Also *Pravda* (January 5, 1980) and *The New York Times* (January 6, 1980).

27. For background, see, e.g., *International Affairs* (Moscow), No. 11, 1978; and (Beijing) *People's Daily* (June 8, 1976).

28. See, e.g., "Attempt to Bridge Sino-Soviet Gap," *The Guardian, Washington Post, Le Monde Weekly* (June 17, 1979).

29. Report from Beijing, *Globe and Mail* (February 26, 1980).

30. On the CPC Central Committee meeting of February 29, 1980 see Bryan Johnson from Beijing in the *Globe and Mail* (March 1, 1980) and AP report in the *Chronicle Herald* of the same day; for background see V. Zorza in *The Guardian* (January 27, 1979) and Johnson in the *Globe and Mail* (February 26, and 27, 1980).

6 THE THIRD ACTOR: THE SOVIET FAR EAST–MANCHURIA–JAPAN 'TRIANGLE'

Japan is the joker in the Sino-Soviet pack, the third actor who for geopolitical, economic, and other reasons could become the most crucial external variable affecting the future course of Sino-Soviet relations. The geographically determined triangle of the Soviet Far East, Manchuria, and Japan encompasses the three nations that have been the most successful in enhancing their relative power positions during the post–World War II era. The Soviet Union, a regional power at war's end, acquired true superpower status, developing strategic and global capabilities that offset those of the United States. China, torn by civil war, corruption, and backwardness until well after the war, developed into a formidable regional power and acquired the aura (if not the reality) of a quasi superpower. Japan emerged from shattering defeat to become an economic and technological giant. The history of all three was replete with ethnocentricity and chauvinism. All have tended to view themselves as the guardian of civilized values. Moscow, once "the Third (and last) Rome," now projected herself as the vanguard of a new historical epoch. China, the erstwhile "Middle Kingdom," repository of civilized values, took on the role of trustee of "true" Marxism-Leninism (at least under Mao). Tokyo, seat of another Emperor God, also remained partial to visions of uniqueness, though in this case there was less concensus as to what that uniqueness could or should entail. All three have faced each other in armed conflict within living memory. Each has major outstanding grievances against the other two. Cultural, economic, and ideological differences divide them. And there are vexatious territorial disputes, not only between China and the Soviet Union, but also between China and Japan, and between the Soviet Union and Japan.[1]

The analysis below will first focus on the cultural antipathies that bedevil Japan's relations with the other two. It will address the historical issues and the degree to which different perceptions of these issues continue to generate misunderstanding and distrust. This will be followed by a section on current territorial disputes: their anticedents and their ramifications. Finally, the analysis will delve into geopolitical dictates: the relevance and consequences of Japan's geographical location and her less than favorable allotment of indigenous resources. Japan's need to secure access to continental resources has dictated her actions in the past and remains a major determinant of policy—both domestic and external. It affects economic and energy policy, defence policy, and foreign affairs. A concluding section will trace the more recent evolutiaon of Japan's relations with her neighbors and future prospects.

Contemporary attitudes may be traced back to the early years of the twentieth century and beyond. The first Sino-Japanese war of 1894-95 established the emergence of imperial Japan; through it, she acquired Taiwan (Formosa), the Pescadores, and the Liaotung Penisula in Manchuria (though great power pressure forced her to relinquish the latter prize). She also gained preponderant influence in Korea. Russia's acquisition of Port Arthur and the southern portion of the Liaotung Penisula in 1898 (as a 25 year leasehold) dramatized the emerging conflict between thrusting Japanese interests and those of the Empire of the Romanovs. Accumulating tension exploded in "the first Pearl Harbor," Japan's 1904 attack on Port Arthur, the sweeping victory of Japan's newly emergent Imperial Navy, and the final pushing north of Russia's Manchurian army. The peace treaty gave Japan southern Sakhalin, as well as her now established foothold in Manchuria. Formal annexation of Korea, in 1910, was followed by Japan's 1915 "21 demands" against Beijing (designed to reduce China to a protectorate) and the 1918-22 occupation of Russia's (now the Soviet Union's) Far East. Initiated as part of Allied interventions to secure the defeat of the Bolshevik regime and the victory of "White" forces (there were British and French landings in the Black Sea, British landings along the Baltic coast, British, U.S., Canadian, Serb, and Italian in the north, as well as Japanese and smaller U.S. contingents in the Far East), Japan's presence lingered long after the withdrawal of the others. In fact, her occupation of northern Sakhalin was maintained until 1925. She was plainly reluctant to concede the return of Moscow's authority in the area; the issue was decided by the combination of growing Soviet power, strongly worded U.S. disapproval of continued occupation, and increased domestic opposition.[2]

A liberal-democratic interlude through the remaining 1920s was followed by a return to Japanese militarism and expansionism during the 1930s. In 1931 Manchuria was overrun. The puppet state of Manchukuo was established. Economic and political penetration of China proper followed. In 1936 Japan joined Nazi Germany in the Anti-Comintern Pact against Moscow. The next year she invaded northern China, an invasion that was to lead to occupation of all of China's seaboard and the 1940 establishment of a client Chinese government in Nanjing. To the north the signing of the Anti-Comintern Pact led inexorably to further tension, skirmishes, and, finally, the battles of Lake Khazan and Khalkin Gol (1939). The Japanese defeat here was to propel the Soviet commander, then General Georgi Zhukov, to Moscow and future glory. It also helped ensure that Japan would direct further expansionism southward, ignoring Hitler's plea for a second front in Moscow's rear (a decision symbolized by the Soviet-Japanese nonaggression pact of April 1941).[3]

This second interlude on the northern front of the Sino-Soviet-Japanese triangle ended on August 8, 1945. In accordance, no doubt, with perceptions of self interest, but also with the commitment pressed upon her by her U.S. and British allies at the Yalta conference in January of that year that she enter the war against Japan within three months of Germany's defeat (Germany surrendered May 9, 1945), Soviet forces now swept into Manchuria/Manchukuo. The cream of Japan's remaining armed forces, the Kwantung army, reeling from the domestic blow of Hiroshima's nuclear devastation on August sixth (August ninth was to bring the obliteration of Nagasaki), crumbled in face of the well-prepared Soviet onslaught. The Soviet price was as promised by the Allies at Yalta: return of southern Sakhalin and the Kurile islands (these had been ceded to Japan in 1875 as the quid pro quo for Japan's acceptance of Russia's suzerainty over Sakhalin)[4], an occupation zone in Korea (later North Korea), reestablishment of a Russian/Soviet naval base at Port Arthur, and joint control with China of Manchuria's railroads (these latter prizes were to be relinquished in 1955 by the post-Stalin regime). The September 1951 San Francisco peace treaty, though not attended by the Soviet Union, India, and some other war protagonists, brought Japanese acceptance of Soviet gains and of the post war return of Taiwan and the Pescadores to China.[5] Yet, there remained outstanding issues of import.

Before turning to these outstanding issues, however, some comment must be made on past history's contribution to the development of the cultural antipathies that continue to sour prospects for understanding and accommodation. The legacy of Soviet-Japanese history in particular is made to order for those wishing to manipulate cultural chauvinisms. Japanese anti-Sovietism, or perhaps one should say anti-Russian attitudes, may, as indicated, be traced back to Russia's late nineteenth century posture as rival to and bulwark against the continental aspirations of Japanese expansionism. The tensions and ultimate battles of the late 1930s evoked similar frustration. Of greater importance, however, is the Japanese view that Moscow's August 8, 1945 attack, though dictated by the Soviet Union's obligation to the other Allies, was opportunism of the highest order. The fact that resultant prisoners of war were not returned, a function of the two powers' continued inability to agree to the terms of a formal peace treaty, served to prolong and embitter the consequent resentment.

Soviet unease was cemented by an equally selective reading of the historical record. In Soviet eyes the trend was set by Japan's Pearl Harbor type attack on Port Arthur in 1904 (one should note that Japan's allegation that the sudden attack was precipitated by purported Russian moves towards Korea is dismissed by Western historians). The next piece of "evidence" is provided by the 1918–22 Japanese occupation of the Soviet Far East and the obvious reluctance with which the Japanese forces finally withdrew. The clashes of 1938 and 1939 are seen as testimony to the perseverence of Japanese designs against Moscow's eastern domains; their resolution is seen as evidence favoring the thesis that only Soviet military strength and superiority can guarantee their security. Both sides appear oblivious to the sincerity of the other's prejudice.

On the Sino-Japanese side of the ledger the scales of recent history have been more lopsided, with the result that their legacy as far as current attitudes is concerned is quite different. Only one side, China, felt the threat of and reality of occupation. And although the sometime harsh brutality of Japanese occupation policies left bitter memories, resentment was at least to a degree diffused by the view that this was but the final act of an era of colonial impositions (an era that began in earnest with the failure to stem Britain's opium trading in the 1830s and 1840s). The fact that this most humiliating and extensive finale to a century of victimization was at the hands of an Asian neighbor, in a sense, only underlined the dangers of weakness and the need for modernization. One might add that the major beneficiary of the experience was Mao and his revolutionary forces. The success of the Japanese served both to discredit the Kuomintang regime of Chiang Kaishek and to reinforce yearnings for a strong national government. In conjunction with the appearance of greater "Communist" earnestness in battling the invader, this was to prove a powerful banner around which to rally support for the culminating stages of the civil war in 1948-49.[6] Japan's emergence from defeat as an industrially potent ally of "U.S. imperialism" revived particular memories. But Japan's abstention from physical involvement in the Korean War, her expressed contrition on the subject of past policies, and of course the allure of her technology, sped Chinese adoption of a more benevolent attitude once the perceived threat from Washington receded (with U.S. disengagement from Vietnam).

Japanese opinion polls of the 1970s reflected the different socialization processes through which popular views of Moscow and Beijing had been formed.[7] Russians generally topped the list of least liked ethnic groups; the Soviet Union topped the list of countries seen as a "threat" to Japanese security. By contrast China, whose culture was more ensconced and more appreciated (typically, the Japanese language, distinct in roots, borrowed its early written form from Chinese), scored far more favorably. On the threat question she ranked only third, behind Japan's U.S. ally. The continued and recognized paucity of China's power projection capability, of her navy and her logistics, reinforced feelings of security and presumably contributed to the benevolence of popular opinion. Yet, the views of opinion leaders was startingly different. China was seen as a greater threat than the Soviet Union by a nearly three to one margin. And while the near-term perception of threat from the Soviet Union still remained distinctly stronger than that associated with the United States, the mid and long term views ranked Washington as somewhat more threatening (though these views still saw China as most ominous by a two to one margin). The result suggested a Japanese establishment concensus that Soviet grievances were not such as might fuel aggressive designs. The calculation that Soviet assertiveness would be more likely to draw a U.S. response may also have been present. The poll result also suggests unease about the friction potential of U.S.-Japanese economic rivalry. Finally, the combination of official jitteriness about Chinese potentials and public equanimity provided both a motivation and a favorable political climate for concessionary Japanese approaches to Beijing during the 1970s.

Two legacies of history, however, continued to cloud prospects for the future: the disputed ownership of the "northern islands" and of the Senkakus in the East China Sea. As concerns the northern dispute, it should be emphasized that the status of Sakhalin and the Kurile chain proper was not in contention. Their Soviet status was confirmed with Japan's signature to the San Francisco treaty (it codified the Potsdam agreement clause, which awarded these terri-tories to the Soviet Union as recompense for her Far Eastern war effort in accordance with the terms of Yalta). Both Sakhalin and the Kuriles had experienced considerable, if varying, degrees of Japanese association and activity.[8] Their murky history might well have provided fertile ground for chauvinist claims and counterclaims. Japan's renunciation of irredentist aspirations therefore exorcised the potentially most vexing, insoluble, and tension-inducing problem complex.

The dispute that remained centered on four islands: Iturup, Kunashiri, Shikotan, and Habomai. It revolved around the question as to whether they were to be considered the southernmost islands of the Kurile chain, or natural extensions of Hokkaido and Japan. Japan insisted on the latter intepretation. Although she had established her presence on the islands at the end of the war, as part of her Yalta and Potsdam decreed assertion of Kurile sovereignty, and although she professed possession of older Japanese maps that marked the islands as belonging to the Kuriles, Moscow nevertheless chose at least at first to present herself as flexible on the issue.

When she resumed diplomatic relations with Tokyo in 1956 Mos-cow stated that Shikotan and Habomai would be returned to Japan upon the signing of a peace treaty, while the future of Iturup and Kunashiri was open to negotiation.[9] But prospects for accomodation receded as Japan pursued her military and economic ties with the West. The signing of the new Japanese-U.S. Security Treaty in 1960 was followed by Soviet retraction of her 1956 offer. In a memoran-dum to the Japanese government she stated that she would not return the islands to Japan unless U.S. forces were withdrawn; she would not allow a change of status that might lead to U.S. military bases on or utilization of the islands.[10]

Through the next decade, with Japan's continuing adherence to the U.S. alliance, the Soviet Union adopted and maintained the un-compromising position that the future of the islands had been "settled."[11] She claimed to see Japanese assertions to the contrary as "revanchist," and "not helping" Soviet-Japanese relations.[12] The Soviet Union's general insistence that her borders, as determined by history, were "sacred and inviolable"[13] added to Japanese anxie-ties. There was the danger that the longer the impasse persisted, the deeper would the status quo become ensconced; the longer the islands retained their Soviet status, the more difficult it would be for the

Soviet Union to relinquish them without encouraging the contemporary or future irredentist claims of other nations.

Moscow appeared aware of this danger and of the burden this might pose on prospects for future Soviet-Japanese cooperation. While maintaining a frigid official stance she nevertheless chose through the early 1970s to strive to retain the option of future flexibility. By encouraging leaks, however guarded, that she might yet revert to her 1956 position, she perpetuated the "special status" of this particular dispute.[14]

In the context of the early 1970s' aura of detente, East-West cooperation, and talk of truly gigantic Japanese (and U.S.) investments in Siberian resource extraction schemes, the issue of the islands appeared eminently solvable.[15] But the search for a solution soon floundered on the shoals of misperception. Japan insisted on transfer of the islands as a precondition for more ambitious cooperative ventures, evidently calculating that Moscow's need for foreign investment and high technology inputs would force a conciliatory attitude. The Soviet Union, on the other hand, saw a possible compromise on the status of the islands as the symbolic finale to and capping of the establishment of an era of cooperation. To her a change in Japanese attitudes and the inflow of Japanese investments (and perhaps a loosening of U.S. apron strings) must come first. The Soviet Union was clearly convinced that Japan's need for Siberia's resources was greater than her own need for investment from abroad.[16]

To an extent, the remainder of the decade proved Moscow right—or, rather, it proved that Moscow remained persuaded of the soundness of the premise. By the end of the decade the islands remained Soviet. Soviet-Japanese relations soured. The more grandiose cooperative schemes were forgotten. The incidence of Japan handing over a defector's MIG for U.S. analysis, in a glare of publicity, was symptomatic of a policy posture that appeared designed to grate on Soviet sensibilities. In turn, Soviet terms for Siberian resource extraction hardened. Yet, as the 1980s dawned, and notwithstanding such irritants as a Japanese government statement favoring U.S. President Carter's boycott of the 1980 Summer Olympics in Moscow, Japanese investment in Siberia continued to increase (even if the pace was considerably more measured than once anticipated).

Before pursuing the question of Japanese resource scarcities and their impact on policy, however, it must be noted, again, that territorial friction is not absent from the Sino-Japanese relationship either. The Senkaku Islands, eight uninhabited and superficially unimpressive pieces of rock 100 miles northeast of Taiwan,[17] were returned to Japanese sovereignty by the United States as an integral part of the Okinawa and Ryukyu island chain reversion. The islands are on the Chinese continental shelf and are claimed by both Beijing and Taipeh as historically Chinese (though Taiwan's position has at times appeared to vacillate somewhat). The historical justification for the claim is categorically rejected by Japan.[18] What makes the dispute potentially volatile is the fact that "the seabed there might be one of the richest oil-bearing areas in the world."[19] To an energy-starved nation with few resources of her own this consideration is not one to be disdained or squandered; on the other hand, neither is the promised bargaining chip without potential benefit to China.

The issue was held in abeyance through the 1970s. It was diplomatically overlooked by the Sino-Japanese communique that followed Prime Minister Tanaka's precedent setting visit to Beijing, and this pattern was repeated in later agreements. The crux would come when or if oil expectations were realized. That eventuality would of course carry significant potential for friction. Whether such friction would ensue would depend on the state of the overall relationship at the time. If the considerations that propelled Japan's early approaches to Beijing were to retain their prominence within Japanese policy-making councils, and if Beijing continued to place the same premium on foreign investment as it did at the turn of the decade, then the course might be set for a compromise.

One could conceive of Svalbard-type solutions for both northern and southern territorial differences. In the Svalbard (or Spitzbergen) case Norwegian sovereignty was confirmed, in return for which all signatories to the Svalbard treaty were to be accorded equal access to the resources of the archipelago, and the archipelago was to be demilitarized. As to the designation of pro forma ownership it might be relevant to point to the trends of recent cartography. *The Times Atlas of World History* "colors" the northern islands Soviet, though it notes that they (only Habomai and Shikotan are specified) continue to be claimed by Japan; this atlas does not address itself to the question of the Senkakus. *The New York Times Atlas of the World* (collaboration with *The Times* of London) also "colors" the northern islands Soviet, but its index differentiates between stated Soviet status for Iturup and Kunashiri and does not mention Habomai and asserted Japanese status for Shikotan; the Senkakus are acknowledged to be Japanese by both color plate and index. The *Time-Hammond World Atlas* distinguishes between acceptance of the Soviet nature of the larger Iturup and Kunashiri Islands and acceptance of Japanese claims as concerns Habomai and Shikotan; again, the Senkakus are acknowledged as Japanese. The trend among Japan's allies is thus to accept Japanese sovereignty over the Senkakus and Soviet sovereignty over Iturup and Kunashiri, while attitudes as concerns the status of Habomai and Shikotan appear to range from ambivalent to lukewarm support for Tokyo. But the issues will of course not be decided by Western cartographers, however eminent. Perceptions of national interest (weighing emotion against colder calculations of economic, defence, and other requirements) in the capitals concerned will be the decisive determinant.

The single most important element in that calculation of national interest is, at least in Japan's case, likely to be economic. The startling fact about this nation whose GNP per capita stood on the verge of becoming the highest in the world by 1980 was the degree to which it remained seriously deficient in natural resources. Its prosperity hid extraordinary vulnerability. Its industries' dramatic dependence on foreign raw materials translated into the simple fact that continued prosperity could only be guaranteed through secured access to foreign resources. The other side of this coin lay in the fact that such purchases had to be paid for through significant surpluses on other trade accounts (that is, once the "answer" of military expansionism and colonialism was ruled out as no longer viable); Japan was therefore vitally dependent also on continued access to foreign markets.

Comfortable assumptions of the past were severely jolted by events of the early 1970s. The decade opened (as it ended) with a tense Middle East and with Arab promises that oil access and oil price would henceforth be determined by their own perceptions of national interest and that neither could be taken for granted any longer. Then there were the Nixon "Shokku" of 1971 and 1972, the Smithsonian Agreement, devaluation of the dollar, revaluation of the Yen, the Nixon visit to Beijing, and talk of U.S. protectionism. The "Shokku," engineered through dramatic unilateral policy decisions to which Japan, though drastically effected, was nevertheless not privy, inevitably kindled unease in Japan.[20] In some quarters the unease sparked an effort to reestablish and solidify old ties with Washington. In others it led rather to a reevaluation of old dependencies and a search for alternative anchors.

The two schools of reaction found common cause in new approaches in Beijing and Moscow. There was the point that if the United States could negotiate with China and the Soviet Union and yet expect to maintain its good relations with Japan, then why could not Japan make similar overtures without fear of U.S. repercussions?[21] There was also the more positive consideration that was to underlie many joint proposals: U.S. bankers favored spreading the economic risk; Japanese politicans sought to spread the political commitment that might be entailed.

Japanese-Soviet trade (as also U.S.-Soviet trade) prospects appeared to flourish. Relaxation of East-West tensions during the 1960s had led to significant and increasing levels of trade and economic cooperation, as exemplified by the 1968 agreement exchanging "equipment, machinery, and other goods for the development of the lumber industry" for "deliveries of lumber to Japan" and the 1970 agreement on Japanese help in constructing a new port at Wrangel Bay.[22] But the above-described constellation of the early 1970s brought new urgency and new scope to the proposals being discussed. 1971 saw agreement on the sale of Japanese technology and equipment, "iron and steel products, textiles, and chemicals," in return for "crude oil, cotton, pig iron and iron ore," industrial wood chips, and deciduous pulpwood logs.[23] 1972–73 saw negotiations envisaging ever more extensive deals. There was talk of a 2.5 billion dollar Japanese investment in Tyumen alone, with supplies to Japan of 10 billion cubic metres of natural gas a year; another proposed venture would have seen annual delivery of 2.4 billion cubic meters of gas from Sakhalin guaranteed for 20 years.[24] Paralleling these vistas were Soviet-U.S. talks that projected U.S. 1980 imports from the Soviet Union at 721 billion cubic feet (20.4 billion cubic meters), the equivalent of roughly 80 percent of total U.S. 1971 imports from all countries.

By 1971 a number of prominent Japanese were voicing the opinion that a furthering of economic ties with the Soviet Union ought to be pursued regardless of the status of the "northern territories." Business-inspired impatience with the impasse created by Japan's insistence on the islands' unconditional return complemented the pursuasion of some representatives of the media and even of certain members of the ruling Liberal-Democratic Party that the islands' return would indeed be more likely as an outgrowth of improved relations than as a precondition for such. They advocated that "The Japanese Government should show the Soviet Union its sincerity (by agreeing to) a large expansion of trade between the two nations and Japan's technical cooperation in the development of Siberia."[25] Their optimism and their perception of the order of priorities required for satisfaction of Japanese interests appeared well founded. The mushrooming of actual and envisaged agreements led to renewed Soviet assertions of flexibility on the territorial issue. Not only did Moscow once again suggest that Habomai and Shikotan would be returned upon the conclusion of a peace treaty, but she also suggested that the status of Iturup and Kunashiri might still be open to negotiation.[26]

1972 was equally a watershed for Sino-Japanese relations. Caught off guard by U.S. President Nixon's visit to Beijing, Japan clearly resolved not to be disadvantaged. Jettisoning her political ties with Taiwan, she extended "apologies for all Japan did to China in the last war,"[27] offered Export-Import Bank credits for joint economic ventures, and rushed to extend formal diplomatic recognition.[28]

It appeared that Japan had succeeded in establishing a firm foothold of economic cooperation with both of her continental neighbors. Japan offered high technology exports that might stimulate their further economic development, while they in turn promised long-term access to raw materials vital to Japanese industry. The balances of advantages and disadvantages appeared perfectly complementary. But the rosier vistas soon proved ephemeral. 1972 was unique (though possibly a harbinger of the future). In Moscow it saw the culmination of the detente process, symbolized by the signing of the first Strategic Arms Limitation Talks agreement and a plethora of economic and cultural accords between the Soviet Union and Western capitals. In China Zhou Enlai's moderate policies had captured center stage.[29] Sino-U.S. rapprochement cleared the decks for initiatives by Japan and others. Moscow and Beijing both oozed mellowness. Decreased prominence of Mao Zedong and his personalized anti-Sovietism also encouraged hopes that Sino-Soviet antogonism might at least abate, a soothing prospect to those Japanese who feared being squeezed between conflicting demands and expectations.[30] 1973, however, saw increased U.S. Congressional opposition to the Soviet-U.S. trade bill signed by Nixon the previous year and a general chilling of the Soviet-U.S. relationship. It also brought the Tenth Congress of the Chinese Communist Party and a resurgence of Maoist influence and xenophobia.

The rest of the 1970s saw steady growth in Japan's trade with the Soviet Union and China, but the more optimistic prognoses of the early 1970s drifted into memory. There were many reasons for this. Reinvigorated anti-Sovietism in Beijing encouraged a more cautious Japanese stance vis a vis Moscow. Siberian opportunities might beckon, but so did Chinese potentials, and too vigorous a pursuit of the former might torpedo prospects associated with the latter. The U.S. Congress' refusal to ratify the trade and credit provisions of the 1972 Moscow agreement also meant that Siberian investment ventures would be bilateral rather than trilateral. Possible economic and political risks could not be spread as previously envisioned. Yet another consideration sprang from renewed optimism on the energy procurement front. This was a function of optimism that conservation might serve to lower future requirements, a bullish view of nuclear reactor potentials and the extent to which nuclear energy might alleviate full import needs,[31] the signing of the first contracts with Arab oil producing nations that cut out the middleman role of U.S. multinationals and hence lessened Japan's vulnerability to possible embargos against U.S. interests,[32] and increased access to non Middle East oil from Third World countries such as Indonesia.

The latter point was a reflection also of another trend, a trend that provided a new cushion against U.S. and West European protectionism and that thus lessened the immediate need to seek Soviet and Chinese market alternatives. The 1970s saw dramatic expansion of Japan's export-import ties with developing countries. Whereas Japan's trade with industrialized nations dropped from over 50 percent of its total to about 35 percent, her trade with less-developed countries rose from 35 percent to 48 percent.[33] By the end of the decade Japan's trade with South Korea, Taiwan, and Hong Kong alone reached 90 percent of her total trade with all the countries of the European Economic Community.[34] The Third World trade cushion looked more uncertain with the approach of the 1980s what with the less-developed nations' generally worsening credit status (due in part to the burden of ever-increasing energy import costs) and political instabilities (as exemplified in the 1979 overthrow of the Park regime in Seoul). It had diffused the urgency that might otherwise have been associated with Tokyo's desire for an expansion of her economic ties with Moscow and Beijing. Yet, the economic argument arising from the natural complementarity of the Japanese economy and those of the Soviet Union and China beckoned just as luringly in 1980 as it had in 1970.

There was one other reason for the demise of the hopes of the early 1970s that needs to be mentioned, however. As concerns Japanese-Soviet ventures Japan overplayed her hand, insisting on terms that the Soviet Union would not accept. Ignoring advice to the contrary the Japanese government reaffirmed its earlier position that the settling of the territorial issue (to its satisfaction) must be a precondition for substantive rapprochement. Moscow reacted by hardening its stand, moving from her position of suggested flexibility to one that coldly asserted that the issue was settled. Japan demanded longer-range and more extensive delivery commitments as concerns energy and other resources than Moscow was willing to offer. Moscow reacted by lowering her offers.[35]

To some extent the Japanese stance no doubt reflected the lessened sense of urgency explained above. But it also reflected the same miscalculation that infected U.S. Congressional policy makers, namely, overestimation of the Soviet perception of need and hence overestimation of the Soviet willingness to make concessions in order to meet the need. One thinks of the Jackson-Vanik amendment that tied Congressional ratification of the U.S. Soviet trade bill to explicit Jewish emigration numbers; Moscow chose to forego the benefits of the bill and cut the emigration rate. There was scant appreciation of the fact that even 6 billion dollars, the figure then viewed by Western bankers as the maximum that could be made available for investments in Siberia, would have constituted no more than about 3 percent of indigeneous annual Soviet investment efforts (Harvard economists calculated that such a sum, even presuming high new technology content, would up the otherwise expected Soviet growth rate by no more than a few tenths of 1 percent.)[36] In the mid 1970s Japanese spokesmen appeared convinced that the Soviet Union would not be able to proceed with the awesome BAM project to construct a second more northern trans-Siberian railway line without their aid;[37] the negotiations broke down, yet the end of the decade saw the project well advanced.

With the approach and arrival of the 1980s Soviet-Japanese relations remained hostage to differing premises spawning mistrust and misunderstanding across the political and security-related spectrum. These will be returned to below. The final years of the 1970s, with the ensconcement in Beijing of the Hua Guofeng-Deng Xiaoping successor regime, did see renewed vigor in the Sino-Japanese (as also Sino-U.S.) relationship.[38] The emergence of dominant Deng influence in Beijing was seen by some to augur well also for the other two sides of the Northeast Asian triangle, in view of his previous history of relatively amicable relations with Moscow. But that augury was sidetracked by the sweep of the East-West polarization process that accompanied the sharp 1979-80 increase in Soviet-U.S. antipathy and rancor (that the sweep drew in China, chilling also Sino-Soviet ties, was a consequence of the preceding years' process of Sino-U.S. rapprochement).[39] 1980 thus saw the realization of hopes for favored Japanese access to Chinese potentials, but within a context that at least temporarily ruled out ideas of equidistance (the ideal that Japan's relations with her continental neighbors should be balanced, to circumvent fear that the favoring of one would be seen as threatening to the other).

Yet China's long-term potential for satisfying Japanese requirements was questionable. Although growing quite rapidly China's oil production towards the end of the 1970s stood at no more than 18.2 percent of the still expanding Soviet figure.[40] China's oil export to Japan was able to meet only 4 percent of Japan's need.[41] And while China's political leadership appeared to favor increased future deliveries, Japan's requirements were also growing apace. Notwithstanding the effects of conservation, a projected five-fold increase in nuclear generating capacity between 1975 and 1985, and increased use of coal and all-too-limited domestic supplies of oil and gas, Japan's oil import requirements was still expected to grow by 51 percent over the same ten year period (from 73.3 percent of a 1975 energy consumption of 286 million cubic meters to 65.5 percent of the 1985 consumption estimate of 432 million cubic meters). The Chinese market's potential as far as Japanese needs are concerned was muddied by a scissor-type phenomenon. On the one hand, Chinese success in the implementation of current modernization plans would greatly increase Chinese domestic requirements and hence squeeze the exportable surplus. On the other hand, failure to generate hoped-for modernization would limit China's ability to absorb high technology imports and hence squeeze Japan's ability to offset the effects of protectionism elsewhere through increased sales to Beijing.

A closer look at the nuclear alternative (on the question of energy supplies) will serve as conduit to our final survey of Japanese security concerns and their impact on Tokyo-Moscow-Beijing relations. During the late 1960s nuclear energy gained acceptance as a vehicle with which to lessen Japan's dependence on imported energy. Continued acceptance of this thesis was reflected in the previously referred to General Energy Council prognosis of a five-fold increase in nuclear generating capacity between 1975 and 1985 (the estimate appeared in the Council's "Tentative Outlook for Long-Term Energy Supply and Demand," a revised update of the August 1975 "Long Term Plan for Supply and Demand" report, which had been criticized as too optimistic).[42] As early as 1971 Japan proved able to limit the foreign input needed to construct a nuclear plant to 7-8 percent.[43] A 30-year agreement for U.S. delivery of uranium, signed in 1968,[44] plus plans to realize domestic Japanese production of enriched uranium by 1985,[45] brought confidence that the nuclear share of the energy equation was secure and not as exposed to the uncertain vagaries of international politics as was oil and gas.

The confidence was undermined by events of the 1970s. Increasing U.S. Congressional and Canadian (and to a lesser extent Australian) concern about the dangers of nuclear weapons proliferation brought demands that reactor and uranium sales be accompanied by stringent inspection and control provisos and that sales be embargoed where the recipient proved unwilling to comply.[46] It became clear that nuclear generating capacity was as dependent on foreign supplies as was oil fuelled energy production and that future uranium supplies might be equally vulnerable to the flux of politics in foreign capitals. Receding expectations as concerns fast breeder reactor break-throughs that might dispense with the uranium import requirement of established technologies further undermined hopes that the future supply situation might be more secure. The dawning realization of uncertainties of supply and of technological capacity was to be joined by yet another obstacle to nuclear reliance, namely, the emergence of an environmentalist lobby.

In the meantime the original shoal-scraping nuclear energy ambitions, that of potential weaponry fallout, remained a centerpiece of Japan's defence policy debates.[47] As early as 1968 it was reported that Japan's still putative nuclear reactor capabilities already produced enough plutonium "waste" to make one nuclear bomb each month.[48] Japan was said to have the capacity to proceed from the political decision to the weapons testing stage "within three years."[49]

Those who argued that Japan must develop nuclear arms (whether for symbolic reasons to confirm its status in the forefront of nations, or as necessary to insure a modicum of independence in the field of national security decision making) found their arguments bolstered during the 1970s. The very fact of rapidly expanding nuclear reactor and research capabilities helped their case; it advertized Japan's nuclear reliance and nuclear mastery, while inherently diffusing the "nuclear allergy" legacy of Hiroshima. The status argument was not strengthened by Japanese opinion polls after India's 1974 "peaceful nuclear explosion"; respondents did not believe that India's status had been enhanced.[50] But the argument received a new lease on life when Washington agreed to give China's (permanent) United Nations Security Council seat to the representative from Beijing, thus effectively ousting Taiwan. With Beijing's admittance the elite club of five permanent Security Council members, those with veto rights, became synonymous with the rollcall of the world's established nuclear weapon powers. The exclusion of Japan might once have been ordained by defeat in war, yet with her GNP now surpassing that of all but one or two world economies there were those who pointed to nuclear bomb abstinence as the major reason for Japan's continued exclusion. Nuclear weapon possession alone might not guarantee access to the inner circle of privilege, but it did suggest itself as one precondition.[51]

Nuclear weapons advocates also drew strength from the attempt by nuclear have nations to maintain their monopoly preserve through restrictive trade practices and legislation; these policies were clearly considered gratuitous or insulting even by Japanese opponents of

indigeneous efforts. But the most telling support for the argument
of the advocates derived from the 1970s' phenomenon of proliferation of weapons possession and weapons potential.[52] The Indian
detonation was followed by reports that Israel and South Africa
had also acquired limited nuclear weapons arsenals (though these
remained untested, at least until early 1980, when it appeared that a
joint test may have been conducted in the South Atlantic).[53] By the
end of the decade Pakistan was said to be nearing the testing stage of
a Libyan financed "Islamic bomb," an event sure to fuel further
development of India's weapons program.[54] Closer to home, there
were reports that both Taiwan and South Korea had amassed the
plutonium and technological expertise required to cross the threshhold within short periods of time. In view of outstanding territorial
and other disputes that might one day exacerbate relations between
these nations and Japan it was inevitable that their progress would
cause nervous flutters in Tokyo.

But opposition to a possible Japanese nuclear weapons program
remained formidable. Such opposition is a basic tenet of government
policy, a reflection of the Constitutional prohibition against the
maintenance of armed forces (Article 9). The Constitutional stric-
ture had admittedly been diluted somewhat through the establishment of limited but potent "self-defence forces" and a national
"Defence Agency" (not of Ministry rank). Notwithstanding a certain
flexibility of interpretation, however, the concensus against offensive
force capability in general and nuclear arms in particular stood firm.

And the opposition was not merely a reflection of government
policy and constitutional diktat. After all, policies change and consti-
tutions are amended. The most unyielding deterrent arose rather
from the geopolitical constraints of Japan's physical shape and location. Her constricted area ruled out advance warning systems. The
ideal locale for early warning radars would be in Siberia and central
China. The reality was that submarines could launch missiles whose
flight time to densely populated Japanese targets would be a matter
of a few minutes. It would be physically and technologically impossible to secure sufficient warning time to activate effective defence
measures. The concept of a Ballistic Missile Defence (BMD) system
was in any case beyond Japan's present technological capabilities.
And there was the point that even if the technological and financial
obstacles to a BMD could be overcome, the proximity of possible
enemy submarine firing stations meant that interception would have
to take place over Japanese territory. This, per definition, meant that
it must take place over populated areas, where a "defensive" nuclear
explosion would have the same effect as if it had been "offensive."

The problems were scarcely less if one focused on the procurement of a deterrent system, as opposed to a true defence system. Restrictions on land availability ensured that land-based missiles would always be vulnerable to enemy "take-out" strikes. And that was not the only obstacle. Apart from the very considerable technological and economic barriers to true Intercontinental Ballistic Missile (ICBM) capabilities, there was the point that even a successful overcoming of these barriers might come to naught in the face of established and evolving Soviet (and to a lesser extent U.S.) BMD capabilities. And mastery of Multiple Independently-targeted Reentry Vehicles (MIRV) technology, something that might provide a better guarantee of defence saturation potential, posed technological and economic problems of a different order of magnitude again. The alternative of Submarine Launched Ballistic Missiles (SLBMs) might circumvent the question of launch vulnerability, although restricted shore lines would give an advantage to enemy tailing designs and hence enemy Anti-Submarine Warfare (ASW) prospects. Submarine launching, furthermore, brought a new set of technological problems. And the question of range and penetration confidence remained. While both Moscow and Washington had overcome the technological obstacles to intercontinental range (and MIRVed) SLBMs, the U.S. system had still not fully completed the testing and development stage by 1980; Japanese emulation would have to pass awesome scientific and financial hurdles.[55]

If opposition to nuclear arms was solely a matter of public aversion, a legacy of Hiroshima and Nagasaki to which Japan's present establishment took exception (whether for reasons of security or what), then the future course of the debate might have appeared less certain. Public opinion is seldom hewn in granite, even when derived from a cataclysmic event like Hiroshima; the passage of time and the manipulative potential of media influence can blur distinctions and convictions of the past. It is relevant to note that India's nuclear weapons development was surreptitiously piggybacked on an extensive civilian nuclear reactor and research program; her delivery capabilities were similarly piggybacked on a "civilian" program pursuing missile and satellite technology for purposes of education (to beam educational material to distant regions) and research.[56] And India's body politic was as fractious and as infused by pacifist ideals as is Japan's. The decisive factor, then, lay rather in the opinion polls' testimony that the groups most opposed to nuclear arms were the young and the military themselves. Military opposition, resting on the nonemotional assessment that Japan's particular geographical circumstances mocked the relevance of nuclear force possession, was likely to ensure that abstinence would remain a central tenet of government policy.

By the late 1970s and early 1980s it was clear that Japanese establishment opinion at least was moving towards a greater emphasis on improved military capabilities. This was a function both of a perception that Washington's commitment to the region's security was less absolute than it once was[57] and unease caused by increased Soviet force potential in the area (an unease exacerbated by continued Soviet-Japanese tension; see below). Defence expenditures remained at just under 1 percent of GNP (although the size of the GNP translated that 1 percent into the world's eighth largest military budget). But the "militarization" of opinion did lead to increased defence outlays, especially in the field of research and development, and expanding commitments as concerned future procurements.[58] Increased urgency was attached to the effort to develop independent research and construction facilities to lessen the technology dependence attendant upon past practices of importation and coproduction.

There was heavy emphasis on pursuit of the technologies currently revolutionizing the potency of "conventional" arms (such as in-flight and terminal guidance for "smart bombs" and cruise missiles).[59] There was also an attempt to leapfrog the nuclear impasse with investments in the field of laser and high energy particle beam technologies. The latter endeavor held some promise in the field of Ballistic Missile Defence for a future intercept system that dispensed with the nuclear element inherent in contemporary concepts. But it was a distant promise at best. The day of Japanese strategic independence remained a vision, a vision that might possibly be realizable by the 1990s but that more probably belonged to the next century.

Finally, one must return to the ambivalences afflicting the Soviet-Japanese relationship. On the one hand, cooperative resource extraction ventures and trade in general had, as mentioned, continued to expand through the 1970s, in spite of the demise of the more ambitious schemes of the early years of the decade. The dominant pattern was one of investment into energy and raw material exploitation, coupled with related infrastructure requirements, in return for payment in produce extracted. But, on the other hand, political and security tensions persisted and thus continued to act as a brake on the realization of optimal levels of economic cooperation.

The Soviet position that the status of the northern islands was settled for the duration of the Japanese-U.S. security embrace was to be a continuous irritant. Its squelching effect on grand designs for joint economic projects on land and off shore has already been dealt with. It was also to complicate agreement on fishery jurisdiction (a question of some considerable importance in view of both nations' dependence on the protein harvest from the seas). The December 1976 Soviet announcement of a 200 mile economic zone was followed by a February 1977 decree that affirmed its applicability to the disputed islands and their environs. This area accounted for 20 percent of Japan's total catch of fish. Fisheries negotiations broke down over a Soviet draft that implied Japanese acceptance of the Soviet sovereignty stand. Agreement was finally reached on a blurring of the offending clause. Mid summer saw the signing of a provisional accord assigning end-year quotas based on past Japanese catch rates off the Soviet-controlled islands and the more modest traditional take of Soviet vessels in Japanese waters.[60] But the dispute simmered.

1978–80 brought a new twist. A Soviet military buildup on Kunashiri and Iturup caused considerable agitation in Japan.[61] It became grist to the mill of those fuelling the previously described "militarization" phenomenon.[62] On the other hand, it also cemented the conviction of those who had resigned themselves to the status quo, at least as concerned these two larger islands. It provided an air of finality to the Soviet stance; the more so when seen in conjunction with the international community's tendency to accept the legitimacy of Moscow's presence. (As shown above, Western sources tended to concede Soviet sovereignty over Kunashiri and Iturup, while reserving their position on Habomai and Shikotan, the smaller islands.)

One is obliged to note that the Soviet contingents on the larger islands could hardly be described as a threat to Japanese security (the effect on Japanese pride is another matter). While they might appear so if seen through jaundiced or ethnocentric lenses, it was clear that the primary rationales for the buildup, in fact, lay elsewhere. On the one hand, it was but a part of Moscow's steady efforts to strengthen her Far East force potential in general, an effort directed at China rather than Japan. On the other, and more specifically, it was an essential component of Moscow's high priority drive to secure the Okhotsk Sea as an inviolable home lake within which some naval strategic forces might safely be withheld from initial strategic exchanges, to serve instead as intrawar bargaining and war termination leverage.[63] Superpower strategic balance calculations provided the sole concern; the position of Japan was of no relevance, except insofar as Japanese policy might abet U.S. counteraspirations.

There was, finally, one other seemingly unconnected incident that helped skewer prospects for Soviet-Japanese relations. In September 1976 a Soviet defector flew a MIG 25 interceptor of the air

defence forces (PVO) to Japan's Hakodate airport.[64] Tokyo's decision
to dismantle the plane and make it available for U.S. inspection
infuriated Moscow. The Japanese action did indeed suggest deliberate
provocation, since standard practice (observed even by NATO nations
when confronted by analagous situations) decreed the prompt return
of the plane. The fact that the MIG 25 was not new and embodied
only the technology of the 1960s added a gratuitous element.
Clearly, Tokyo's course reflected frustration, frustration presumably
caused, in part, by receding expectations on the issue of the northern
isles and possibly, in part, by Moscow's hard stance on economic and
other issues. Be that as it may, when the reassembled plane was
finally handed back the dispute continued to simmer. The Japanese
demanded compensation for damage to a control tower that they
claimed resulted from the MIG's original landing. Moscow pressed a
larger claim, to cover alleged damages brought about by the dis-
mantling and reassembling (the fighter was said to have been effectively destroyed). Both nations ignored the claim of the other. The
fallout from the affair was significant. The rest of the decade saw a
further hardening of Moscow's negotiating position: on the islands,
on fisheries, across the board. Improving Japanese ties with China
brought no concessions from Moscow, only the solidifying of an
unyielding official posture that portrayed Japan as a tool of the
other superpower. Greater Japanese defence efforts, invigorated by
the failure of established systems to track the incoming MIG, were
decried as but a symptom of the same malady.

Prospects for the 1980s and future Soviet-Japanese cooperation
obviously labored under severe handicaps, deep distrust, and a considerable degree of mutual ignorance—compounded by mutual
disinclination to break out of established molds. That commercial
ties nevertheless survived and, in fact, strengthened testified to continued and mutual appreciation of the potentials that improved
relations might bring. They served as a lifeline to the day when rancor
might abate, and estrangement might wane. They signalled that
political antipathies had not been allowed to completely smother
the lure of economic advantage.

The Northeast Asian triangle of giants entered the 1980s with
smoother sailing along its Sino-Japanese leg, but with the other two
sides mired in ambiguity. Both the Japanese-Soviet and the Sino-
Soviet relationship appeared schizophrenic: veering between antagonism and accommodation, pulled alternately by haunting memories
and alternately by the uncertain fears and hopes of the future.

NOTES

1. For background, see C.G. Jacobsen, *The USSR-China-Japan: Strategic Considerations Affecting the Triangle of the Soviet Far East-Manchuria-Japan*, Columbia University Russian Institute Report, March 1973, published as Canadian Department of Defence DRAE Memorandum, Spring 1974. See also J.K. Fairbank, E.O. Reischauer, and A.M. Craig, *East Asia: The Modern Transformation* (Boston: Houghton Mifflin, 1965).

2. Fairbank, Reischauer, and Craig, *East Asia*, pp. 563–8.

3. Ibid., pp. 597–601, 606–610.

4. "The Expansion and Modernization of Japan 1868 to 1918," *The Times Atlas of World History* (London: 1978) pp. 242–3.

5. *The New Columbia Encyclopedia* (New York: Columbia University Press, 1975) p. 1400.

6. J.W. Strong, "Sino-Soviet Relations in Historical Perspective," in *Communist States at the Crossroads*, ed. A. Bromke, (New York: Praeger, 1965) provides an excellent summary of the period.

7. Most of the survey results referred to may be found in Herbert Passin's fine analysis of "Nuclear Arms and Japan," in *Asia's Nuclear Future*, ed., W.H. Overholt, (Col: Westview Press, 1977) pp. 67–132. See also *Gakushuin Daigaku Hogakubu Kenkyu Nempo*, No. 9 (1973) p. 127, and *Chosa Geppo*, No. 9 (1974) p. 30.

8. John J. Stephan, "Sakhalin Island: Soviet Outpost in North-East Asia," *Asian Survey* (December 1970).

9. *Soviet-Japanese Joint Declaration*, accompanying the resumption of diplomatic relations (October 19, 1956).

10. *Voprosi Istorii*, Nos. 3 and 4 (1971), see especially pp. 130–156 of No. 4.

11. Ibid.

12. *Pravda* (March 31, 1971) L. Brezhnev's report to the Twenty-fourth CPSU Congress.

13. *Mezhdunarodnaya Zhizn*, No. 6 (1972) article by L.G. Beskrovny, S.L. Tikhvinskii, and V.M. Khostov.

14. See *Japan Times Weekly* (November 6, 1971) for comments made by JCP Chairman Miyamoto upon his return from Moscow (note also coverage of same in JCP's organ, *Akahata*).

15. *Japan Times Weekly* (March 9, 1972), *Le Monde* (April 10, 1972) quoting sources associated with the Japanese Embassy in Moscow, *Financial Times* (London) (July 18, 1972) quoting sources in the Japanese Foreign Ministry.

16. C.G. Jacobsen, "Japanese Security in a Changing World: the Crucible of the Washington-Moscow-Peking Triangle?" *Pacific Community*, Tokyo, (April 1975). See also *Voprosy Istorii*, No. 4 (1971): 130–156.

17. *The Guardian* (May 26, 1972).

18. *Le Monde* (March 25, 1972), as corrected by *Le Monde* (March 30, 1972).

19. *The Guardian* (May, 26, 1972).

20. Jacobsen, *The USSR-China-Japan*.

21. Note also analysis in *Le Monde* (March 30, 1972).

22. *Izvestia* (January 14, 1972).

23. Ibid. See also *The Japan Economic Review* (October 15, 1971).

24. *The Christian Science Monitor* (February 19, 1970) and *The Japan Economic Journal* (May 16, 1970).

25. *Japan Times Weekly* (November 6, 1971) quoting Tokusaburo Kosaka, a Liberal Democratic Dietmember, who furthermore asserted that: "The argument that improvement in Japan-Soviet relations will aggravate relations between Japan and the US and hamper the normalization of diplomatic relations between Japan and mainland China is utter nonsense."

26. Ibid.

27. Statement by Finance Minister Takeo Fukuda to Tokyo Press Conference, June 20, 1972.

28. *Japan Times Weekly* (March 11, 1972) and *International Herald Tribune* (July 8, 1972).

29. See Chapter 3.

30. For background and comparison, see. e.g., *Beijing Review* (June 13, 1969). See also *Le Monde* (March 30, 1972).

31. *Japan Economic Journal* (December 14, 1971) and *Japan Times Weekly* (December 18, 1971). See also, e.g., *Japan Weekly* (November 9, 1968).

32. *The Times*, Business News, (February 8, 1972), covers the original February 7, 1972 Japanese agreement to buy crude directly from a Mid East oil producing country, Abu Dhabi.

33. Kyung-Won Kim, in *Strategy and Security in North East Asia*, eds., R.B. Foster, J.E. Dornan Jr., and W.M. Carpenter, (New York: Crane, Russack, 1979) p. 249. See also review in *The Bulletin of the Atomic Scientists* (May 1980).

34. Ibid.

35. Jacobsen, "Japanese Security in a Changing World."

36. Ibid., pp. 357-8.

37. As evident in debate that followed this author's Japanese Ministry of Foreign Affairs' sponsored lecture, Imperial Hotel, Tokyo, June 14, 1974. See *Tokyo Association of Asian and European Affairs Report No. 69*, (Fall 1974).

38. For a Soviet commentary, see *International Affairs* (Moscow), No. 2 (1978) especially p. 49, and No. 8 (1979) p. 70.

39. C.G. Jacobsen, "Afghanistan: Ice and Fire," *The Bulletin of the Atomic Scientists* (March 1980).

40. *The Europa Year Book 1979: A World Survey* (London: Europa Publications Ltd., 1979) pp. 123 and 1241.

41. Koichi Saito, "Oil and Energy in Northeast Asia" in *Strategy and Security in Northeast Asia*, p. 309.

42. Ibid., p. 306.

43. *Japan Economic Journal* (December 14, 1971).

44. *Japan-US Atomic Agreement*, signed in Washington, D.C. on February 26, 1968.

45. *Japan Economic Journal* (December 14, 1971) and *Japan Times Weekly*, (December 18, 1971). And see, e.g., *The Financial Times* (London), (March 17, 1967).

46. For an early indicator of the trend, and of Japan's reaction, see *Washington Post* (November 14, 1970).

47. "National Security Experts Analyze Japan's Defence, Nuclear Issues," *Asahi Evening News* (April 26, 1967). See also *Japan Times Weekly* (February 10, 1968), and *The New York Times* (August 24, 1968).

48. *Christian Science Monitor* (April 29, 1968).

49. See *Washington Post* (July 18, 1968) quoting Japanese Defence Agency study *The Security of Japan and Prospects for 1970* (prepared by the Security Research Council).

50. *Sankei* (May 23, 1974).

51. *Chosa Geppo*, No. 2 (1975): 35.

52. Overholt, ed. *Asia's Nuclear Future.*

53. For an early report, see *Science* (November 30, 1979) pp. 1051-52. Note also *CBC Evening News*, February 21, 1980, and followup coverage in *The New York Times* (February 23 and 25, 1980).

54. C. Smith and S. Bhatia, "Stealing the Bomb for Pakistan," *The Observer* (London) (December 9, 1979).

55. See Chapter 1 and this author's *Soviet Strategic Initiatives: Challenge and Response* (New York: Praeger, 1979) especially Chapters 1 and 2.

56. Onkar Marwah, "India's Nuclear Program: Decisions, Intent and Policy, 1950-1976," in *Asia's Nuclear Future*, pp. 161-196.

57. Popular opinion was never overly sanguine. See, e.g., survey results in *Asahi*, (October 1, 1969) and *Yomiuri* (October 19, 1971) less than a third of respondents expected "that in case of emergency, America will defend Japan under the US-Japan Security Treaty."

58. *The Economist* (London) (July 29, 1978), and *Atlas* (November 1978) special report on "Japan's New Nationalism." And see *Aviation Week and Space Technology* (January 21, January 28, February 4, and February 11, 1980). For a Soviet commentary, see *Pravda* (September 19, 1979).

59. *Aviation Week and Space Technology* (January 28, 1980) especially article, "Broad Military Technology Base Sought."

60. D.R. Jones, ed., *Soviet Armed Forces Review Annual* (SAFRA) 2, Academic International, 1978, pp. 271-2.

61. *Aviation Week and Space Technology* (January 21, January 28, February 4, and February 11, 1980) for special reports on "Japan's Growing Strategic Role."

62. Ibid.

63. See Chapter 1.

64. D.R. Jones, ed., *SAFRA.*

Kurile
Islands

Sakhalin
Island

USSR

Iturup

Kunashiri
Shikotan
Habomai

Hokkaido

Senkaku

Okinawa

CHINA

Islands

Ryukyu Islands
(JAPAN)

TAIWAN

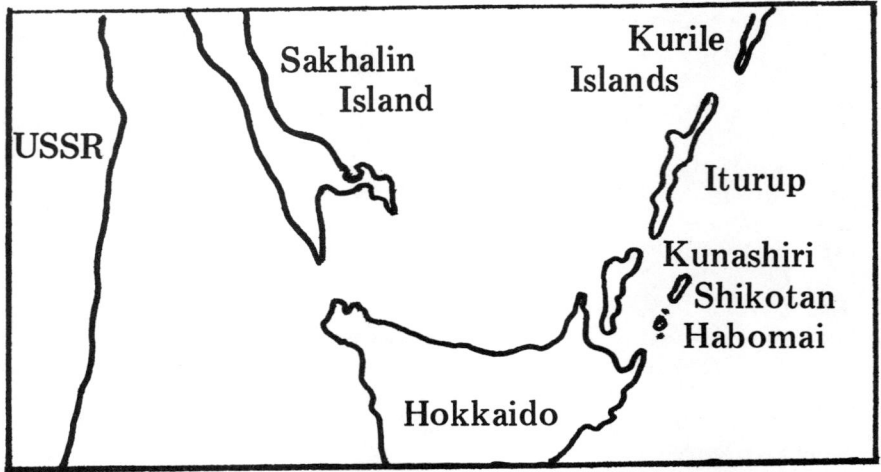

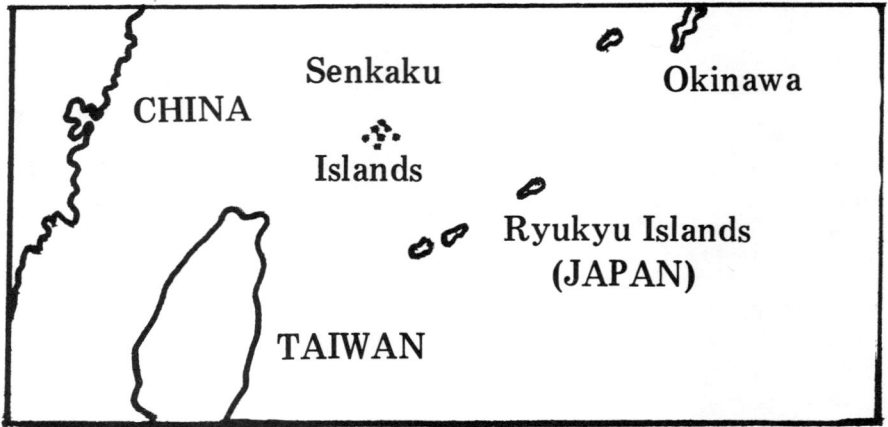

Disputed Islands

MAP 8.   Disputed Islands

CONCLUSION   FUTURE PROSPECTS

Any realistic discussion of future eventualities must perforce rest on a thorough understanding of the present, so also with the question of the probable future course of Sino-Soviet relations. In view of the evidence of preceding chapters of the extraordinary degree to which Sino-Soviet relations of the 1960s and 1970s remained hostage to the vagaries of internal politics, particularly in Beijing, it would appear appropriate to begin this concluding chapter with a review of the respective domestic scenes, anno 1980, at least insofar as they remain relevant to our larger purpose. The viciousness of the preceding decades' struggle for the body and soul of China's ruling Party and the intimate relationship that developed between particular factional positions and certain aspects of both the substance and the conjectured symbolism of ties with Moscow requires that one focus first and foremost on Deng Xiaoping's China.

China at the dawn of the 1980s did indeed look to be Deng's preserve. His old nemesis, Mao Zedong, was dead; Mao's radical followers appeared cowed, their leaders arrested. After two and a half years' uneasy duomvirate with Hua Guofeng, Deng managed in early 1980 to tilt the scales of power dramatically and perhaps decisively in his own favor. As described in Chapter 5, February 29, 1980 saw the promotion to the Standing Committee of the Politburo of two of Deng's closest associates and proteges, Hu Yaobang and Zhao Ziyang, with Hu confirmed also as the new Secretary General of the Party and hence head of its Secretariat. It was, furthermore, announced that four Politburo members presumed still to harbor sympathy for Maoist concepts and aspirations had been purged, thus leaving Hua as the only member with any ties to the former regime. To underline the change Mao's ouster of then Premier Liu

Shaoqui a decade and a half earlier (he had castigated Liu as a "renegade, traitor, and scab") was officially termed "the biggest frameup our Party has ever known." As if that was not enough, it was announced that the Four Freedoms inscribed in Mao's Constitution—to "speak out freely, air views fully, hold great debates, and write big character posters"—would be abolished.[1]

The February Party decisions were duly accepted and confirmed six weeks later by China's de facto Parliament, the 120 member Standing Committee of the National People's Congress, and forwarded for final ratification by the next full Congress session scheduled for August.[2] The confirmation was accompanied by the news that Zhao had also been appointed Vice Premier.[3] Through interviews with Western press representatives Deng conveyed an image of supreme confidence. He encouraged speculation that Zhao was being groomed for the Premiership to complement Hu's emergence as day to day manager of Party affairs and suggested that he himself expected to be able to retire to a more leisurely supervisory role within five years.[4]

Yet the eery fact was that, although the will had been read and the successors annointed, the body was not yet dead. There could be little doubt that the events of the spring had seriously undermined Hua Guofeng's power and influence, but he still retained the titles of Party Chairman and Premier. The apparent hollowness of Hua's titular prominence revived memories of his anomalous rise to high office after Zhou Enlai's death in January of 1976. His appointment then as Premier had been described as a moderate, compromise, and perhaps temporary choice that signalled Mao's veto against the heir presumptive, Zhou's Deputy, Deng Xiaoping, and foreshadowed Deng's imminent disgrace. To some observers the appointment had indicated a recognition on Mao's part that he did not possess sufficient power and will to force acceptance of a more radical figure. To others who remembered his original support for Zhou and his belief that it was advisable to have a pragmatic hand on the management rudder to balance the impetuousness of more utopian advocates, it suggested the perseverance of the Maoist insistence on the need for unity of opposites, for "red and expert." Both interpretations, that which saw Mao as resigned to the appointment and that which saw him as supportive of it (the truth probably lay in between, with the idea of "putting the best face forward" not altogether absent), echoed the constellation of 1965 at the start of the Cultural Revolution. That effort had seen Mao's stature and authority powerful enough to bulldoze through the dismissal of his immediate foes, Liu and Deng (who had been Party Secretary General), yet without the sustaining strength to ensure also the ouster of their followers who remained entrenched within the Party apparat.[5] It had been a pyrrhic victory resting on an enforced compromise that only postponed the resolution of the fundamental differences that had spawned the upheaval.

The Hua-Zhou analogy is attractive. Yet, the implication of original Mao support for Hua's candidacy is somewhat undermined by Mao's disenchantment with Zhou's later support for Deng and the evidence that only Zhou's death thwarted a concerted Maoist assault on his authority. It would seem logical to presume that, notwithstanding his theoretical predisposition, Mao would likely have entertained a certain reluctance at the thought of another "pragmatist" in the Premiership, even one as apparently innocuous as Hua. Certainly such unease would have received superficial vindication after Mao's death some months later when in a sense Hua began where Zhou left off, when he orchestrated (or appeared to orchestrate) the arrest of the radical "Maoist" leadership, the Gang of Four. On the other hand, that particular leading role may have been scripted or dictated by the pragmatic judgment that without Mao's authority to shield them the radicals were foredoomed to defeat by the Party apparat, that the balance of bureaucratic power within the Party, government, and armed forces now made a Deng return to authority inevitable, and that self-preservation required accommodation and perhaps anticipation of this eventuality. The point is, of course, that Hua subsequently reverted to a position more akin to that of Zhou in earlier years. Having retained a measure of power through the process of Deng restoration Hua began to sound more appreciative of Mao's old dictum that the preservation of the revolution necessitated a guiding role for "red" aspirations. While Deng proceeded to try to purge remaining radical supporters, Hua increasingly appeared to be calling for their support.[6] It was in this context that Hua's survival in the immediate aftermath of the February 1980 decisions, an aftermath that brought Deng insistence that the Gang of Four stand formal trial (and advance Deng assertion that they would without doubt be convicted of "extremely grave crimes"),[7] was particularly interesting and intriguing.

The thesis of general Deng preeminence was unassailable.[8] The final years of the 1970s and early 1980 saw the reversal of Maoist policies across the entire sociopolitical and economic gamut. In the fields of ideology, culture, economic, and Party management, government organization, and foreign trade Deng's ingrained and historical preference for what is best described as the early Stalinist model (see Chapters 2, 3, and 5) prevailed. The order of the day called for strict discipline that brooked no opposition, with all efforts to be focused on an ambitious centrally directed program of enforced development (the "Four Modernizations"). It was an economic program that relied for incentives on a mixture of brute authority, increased financial differentiations, stratification, and bonuses, and a more impatient attitude to the social and human costs that might be incurred. The official rationale for the change of course rested on the asserted inefficiency of Mao's more utopian social designs, designs seen as unrealistic and disruptive. Prima facie evidence was found in the chaos precipitated first by Mao's Great Leap Forward, then by his Cultural Revolution campaign.

Deng's rationale, the raison d'être for his stewardship of the nation, and the foundation for his apparent (presumed might be a better word) support also among the wider strata of the populace appeared somewhat frayed by 1980. The realities of China's continued underdevelopment were such that rising expectations could not easily be met, at least not in the shorter run. The economic record of the final years of the 1970s, in fact, proved decisively and embarrassingly inferior to that which had been attained during the years of Maoist "chaos."[9] The argument that continuing problems were due to the sabotage of the Gang of Four was, furthermore, wearing somewhat thin nearly four years after their arrest. Deng's response was to scale down previously announced targets, consolidate his political power (viz. above), call for still tighter discipline, and in general speed the further consolidation and impetus of his Soviet-derived model.[10]

Deng's emulation of the early Stalinist model (one also pursued by Stalin's successors in Moscow) did, as previously discussed, extend also to the concept of "socialism in one country." In effect this concept is a declaration of self-sufficiency, connoting a program of self-interest and self-reliance, of deideologized and supremely pragmatic search for advantage (one might even call it "Gaullist"). In the sphere of foreign affairs it suggests a willingness to tailor policies so as to extract maximum advantage from opportunities of the moment. Alliances are viewed without emotion, as tools to be used when opportune for the furthering of one's own interests and security calculations. Seen in this light, Stalin's pact with Nazi Germany in 1939 became an essential tool for the postponing of looming conflict, once it became clear that Britain and France were not prepared at that time to commit themselves to joint defence with Moscow. China's quasi alliance with Washington was similarly dependent on Beijing's perception of U.S. willingness and ability to satisfy Chinese needs—developmental needs and security needs—and it was dependent on a Chinese judgment that these could not be better served through different alignments.

China's so-called moderates, or pragmatists, had always criticized the emotionalism of Mao's anti-Soviet phobia as counter productive and dangerous. The element of danger arose from their perception of the historical legacy, namely, that Sino-Soviet border issues encompassed a number of potential "Berlins"—friction points, which if approached emotionally or dogmatically could all-too-easily spill over into much wider and less manageable confrontations. The counter-productive argument, however, extended also well beyond matters of security. There was deep conviction that a freezing of ties with Moscow was not in China's developmental interest. There was considerable economic complementarity between the differing developmental stages of the Soviet and Chinese economies. Soviet technology and machinery might in many cases not be up to the most advanced Western standards of sophistication. But though sometimes simpler, Soviet products were often "sufficient"; furthermore, it could be argued (and was argued) that their very simplicity made them better suited to less developed regions, easier to operate by less educated personnel, and in general easier to absorb into the structure of local knowledge and requirements. The argument echoed the more general Third World critique of most Western aid programs, that too high a degree of product sophistication often proved more disruptive than helpful and that the primary emphasis ought to be on projects and technology that could be integrated into the existing socioeconomic structure. Finally, the point must be made (again) that these Chinese leaders had been trained and socialized to see the Soviet model of economic development and political control as the most effective generator of progress. This was the persuasion that had formed the core of their arguments against Mao during the 1950s and through the subsequent decades. Deng's policy prescriptions of 1980 were faithful to the course he had helped Liu Shaoqui implement during the early 1960s; their philosophical debt went back to the 1920s and 1930s.

Deng's personal history evinced a lifelong familiarity with and preference for Soviet sociopolitical and economic structures and a consequent belief that Sino-Soviet negotiations could and should be conducted as between people who at least speak the same language—no matter how vexatious the particular differences that separate them might be. Deng's posture towards the end of the 1970s, especially at the time of the 1979 Sino-Vietnamese War and its aftermath (preempting the anti-Soviet rhetoric of his Maoist opponents, Deng assumed the role of prime spokesman for anti-Moscow phobia), jarred sharply with that of his past. In light of his subsequent reversal to a posture more in keeping with his earlier stance towards Moscow, one is tempted to see his aberrant record in part as a tactical response to Hua's maneuvering of 1978-79. Deng would not have failed to appreciate that his stand might serve, whether coincidentally or not, to undercut any putative rapprochement between Hua and the radicals.

Deng's early 1980 success in finally asserting and solidifying his preeminence within policy-making councils was quickly followed by a certain cooling of official attitudes to Washington and a signalling to Moscow that Beijing would not veto renewed negotiations. The change was heralded already in a speech of January 16, when Deng noted that the Soviet Union "has nothing to brag about in the way it pursued socialism," but pointedly refrained from the usual incantation that Moscow had ceased to pursue socialist goals. March saw wide dissemination provided to the text of a speech given by Zhang Guangdou, Vice President of Peking's Quinghua University, after a two-month visit to the United States. He reported that "The United States is a capitalist hell where corrupt millionaires rig the elections, human rights are trampled underfoot, blacks are without representation; in the future the American people and the Japanese will change color. They won't care for you after you have no more resources; what we are doing now is tactical. We don't want to believe that, because America has become our friend, everything is friendly...we don't want to entertain any illusions."[11] Other straws in the wind during March included a memorial service at which China's leadership honored the memory of two revolutionary veterans who had enjoyed particularly close ties with Moscow and a number of meetings "held to discuss a more favorable view of the Soviet Union as basically a Socialist country which may still have something to offer."[12] The end of the month saw the return to Beijing of a principal Soviet negotiator, for discussions with Moscow's embassy officials on the spot.[13] By early April, though affirming the belief that Soviet policy was expansionist (in view of the continuing Soviet military presence in Afghanistan he could hardly have done otherwise without jeopardizing Beijing's other interests), Deng was telling Western newsmen that renewed talks with Moscow was a distinct possibility ("at an appropriate time, when it is necessary").[14]

The next bellwether appeared to be the prominent display and sale in Beijing of an otherwise obscure provincial journal. It centerpieced a remarkably pro-Soviet article (under the guise of reporting a Heilongjiang conference on Soviet society). The article affirmed that Soviet "economy, science, and technology have made considerable progress, and the livelihood of the people has improved," and concluded approvingly: "internal policies are basically socialist and, compared with Stalin's time, there (has) not been much qualitative change."[15] A Western diplomat commented: "it has become embarrassing for the current leadership that the Russians are considered 'revisionist,' There is too much similarity now with Deng Xiaoping's own economic policies and there had to be some kind of official meeting where Russian economics (was) given the okay."[16] April also saw the leaking of "news" of a report by a Chinese trade delegation that had recently returned from Moscow; it "apparently supports the Soviet centralized system and claims that it "works very well."[17]

Deng was clearly orchestrating a climate favoring substantive Sino-Soviet negotiations.[18] Anti-Soviet propaganda had not been totally displaced. But Hua Guofeng was allowed to reclaim the role as the main fountain of anti-Soviet sentiment.[19] The fact that he was allowed to do so was thought by many observers to be suggestive of Deng confidence. A Deng desire to ensure that established bridges not be burnt before new ones were in place (and preferably not at all) might also be presumed to have been involved. There could be no question of the dominant trend of spring 1980. But the constellation both of domestic power and of current policy preferences was not hewn in granite. *The Economist*, of London, put it succinctly: "Recent Chinese history provides too many lurid examples of slip between anointment and appointment to take any succession formula for granted."[20]

There were two external obstacles to Deng's unfettered pursuit of his personal inclinations. One lay in the Cold War type atmospherics that in 1980 again threatened to petrify established alignments and perceptions. Deng might wish to improve state to state and perhaps Party to Party ties with Moscow, but much had been invested in improved relations with Washington, and their disruption was a price that Deng was loath to pay.

The other external obstacle arose from the uncertainties of succession in Moscow. Secretary General Brezhnev was seriously ailing, yet no succession script looked either secure or lasting. On the other hand, while many concerns separated and distinguished the jockying factions, there was no evidence of significant differences of attitudes towards China. There was every reason to believe that the concensus remained as it had been in 1964, when the charge that irrational emotionalism was affecting Khrushchev's view of Beijing topped the list of justifications for his ouster. The new and determinedly pragmatic leadership had been as keen to ostracize Khrushchev's personalization of the issues as were Deng and their other Chinese counterparts to eviscerate Maoist emotion. Soviet grievances against Beijing were as real as those of China against Moscow. But the evidence available indicated that all the factions maneuvering to take advantage of post-Brezhnev eventualities felt that resolution of major Sino-Soviet differences was possible and that a Deng-associated regime in China would prove a realistic (if tough) negotiating partner. Yet, that is what they had believed in 1964–65, and that is what they thought in late 1975. On both occasions the Maoists had succeeded in reestablishing dominance. By 1980 Moscow was as hesitant about assuming Deng's third emergence to be permanent as was *The Economist*; Soviet leaders remained acutely aware of the continuing survival in Beijing of those who would be all too happy to engineer a third Deng banishment.[21]

Before turning to a discussion of future prospects, there is one other aspect of Chinese reality that needs to be addressed once more, and that is the phenomenon or perception of China as a world apart, a world within the world. The reluctance of many Western and Soviet observers to concede the apparent permanence of Deng ascendancy and its corollary implication that China's two decade long quasi civil war was finally over was, as previously suggested, due to the sometimes painfully absorbed lessons of the immediate past. But there is a wider dimension that deserves consideration. Hua Guofeng's continued titular prominence in Beijing (however emasculated the substance) after Deng's assertion of dominance in February of 1980 is a case in point. On the one hand, it suggested that Deng's victory was less than complete. And that was a suggestion replete with haunting memories of the vicissitudes of Chinese politics of the 1960s and 1970s; referring again to the earlier analogy pairing Deng and General de Gaulle, it was a reminder that the latter gentleman's imperious rule had crumbled in the face of increased domestic opposition. On the other hand, both Hua's survival of the immediate aftermath of Deng's consolidation of power and the fact that Deng himself had found protection during earlier periods of banishment at the hands of Mao, could be said to echo an abiding facet of Chinese politics. Whether in the days of earlier dynasties or during the more recent "revolutionary" epoch, a strong case can be made for the argument that China has proved too large, populous, and unwieldy to allow for total centralization of control. The war lord period during the first half of the twentieth century was but an extreme manifestation of an enduring pattern of provincial authority diverging from the dictates of the capital. Beijing has nearly always had to concede a measure of local autonomy, at least in some regions.[22]

But whatever the ultimate fate of China's current political course, certain short and medium term predictions do suggest themselves. One derives from the state of the economy and the perseverence of two fundamental problems. The first concerns the admitted impossibility of fully satisfying the demands of rising expectations. The realities of China's continuing underdevelopment ensure that this problem will fester for quite some time.[23] The capacity of China's industrial infrastructure will remain a limiting factor through the remainder of the twentieth century, even with maximum effort being concentrated on its development.

The second related problem arises from the evident fact that foreign investment cannot provide quick escape from this predicament. It is not a panacea. Even if foreign benefactors were to be totally forthcoming, an improbable proposition, the Chinese economic structure just would not be able to digest dramatic infusions of new equipment and technology. The trend established during the first months of 1980 of a lowering of growth targets and a concommitant tightening of discipline and central control looked set for a longer lease on life than its progenitors would have liked to admit. Developmental constraints seemed likely to reinforce the self-perpetuating and extending logic inherent in the Stalinist-type model now being established. This did, of course, not mean that the Chinese version must necessarily inherit the rather horrifying warts and blemishes that its precursor acquired during the 1930s. But it did mean that Chinese society would tend to move closer to the Soviet pattern. The trend promised to enlarge the "common ground" basis for Sino-Soviet negotiations.

There is little doubt that Deng, or a Deng-associated regime, favored and would continue to favor the establishing and retention of whatever foreign ties might be considered to be in China's interest. China's pragmatists had always frowned on confrontation tactics, whether directed towards Washington or Moscow. They had always believed, with the early Bolsheviks and with later "nonaligned" leaders of the Third World, that equidistant cordiality would allow them to squeeze maximum economic and security benefits from foreign power constellations competing for advantage. Courtship by one might be profitable, but it could constrict freedom to maneuver and lead to dependency; courtship by more than one rival promised to multiply material gain, while at the same time diluting the spectre of involuntary dependency.

The point that was not appreciated by those Western observers who extrapolated from the superficialities of the Chinese "pragmatic" policy posture of the 1970s, a posture carefully tailored to the tactical requirements and possibilities of factional infighting in Beijing, was that a longer view of the historical record would encourage different conclusions. The primary stress on ties with Washington was time and situation dependent, a tactical response to a particular conflux of domestic sociopolitical and economic considerations. The longer view clearly suggests that it was a policy posture that was adopted as the lesser of available evils. It was based on minimalist rather than maximalist goals. Although the one-sided approach to the West (Washington, Tokyo, and NATO capitals) was considered less than ideal it was an investment that developed its own dynamism and dependency. In a confrontational international environment such as that spawned by the Afghan crisis of 1980, in which third party freedom of choice was squeezed by more strident superpower insistence on either/or positions, the dependency aspect was bound to come to the forefront; in such an environment the seeking of greater balance inevitably puts strains on and jeopardizes established links. Nevertheless, the full historical record provided powerful evidence of the Chinese pragmatists' desire for more balanced inter-relationships. In fact, there was persuasive evidence that Deng's longer term preference and hence choice, if one had to be made, was for accommodation with Moscow—presuming circumstances that made this feasible. There were also indications that Chinese leaders were less than impressed with the return on their "Western invest-ment." Considering both Deng's personal record in favor of nego-tiations with Moscow and the apparent judgment that the economic and security advantages of China's links with the West were more vital to the latter than to Beijing, one is forced to conclude that a Deng regime sees limited realignment as a feasible and indeed attrac-tive option. Prolonged Deng dominance in Beijing is likely to see continued Chinese interest in improved Sino-Soviet relations and confidence that this interest could be pursued without jeopardy to other relationships.

A return to power or influence of radical Maoist aspirations, however, would entail return to the predisposition favoring a "pox on both your houses" policy. Yet the record suggests that primary antipathy and animosity would be directed towards Moscow. The ideological confrontation with Moscow would again occupy center stage, in part because of ideological commitment, but perhaps more importantly because such a stance would be dictated by the nature of their domestic opposition. It would be a return to the situation of the Cultural Revolution, when Moscow was used as a symbol and synonym for non-Maoist aspirations, and the postulated Soviet threat was used to galvanize patriotic support for the Maoist leader-ship. That, together with the autarkic (self-sufficiency) strain integral to Maoist preference, would further lower the priority attached to ties with the West and hence reinforce the tendency to manipulate these for tactical advantage.

One might conceive also of a future revival of aspirations such as those associated with Lin Biao, aspirations favoring autarky but devoid of the anti-Soviet phobia of Maoism. This admittedly unlikely eventuality would see an inward-looking China regularizing but minimizing relations with both Moscow and Washington. It would be a China that turned away from the insistence on rapid industrial growth epitomized by Deng, as well as from the insistence on continued social transformation that had been espoused by Mao. Already achieved levels of economic and social development would be viewed with more satisfaction. Further sweeping changes would be deferred in favor of consolidation. A gradualist approach would focus in the domestic arena on decentralization and rural rather than urban priorities; the security preference, on the other hand, would echo the Maoist emphasis on People's War capabilities, combined with a minimum deterrence, "force de frappe" posture vis a vis the outside world.

Lines of allegiance are of course neither clearcut nor simple, either within the Party organization or in other state structures. While some functional groups have been generally identified with one or other political tendency (thus one prominent observer has argued the case that army leaders have tended to favor the pragmatists, while navy and air force personnel leaned to the Maoists), there are also no doubt considerations that cut across functional lines (the observer quoted above also presents evidence that northerners tend to be more sceptical of Soviet intentions and therefore less inclined to pursue ties with Moscow than southerners).[24] But information on such matters is usually circumstantial and inferential. Thus rumors of air force support for Biao's alleged coup attempt in 1971 received indirect confirmation from reports that the air force had subsequently been grounded for some 28 days.[25] Yet, the story of that crisis remains a morass of assertion and insinuation splendidly devoid of documentation of substance.

China remains a country or world of strict censorship, both official and unofficial. Neither instant "news" derived from permitted interviews nor more conscientious analyses of information provided by the official media—radio, television, or print, provincial or central—can be accepted as more than isolated pieces of a jigsaw puzzle, most pieces of which are hidden. The verbal promulgations and "confidences" of officials must be presumed to be as controlled and selective as are broadcasts and the written word; and while the testimony of refugees or emigres might be a barometer of the attitudes of a segment of popular opinion, it cannot by any stretch of the imagination be used as a guide to state policy or thinking. Thus, even if one had the resources to collate every possible strand of available evidence, the apparent detail that could be extracted would likely be as deceiving as it was informative. A work purporting to be a detailed history of modern China could be written, but it could not be definitive or indeed pursuasive.

The effort that can be undertaken, and that this book was designed to contribute to, is the identification of the major themes and concerns of policy. It is the search for understanding and context, a tracing of abiding aspirations and constraints. The endeavor must eschew the shorter view and perceptions of the moment and focus instead on what can be gleaned from an investigation of the formative background of people and events; the clues of history must be sought first as the essential foundation for realistic analysis. Having sought the legacy of history, however, it is equally vital that one pursue the investigation conscious of the need to employ an interdisciplinary approach. The information available would not suffice to satisfy and validate the narrowly specialized and rigorous requirements of single-profession analysis, be it that of political science, economics, sociology, or any other discipline. Yet, when the various strands of evidence from different disciplines and perspectives are collated, one can at least hope to acquire a sense of background and context. The resultant sketch will still be too hazy to allow one to identify every piece of the puzzle. But it can be trusted to help determine whether a stray piece, a snippet of information, might be relevant at all, or whether it can be disregarded a priori as incompatible with established points of departure or established trends.

The acknowledgement that details of events and personalities are unknown and that one must therefore focus rather on larger themes and trends carries with it the corollary truth that names must on occasion be used as short-hand for more general phenomena, movements, and aspirations. It is illusory to believe that one can fully account for the complex private thoughts, ambitions, hopes, fears, and insecurities of a Mao, a Deng, a Stalin, or of any man or woman; even the strongest willed has on occasion to bow to circumstance and conform to dictates of the environment. The point is that the personal inclinations of an individual may or may not always conform fully to the momentum of the movement with which their names are associated, but as long as the association is maintained, the idiosyncracies of the soul are less relevant than the effective symbolism of the name and the cause that it serves.

Finally, one must also return to the single most insistent lesson of the 1960s and 1970s, that dominant power constellations are never as secure as they appear, or would like to be. The lesson was driven home again in May of 1980, less than three months after Deng's assertion of preeminence, when the *People's Daily* published a speech by Hua Guofeng containing sharp criticism of some of

Deng's policies.[26] Hua's references to Deng's policy on material incentives were scathing: "No good results would be achieved if undue emphasis is placed on economic methods and material rewards while political work and efforts to raise the people's ideological awareness are relaxed." That statement echoed the quintessential Mao, as did the followup admonishment: "It is imperative to strengthen, not weaken, political and ideological work now and in the future." It was immediately clear that even if the speech proved to be Hua's swan song (a prospect suggested by the fact that other evidence of the time tended to confirm continued Deng dominance), the publication of the attack in such a prominent organ was graphic testimony that the Party was not united.

The publicity granted to Hua suggested that significant sectors of the Party remained either adverse to or sceptical of the policy course charted by Deng. Whether the strength of residual opposition could be equated with potential support for "Maoist" prescriptions was another matter. Deng's brusque arrogance had in earlier years also alienated certain segments of the "pragmatic" constituency. There was no evidence that the opposition to his policies was itself united. The Maoist focus of the Hua attack might be indicative of wider preferences. But it might equally be a tactical response to the fact that Deng's incentives policy had stirred a measure of public resentment, and that it therefore constituted an area of peculiar vulnerability.[27] Deng's ship of state might be moving under full sail, but there were still treacherous waters to navigate before it could reach the open sea; so is it also with the possibility of Sino-Soviet accommodation.

September saw the formal resignation from government posts of Hua, Deng, and five other Deputy Prime Ministers, and the official elevation of Zhao Ziyang to the Premiership. Hua retained his position as pro forma Party Chairman (though General Secretary Hu Yaobang was presumed to have usurped much of his authority), and Deng remained Party Vice-Chairman and *eminence grise*. The events appeared to confirm that Deng had finally succeeded in orchestrating a handing over of power to men of his choice. The subsequent announcement that the long awaited trial of the Gang of Four was to be postponed no more buttressed that interpretation. Yet there clearly remained more murky undercurrents, even if the surface seemed calm and bereft of ripples. During the preceding months Deng had repeatedly reiterated his intention to resign and his belief that the younger generation must now be brought to the fore. "Rumors" that Hua would also resign multiplied. It was implied that he would resign from both Premiership and Party Chairmanship. The fact that he relinquished only the former post, at least in the first instance, and that Deng chose also to retain his official Party status suggested a degree of compromise (as did rumblings that the army leadership was less than enthused about the scope and pace of the drive to assign Mao to "the dustbin of history").[28] One might also note that while Hua evidently finally had to concede to Deng's insistence on a quasi-public trial of the Gang and to Deng's pre-judgement of the question of guilt—another echo of Stalinist Russia of the 1930s—Hua apparently retained enough influence to veto the death sentence.[29] Whether the residual opposition to Deng would also continue to be able to affect policies vis a vis Moscow and, if so, for how long, could be answered only by those in possession of a crystal ball. Deng had won the battle. Whether he had truly won the war was a question only the future could answer.

NOTES

1. See Chapter 5 and *Beijing (Peking) Review* March 10, 1980 on "5th Plenum of the CPC 11th Central Committee." Also, e.g., articles on Liu in *China Reconstructs* (Beijing), June 1980, and in *Beijing (Peking) Review* (March 24 and 31, 1980).

2. *Radio Beijing* announcements, April 14 and 16, 1980.

3. Ibid. April 16, 1980. See also, e.g., report in *The New York Times* (April 20, 1980).

4. UPI report, the *Ottawa Journal* (April 17, 1980). And see *The New York Times* (March 23, 1980).

5. See Chapter 2.

6. See the final section of Chapter 3, and Chapter 5.

7. Deng Xiaoping interview with Associated Press, in *Globe and Mail* (April 12, 1980).

8. Ibid. See also, e.g., report in *The Economist* (March 8, 1980).

9. See John Gitting's analysis in (London and Manchester) *The Guardian* (April 27, 1980) and note the evidence presented by Charles Bettelheim in his lengthy and impressive dissection of "The Great Leap Backward," *Monthly Review* (July-August 1978).

10. See, e.g., analysis in *The Economist* (April 26, 1980) though their suggestion that the "tried and tested...methods of political control" being implemented by Deng were "Leninist" is historically incorrect; the particular model now in vogue in Beijing was, as previously noted, distinctly "Stalinist."

11. Beijing correspondent Bryan Johnson, "US a 'capitalist hell,' Chinese told," *Globe and Mail* (April 1, 1980). In an interview with Associated Press' John Roderick Deng subsequently chose to disassociate himself from Zhang's verbal extremism (see *The Guardian*, May 11, 1980). Yet, as evident in the text, there can be no doubt that Zhang's message conformed with Deng-manipulated trends.

12. John Gittings, from Beijing, "China rehabilitates pro-Soviet leader," *The Guardian* (March 30, 1980).

13. Ibid.

14. AP report, in *Globe and Mail* (April 12, 1980).

15. Bryan Johnson, from Beijing, "China voices approval of Soviet internal plans," *Globe and Mail* (May 3, 1980).

16. Ibid.

17. Ibid. The article's assertion that such views are at variance with those of Deng Xiaoping betrays a lack of familiarity with Deng's past and acquaintance only with the public posture affected by Deng during 1978–79.

On the question of positive Chinese feelers to Moscow, see also, e.g., Andre Fontaine's "The Shortest Road from Peking to Moscow," *Le Monde* (April 24, 1980) though the analysis credits only security-related motivations, ignoring the more "positive" considerations of economic and socio-political complementarity.

18. Ibid.

19. See, e.g., Reuter report of Hua's welcoming banquet speech, to visiting Pakistani President Zia ul-Hag, in *Globe and Mail* (May 3, 1980).

20. *The Economist* (April 26, 1980).

21. For an example of Soviet fears, see N. Nikitin's article in *Pravda* (January 15, 1980).

22. One manifestation of this phenomenon, concerning Fujian province, is related by Bryan Johnson in the *Globe and Mail* (April 8, 1980).

23. In 1980 China's State Statistical Bureau put per capita, average income at U.S. \$225; *The Economist* (May 10, 1980) contains a summary of the Bureau's data on recent Chinese economic performance.

24. Bill Whitson. See C.G. Jacobsen's *Summary Report of China Workshop*, PSIA, Harvard University; March 1974. Southerners bore the brunt of colonial impositions during the nineteenth century, they were exposed to the worst atrocities committed by Japanese troops during the Second World War, and they constituted the front line against the later perceptions of threat from a U.S.-backed Taiwan.

25. See Alan Whiting's presentation in *Summary Report* (above).

26. *The People's Daily* (Beijing) (May 13, 1980).

27. See, e.g., Jay Mathews' analysis in the *Washington Post* (May 14, 1980).

28. See, e.g., *The New York Times* (August 26, September 4, and September 5, 1980).

29. See *The New York Times* (September 18, 1980).

SUGGESTED READINGS

I. Alexandrov. *Peking's Policy—A Threat to Peace*. Moscow: Novosti, 1978.

Charles Bettelheim. "The Great Leap Backward." *Monthly Review*. (July-August, 1978).

O.B. Borisov and B.T. Koloskov. *Soviet-Chinese Relations 1945-70*. Moscow: Mysl, 1972.

J. Bredsdorff. *Revolution: There and Back*. London: Faber and Faber, 1980.

Jerome Chen, ed. *Mao Tsetung*. Oxford University Press, 1970.

A.D. Coox and H. Conroy, eds. *China and Japan: search for balance since World War I*. Cal: ABC-Clio Books, 1978.

J.K. Fairbank, E.O. Reischauer, and A.M. Craig. *East Asia: The Modern Transformation*, Boston: Houghton Miffling, 1965 (vol. 2 of *A History of East Asian Civilization*).

H. Gelber. "Nuclear Weapons and Chinese Policy." *Adelphi Papers*, No. 99, London: IISS, 1973.

J. Gray and P. Cavendish. *Chinese Communism in Crisis: Maoism and the Cultural Revolution*. New York: Praeger, 1968.

C.G. Jacobsen. *Soviet Strategic Initiatives: Challenge and Response*. New York: Praeger, 1979.

———. *Soviet Strategy—Soviet Foreign Policy*. Glasgow: The University Press (Robert MacLehose), 1972, 74.

———. *The USSR-China-Japan: Strategic Considerations Affecting the Triangle of the Soviet Far East-Manchuria-Japan*, (Canadian) Dept. of National Defence DRAE Memorandum, Spring 1974.

D.R. Jones, ed. *Soviet Armed Forces Review Annuals*. No. 1-4, Academic International, 1976-1980.

R.C. Kingsbury and R.N. Taaffee. *An Atlas of Soviet Affairs.* New York: Praeger, 1965.

Moshe Lewin. *Lenin's Last Struggle.* New York: Pantheon, 1968 (also Vintage Press, 1968 and 1970, and Monthly Review Press, 1979).

V.P. Lukin. "Vashington-Pekin: Kvazisoiuzniki?" *S.Sh.A.*, (Moscow), December, 1979.

Mao Tsetung in the Scales of History. Cambridge University Press, 1979.

The Military Balance (annual), International Institute for Strategic Studies, London.

W.H. Overholt, ed. *Asia's Nuclear Future.* Boulder, Colorado: Westview Press, 1977.

J.J. Stephan. "Sakhalin Island: Soviet Outpost in North-East Asia." *Asian Survey.* (December, 1970).

J.W. Strong. "Sino-Soviet Relations in Historical Perspective." In *Communist States at the Crossroads.* A. Bromke, ed. New York: Praeger, 1965.

N.S. Sukhanov. *The Russian Revolution.* Oxford University Press, 1965.

P.M. Sweezy. "Theory and Practice in the Mao Period." *Monthly Review.* (February 1977).

D.S. Zagoria. *The Sino-Soviet Conflict 1956–1961.* Princeton, New Jersey: Princeton University Press, 1962.

INDEX

ABOUT THE AUTHOR

DR. C.G. JACOBSEN is a Professor and Director of Soviet Studies at the Center for Advanced International Studies, University of Miami and Adjunct Professor of the Institute of Soviet and East European Studies, Carleton University, Ottawa.

A frequent government consultant, he is the author of numerous articles and books on Soviet foreign policy, Soviet strategy, Soviet-Chinese relations, and arms control (his most recent book, *Soviet Strategic Initiatives: Challenge and Response*, was published by Praeger in October 1979). Dr. Jacobsen completed his doctoral thesis on *Strategic Factors in Soviet Foreign Policy* in 1970 at the Institute for Soviet and East European Studies, Glasgow University, Glasgow, Scotland. A year in Moscow on a British exchange fellowship was followed by appointments with Carleton University, Columbia University, New York, and Harvard University, Cambridge, from whence he returned to Carleton University in 1975 as Visiting Professor of Soviet and Strategic Studies. From 1976 to 1980 Dr. Jacobsen held the Canadian government funded Chair of Strategic Studies at Acadia University, Nova Scotia.